SPEAKING THE TRUTH

Zionism, Israel, and Occupation

edited by Michael Prior
foreword by Archbishop Desmond Tutu

OLIVE
BRANCH
PRESS

An imprint of Interlink Publishing Group, Inc.
Northampton, Massachusetts

First published in 2005 by

OLIVE BRANCH PRESS
An imprint of Interlink Publishing Group, Inc.
46 Crosby Street, Northampton, Massachusetts 01060
www.interlinkbooks.com

Library of Congress Cataloging-in-Publication Data available
ISBN 1-56656-577-4

Printed and bound in Great Britain

CONTENTS

CONTRIBUTORS

Naseer Aruri is Chancellor Professor (Emeritus) of Political Science at the University of Massachusetts at Dartmouth. He is Chair of the Board of Directors of the Trans-Arab Research Institute (Boston), a member of the Executive Committee of the Center for Policy Analysis on Palestine (Washington, DC), and a member of the Board of the International Institute of Criminal Investigations (The Hague). He is a member of several organisations protecting human rights internationally, and was a member of the Board of Directors of Amnesty International, USA, 1984–1990. He is a member of the editorial board of *Third World Quarterly*. His publications include *The Palestinian Resistance to Israeli Occupation* (1970), *Enemy of the Sun: Poems of Palestinian Resistance* (with Edmund Ghareeb, 1970), *Occupation: Israel Over Palestine* (1983), *The Obstruction of Peace: The US, Israel and the Palestinians* (1995), and *Palestinian Refugees: The Right of Return (2001), and Dishonest Broker: The US Role In Israel and Palestine* (2003).

Elizabeth (Betsy) Barlow was Outreach Co-ordinator at the University of Michigan's Center for Middle Eastern and North African Studies. She wrote 'Educating Myself—and Others' in *They Came and They Saw* (ed. Michael Prior, 2000), 'Teaching About the Middle East', *The Link* 28 (1995), no. 4, and is the editor of *Evaluation of Secondary-Level Textbooks for Coverage of the Middle East and North Africa* (a project of the Middle East Studies Association and the Middle East Outreach Council) 1990, 1991 and 1994. She wrote a regular column on Education for the *Washington Report on Middle East Affairs* (1995-2000).

Paul Eisen is a director of *Deir Yassin Remembered*, and is on the Executive Committee of Friends of *Sabeel* UK.

Daniel McGowan is the Director of *Deir Yassin Remembered* www.deiryassin.org. He is a Professor of Economics at Hobart and William

Smith Colleges in Geneva, New York. He is the co-author of *The Saga of Deir Yassin: Massacre, Revisionism, and Reality* and the co-editor of *Remembering Deir Yassin: The Future of Israel and Palestine.*

The Revd Dr **Duncan Macpherson** was Principal Lecturer in Theology and Religious Studies at St Mary's College, Strawberry Hill (University of Surrey, UK). He is the editor of *Living Stones Magazine*, the journal of the Living Stones of the Holy Land Trust. His publications include *Accessing Hinduism*, co-authored with Helen Kanitkar (1998), *A Third Millennium Guide to Pilgrimage to the Holy Land* (editor and contributor, 2000), and is the author of *The Pilgrim Preacher. Palestine, Pilgrimage and Preaching* (2004).

The Revd **Peter J Miano** is Executive Director of The Society for Biblical Studies, 661 Massachusetts Avenue, Suite 40, Arlington, MA 02476, USA (www.sbsedu.org). He has been involved in education and mission in the Holy Land since 1992 and has developed distinctive travel study programmes in contextual study of the Bible. He did graduate studies in New Testament and missiology at Union Theological Seminary, Harvard Divinity School and Boston University School of Theology. He is the author of *The Word of God and the World of the Bible. An Introduction to the Cultural Backgrounds of the New Testament* (2001).

Ilan Pappé is Senior Lecturer in the Department of Political Science, University of Haifa, Israel and the Chair of the Emil Touma Institute for Palestinian Studies (Haifa). He is the author of several books, including *Britain and the Arab-Israeli Conflict 1948-1951* (1988), *The Making of the Arab-Israeli Conflict, 1948-1951* (1992) and *A History of Modern Palestine* (2004)

Revd Dr **Michael Prior**, CM, is Professor of Bible and Theology at St Mary's College, Strawberry Hill (University of Surrey, UK), where he is also Senior Research Fellow in Holy Land Studies. He is author of *Paul the Letter Writer and the Second Letter to Timothy* (1989), *Jesus the Liberator. Nazareth Liberation Theology (Luke 4.16-30)* (1995), and *The Bible and Colonialism. A Moral Critique* (1997). His books on the Holy Land include *Christians in the Holy Land* (1994), *Western Scholarship and the History of Palestine* (1998), *Zionism and the State of Israel: A Moral Inquiry* (1999),

Holy Land—Hollow Jubilee: God, Justice and the Palestinians (1999), and *They Came and They Saw. Western Christian Experiences of the Holy Land* (2000). He is the editor of *Holy Land Studies: A Multidisciplinary Journal.*

Rosemary Radford Ruether and Herman Ruether are the co-authors of *The Wrath of Jonah: The Crisis of Religious Nationalism in the Israeli-Palestinian Conflict* (2002, 2nd ed.). Rosemary Ruether is the Carpenter Professor of Feminist Theology at the Graduate Theological Union in Berkeley, California. Herman Ruether is a retired professor of Political Science and Asian Studies.

Stephen Sizer is a visiting lecturer at Wycliffe Hall, Oxford and Oak Hill College, London. He is the vicar of Virginia Water, Surrey and chair of the International Bible Society UK. He is the author of *In the Footsteps of Jesus and the Apostles* (2004) and *Christian Zionists on the Road to Armageddon* (2004).

Desmond Tutu was Bishop of Lesotho (1976-1978), Secretary General of the South African Council of Churches (1978-1985), Bishop of Johannesburg (1985-1986), and Archbishop of Cape Town (1986-1996). He won the Nobel Peace Prize (1984), being cited as 'a unifying leader figure in the campaign to solve South Africa's apartheid problem by peaceful means'. He chaired South Africa's Truth and Reconciliation Commission (1995-1998). He is the author of several books, including *Crying in the Wilderness. The Struggle for Justice in South Africa* (1982), *The Rainbow People of God: The Making of a Peaceful Revolution* (1994), and *No Future Without Forgiveness* (2000).

Jean Zaru, a Palestinian woman living under Israeli military rule and in a traditional culture, devotes her life to the struggle for liberation, for Palestinians, for women, and for all peoples. She is acclaimed internationally for her work in interfaith dialogue and human rights issues. She was a Fellow at Hartford Seminary (1992) and Dorothy Cadbury Fellow to Selly Oak Colleges (1993). She was a member of the Central Committee of the World Council of Churches (1975-1983), and a member of the WCC Working Group on Interfaith Dialogue (1981-1991). She was the Vice President of the World YWCA (1983-1991), and was a member of the International Council of the World Conference

for Religion and Peace. She has contributed to several books. She is the presiding clerk of the Ramallah Friends Meeting, and taught religion and ethics at the Friends Schools there. She is a founding member and Vice-Chair of Sabeel, and is a board member of Wi'am Conflict Resolution Center in Bethlehem.

FOREWORD
Archbishop Desmond Mpilo Tutu

The affairs of the Holy Land have long been a concern for Christians world-wide, and we in South Africa take a particular interest in them. The two countries have so much in common, and the forms of oppression in each demonstrate remarkable similarities. Over the last several years during which our problems in South Africa have diminished, matters in the Holy Land have got increasingly worse, and the human tragedy has been multiplied. In a context of spiralling violence human optimism is severely strained. And, yet, the human spirit holds on to hope for a better future. For those of us who are inspired by the message, life and death of Jesus, hope is never frustrated—not even by death. The transformation in South Africa culminating in the liberation of the 1990s should encourage all those who strive for justice and peace in the Holy Land.

For many years in South Africa it looked to some as if we could never emerge as a single people. Years of White domination of the Blacks and Coloureds was underpinned by the whole system of government. For a period, indeed, proponents of racial supremacy had the support of several of the theological strands within some of the mainstream Churches. It took even the Churches time to realise that it was not within God's plan that one people should dominate another, and, ultimately, to see that *Apartheid*, the official policy of domination, was indeed a heresy. The process of healing, of course, could only follow when people began to know the truth, much of it particularly uncomfortable.

In our struggle against *apartheid* Jews were among our greatest supporters. It seemed as if they were instinctively on the side of the disenfranchised, the voiceless, forever fighting injustice, oppression and evil. I continue to feel strongly with the Jews, and am patron of a Holocaust centre in South Africa. I find all the more perplexing, then, what the Jewish state has done to another people to guarantee its existence.

I was profoundly distressed by my visits to the Holy Land. They reminded me so much of what happened to us black people in South Africa. I saw the humiliation of the Palestinians at checkpoints and

9

roadblocks, just like our people who continued to suffer when young white police officers prevented us from moving about. On one of my visits to the Holy Land, in particular, I drove to a church with the Anglican bishop in Jerusalem. As I saw the encroaching Jewish settlements, I reflected on the Palestinians who had lost their land and homes. Later in his hometown Beisan (now Bet Shean) Canon Naim Ateek (Director of the Sabeel Ecumenical Centre in Jerusalem) pointed in a particular direction, saying, 'Our home was over there. We were driven out of our home; it is now occupied by Israeli Jews.'

The sufferings of the Palestinians, which I saw at first hand, brought me back to my address on receiving the Nobel Peace Prize (1984):

> In pursuance of apartheid's ideological racist dream, over 3,000,000 of God's children have been uprooted from their homes, which have been demolished, whilst they have then been dumped in the bantustan homeland resettlement camps. I say dumped advisedly: only things or rubbish is dumped, not human beings. Apartheid has, however, ensured that God's children, just because they are black, should be treated as if they were things, and not as of infinite value as being created in the image of God. These dumping grounds are far from where work and food can be procured easily. Children starve, suffer from the often irreversible consequences of malnutrition—this happens to them not accidentally, but by deliberate Government policy. They starve in a land that could be the bread basket of Africa, a land that normally is a net exporter of food.

My heart aches as I see similar treatment meted out to the Palestinians by the State of Israel. Much of the suffering is the same. Only the numbers are different. Why, I ask myself, are human memories so short? Have our Jewish sisters and brothers forgotten their humiliation? Have they forgotten so soon the collective punishments, the home demolitions of their own history? Have they turned their backs on their profound and noble religious traditions? Have they forgotten that God cares deeply about the downtrodden?

Our experience in South Africa assures me that Israel will never get true security and safety through oppressing another people. A true

peace can ultimately be built only on justice. We condemn, of course, the violence of suicide bombers, and we condemn the corruption of young minds taught hatred; but we also condemn the violence of military incursions in the occupied lands, and the inhumanity that won't let ambulances reach the injured.

The military actions of recent times, I predict with certainty, will not provide the security and peace Israelis want; it will only intensify the hatred. Israel has three options: revert to the previous stalemate situation; exterminate all Palestinians; or—and I hope that this one will be chosen—to strive for peace based on justice, based on withdrawal from all the occupied territories, and the establishment of a viable Palestinian state on those territories side by side with Israel, both with secure borders. That, at least, would provide partial justice.

* * *

Speaking the truth, we realised quickly in South Africa, would be a pre-requisite for any long-term reconciliation. Furthermore, we learned over the years that seeking and speaking truth required the most serious interrogation of ideologies and racial identities that were long cherished. Some of the core assumptions of the dominant culture had to be challenged. Theories of racial supremacy, mythologies of nationalisms, and naive biblical interpretations had to be examined critically.

In *Speaking the Truth about Zionism and Israel*, a variety of authors examine some of the 'hard truths' about Zionism and Israel. Dr Michael Prior has assembled authors from Israel, Palestine, the US, the UK and Ireland, women and men, Jews, Christians and Muslims, each of whom has a distinguished record of concern for justice in the Holy Land, and several of whom are Friends of Sabeel.

The Jerusalem-based organisation *Sabeel* (in Arabic, 'The Way') is 'a voice in the wilderness' in these violent times. It promotes liberation and reconciliation through non-violence. The roots of *Sabeel* are in the community of indigenous Christians of the Holy Land. I am honoured to be the *Patron of Sabeel International*. Friends of *Sabeel* in the United States, Canada, the United Kingdom, Ireland, Australia, Scandinavia, and elsewhere advocate in favour of peace in the Holy Land. They work to promote more accurate perceptions of the Palestinians by educating

Christians world-wide about the history and identity of the Palestinian Christians, and by forming bonds of friendship between Western Churches and the ancient Mother of All Churches in the Holy Land.

World-wide commitment to peace in the Holy Land is vital. I welcome this book which sets out to question some of the assumptions underpinning the Israeli oppression of the Palestinians. It brings to a concerned world-wide public the reflections of distinguished authors. *Speaking the Truth about Zionism and Israel* is a certain *Voice of the Voiceless*. We in South Africa remember with gratitude the extraordinary phenomenon of the world-wide movement against *apartheid*. And, after years of tribulation, here we are, finally, free! South Africa, once a pariah state, and an embarrassment to many is now a blossoming democracy. And all because people around the world prayed for us, supported us, and were even willing to go to jail for us.

Now, alas, we see *apartheid* in Israel, complete with the 'Separation Wall' and bantustans that keep Palestinians rounded up in prisons. History tragically repeats itself. Yet, injustice and oppression will never prevail. Those who are powerful have to remember the litmus test that God gives to the powerful:'How do you treat the poor, the hungry, and the voiceless?' And God judges accordingly. We need now to put out a clarion call to the government of the people of Israel, to the Palestinian people, saying, 'Peace is possible. Peace based on justice is possible. We will do all we can to assist you to achieve that peace, because it is God's dream, and you will be able to live amicably together as sisters and brothers.'

We in South Africa had a relatively peaceful transition. If the madness which oppressed us could end as it did, it must be possible for the same to happen everywhere else in the world. If peace could come to South Africa, surely it can come to the Holy Land. Somehow, the Israeli government is placed on a pedestal in the US, and to criticise it is to be immediately dubbed antisemitic. People are scared in the US, to say 'wrong is wrong', because the pro-Israeli lobby is powerful—very powerful. Well, so what? For goodness sake, this is God's world! We live in a moral universe. The apartheid government was very powerful, but today it no longer exists. Hitler, Mussolini, Stalin, Pinochet, Milosevic, and Idi Amin were all powerful, but, in the end, they bit the dust.

ZIONISM AND THE CHALLENGE OF HISTORICAL TRUTH AND MORALITY

Michael Prior

The generally benevolent assessment of Zionism and the State of Israel in 'the West' is a result of several factors. Part of the background, of course, is the long history of persecution of Jews in European countries, but the more immediate one was the realisation of what Hitler's extermination programme had achieved: some six million Jews were killed, using all the facilities for mass extermination available to an evil national government. The emaciated condition of the mere 500,000 Jews who had survived in the camps helped to instil in the public mind a concern for ensuring the safety of Jews into the future. US President Roosevelt proposed to solve the immediate problem pragmatically but his plan was not well received by those Jews determined on establishing a nation state in Palestine.[1] For its part, the British government was on record since 1917, viewing 'with favour the establishment in Palestine of a national home for the Jewish people', declaring its 'sympathy with Jewish Zionist aspirations', and determined to 'use their best endeavours to facilitate the achievement of this object' (the Balfour Declaration, 2 November 1917).[2]

---

[1] The president had got Britain to agree that both it and the US would receive up to 150,000 survivors each, and, with such a start, he was confident it would not be difficult to accommodate in other countries the remainder of the total half million. Roosevelt had despatched his emissary, Brigadier General Patrick J Hurley, to report directly to him on the conditions in Palestine. Hurley informed the president that the Zionist Organisation there was intent on establishing a Jewish state, embracing Palestine and probably Transjordan, and transferring the Arab population to Iraq. Somewhat fearful, then, that his rescue plan might not be well received, the president sent his envoy, Morris Ernst, to enquire as to whether there might be Zionist opposition to the president's plan. Ernst was 'thrown out of parlours of friends of mine who very frankly said, "Morris, this is treason. You are undermining the Zionist movement"' (Ernst 1964: 170-77). The president had to abandon his plan.

[2] The British government had good reason to know even before the onset of World War II that the realisation of the Zionist aspirations could not be achieved without fatal damage to 'the civil and religious rights of existing non-Jewish communities in Palestine', to say nothing of the other *caveat* of the Declaration 'that nothing shall be done which may prejudice the rights and political status enjoyed by Jews in any other country.'

Western sympathy for the Zionist aspiration is due in no small measure also to the success with which Zionist ideologues and the historiographers of the State of Israel have hidden from the public the real intentions of the Zionist enterprise, and the realities surrounding the establishment of the state in 1948, and the state's behaviour since. Despite the catastrophic consequences for the people of the region, Israeli public relations and propaganda, thanks to one of the most successful disinformation campaigns in modern times, has succeeded in masking the fact that the creation of the state resulted in the dispossession and dispersion of another people, and that that dispossession was the result of formal planning and ruthless execution. In the more bizarre versions of the 'court history' of Israel, the claim is promulgated that the dislodgement of the Arabs was forced by circumstances upon a broadly benevolent, if not indeed altruistic body of Zionists.

The Zionist narrative ('court history') is repeated over and over again. It has, virtually, 'canonical' (fixed, and revered) status, enjoying some of the privileges one associates only with 'sacred texts'. It is presented as if it were above reproach. It constitutes a veritable primordial truth, the very questioning of which is at least presumptuous, if not downright pernicious. Even in the face of overwhelming evidence to the contrary, the Zionist narrative is solemnly promulgated as if with the confidence that the constant repetition of an untruth ensures its perdurance as a truth. The ploy has worked not only in secular contexts but even in religious and theological circles.

The canonical Zionist narrative

In broad terms, the canonical Zionist historical narrative, followed, after the establishment of the state in 1948, by the canonical Israeli one, makes a number of significant claims. The components of the narrative up to 1967 were almost entirely secular, but, coinciding with the changes that took place on the ground in the wake of the June war, religious elements have been inserted into the narrative, assuming ever greater importance since. We shall review in turn the secular and religious elements of the hegemonic Zionist narrative.

The canonical secular Zionist narrative

The hegemonic secular narrative, affirming the innocent intentions of Zionism, and the virtually irreproachable behaviour of the State of Israel since 1948, includes the following elements:

▢ the existence of Jews outside Palestine is the result solely of their total expulsion from Palestine after the crushing in 70 AD of the great Jewish revolt of 66-70 AD, and that under Bar Kochba in 135 AD;

▢ diaspora Jewish life ever since was fundamentally incomplete;

▢ the Jews 'in exile' forever longed 'to return', and prior to the development of Political Zionism lacked only the opportunity;

▢ Zionism's birth was the inevitable consequence of Gentile pressures and persecution in Europe, which were perennial and ubiquitous;

▢ 'the land [of Palestine] was empty'—or, at least, empty of significant people;

▢ most of the Arab inhabitants came to the country only recently, to benefit from the job opportunities afforded by the Zionist settlement;

▢ the Zionists intended no ill to the Arabs of Palestine— their intentions did not necessitate any clash or displacement;

▢ on the contrary, Zionist intentions would be, broadly, beneficent;

▢ nevertheless, Israel was born into an uncharitable, predatory environment, which 'failed to welcome Jews back to their own home';

▢ Zionist efforts at compromise and conciliation were rejected interminably by the Arabs, who, though far stronger politically and militarily nonetheless lost the 1947-49 war;

▢ on the day after Israel's declaration of independence, the country was invaded 'by the armies of seven Arab states' which, being altogether more powerful than the Zionist forces, were likely to suffocate the fledgling state on the very day of its birth;

☐ in the course of the 1947-49 war, the Palestinian leadership ordered its people to quit their homes and villages, thus laying the Zionists and, later, the Jewish state open to charges of expulsion;

☐ in any case, those who left ('emigrated', in the more extreme expressions) had any of several Arab countries to go to—Jews, on the other hand, had only one sliver of land;

☐ on the question of responsibility for 'the refugees' Israel is free; the responsibility for their welfare devolves on the Arab states which, instead of integrating them into their national polities, leave them destitute;

☐ Zionism never damaged, and indeed benefited the natives, who, nevertheless, remain ungrateful—those Westerners who think otherwise are dupes of Arab propaganda;

☐ the few unsavoury actions in 1947-49 were the result of the stresses of war—otherwise the Zionist fighters and their Israeli successors were models of 'purity of arms';

☐ in the new order, the land, neglected for generations by dissolute and lazy Arab interlopers, was redeemed by Jewish labour, which 'made the desert bloom';

☐ Zionism was purely a Jewish liberation movement, and not at all a colonial one;

☐ the Zionists acted independently of interested imperial powers;

☐ the Zionists introduced into the region its sole democracy, being, indeed, a (secular) utopian 'light to the nations';

☐ all Israel's wars and invasions, and its actions against the Palestinians and others, were purely defensive;

☐ the 1967 war was forced upon Israel, which in occupying territory of three neighbouring states was guided exclusively by the imperative of self-defence;

☐ all efforts to reach an accommodation with the Palestinians, most recently 'the generous offer of Prime Minister Barak', were frustrated by them.

The Six-Day War of June 1967 changed not only the political realities of the region but also the rhetoric of the 'court history'. While virtually all of the narrative before then referred to purely secular affairs,

from 1967 on, religious assertions were inserted into it, with the result that now religious and theological considerations form an integral part of the Zionist discourse. This is true for the majority of Jewish religious leaders, even though the prevailing ideology of Political Zionism was repudiated by religious Jews, and on the lips of some religious leaders—e.g., Britain's Chief Rabbi, Hermann Adler, who met Theodor Herzl, the founder of Political Zionism (1860-1904)—was considered to be contrary to Holy Writ and to Judaism. Since 1967 in particular, the hitherto altogether secular enterprise of Zionism was metamorphosed into a religious one, and even for those Zionists not sympathetic to religious matters the religious dimension entered the national narrative in a fundamental fashion, along the following lines.

The canonical religious Zionist narrative

The religious dimension of the canonical Zionist narrative affirms that:

- Zionism is, fundamentally, a religious enterprise;
- the Zionist programme relates to, or derives its legitimacy from the biblical covenant;
- there is ethnic continuity between the Israelites who captured Canaan and the collective of modern Jewry;
- 'biblical archaeology' confirms such continuity;
- Jews returning to *Eretz Yisrael* can be seen to do so in fulfilment of the Scriptures;
- the Zionist perspective on the Jewish diaspora—that Jews everywhere always longed to 'return home', etc.—conforms to historical realities;
- the victory in 1967 was 'miraculous' and confirmed divine support for the Zionist perspective;
- settling 'Judea and Samaria' derives its legitimacy from the biblical narrative;
- to surrender one square metre of the Promised Land would be a betrayal of God's determination.

The Reception of the Canonical Narrative

The narrative outlined above is consistently taught to Israeli children,[3] and, with varying adherence to its secular or religious tenets, has shaped the minds of generations of Israeli and diaspora Jews. It has also moulded the perceptions of foreign governments and much of the international community. This is not to pretend that Zionism was a monochromatic ideology,[4] or that its proponents would sign up to the totality of the tenets of the canonical narrative. In particular, secular Zionists abhor the religious element, and blame it for much of the modern extremism of the state. In general, religious supporters of the project, and those of the more fascist tendencies of the Right, show little concern for, and no sense of guilty conscience about who had to pay the price for the prize of Zion. The main terms of the canonical narrative, however—the innocent intentions of the Zionist project, its 'purity of arms', its appetite for compromise; etc—are either assumed, or are propagated as self-evident facts. In the light of all the evidence that challenges the canonical narrative I continue to be shocked by the naivety—or, perhaps, it is the disingenuousness—of prominent intellectuals (Jewish and Christian) and Church leaders who not only promulgate the canonical narrative, but

---

[3] Suspicious of the possible impact of the biblical narratives on the formation of conscience, the Israeli socio-psychologist, Georges Tamarin, surveyed the presence of prejudices in the ideology of Israeli youth. He was anxious to evaluate the degree to which an uncritical teaching of notions of the 'chosen people', the superiority of monotheistic religion, and the study of acts of genocide carried out by biblical heroes contributed to the development of prejudice. He chose the Book of Joshua, because of its special position in the Israeli educational system. Tamarin concluded that, 'The uncritical teaching of the Bible—to students too young—even if not taught explicitly as a sacred text, but as national history or in a quasi-neutral atmosphere concerning the real or mythological character of its content, no doubt profoundly affects the genesis of prejudices...even among non-religious students, in accentuating the negative-hostile character of the strangers.' His research brought him unsought and unexpected notoriety and led to his losing his professorship in Tel Aviv University. In a letter to the senate he wrote that while embarking on his scholarly investigation he had never dreamt that he would become the last victim of Joshua's conquest of Jericho. Dr Nilly Keren's subsequent research shows that, while knowing a great deal about antisemitism and the *Shoah*, Israeli children, especially those in the religious sector, have little appreciation of other forms of racism. Her research suggests that the deeper the religious factor in education, the more likely ideological extremism (see further, Prior 1999a: 166-68).

[4] Rather, it expressed itself in a variety of colours: e.g., the Political Zionism of Herzl, the Cultural-Historical Zionism of Ahad Ha'am, the Religious Zionism of the Rabbis Kook, the Syndicalist Zionism of Nahman Syrkin, the Marxist Zionism of Ber Borochov, the Fascist Zionism of Jabotinsky, and Labour Zionism, which dominated the Yishuv and prevailed for the first thirty years of the life of the state until the advent of a Likud-led government in 1977.

do their best to ensure that it is not exposed to questioning. Most recently, the minister of education in the Sharon government has ordered the removal of any textbook, or school syllabus, that refers to the *Nakba*, even marginally. Attempts to challenge the canonical narrative composite character, or even in any one of its tenets, meet with considerable opposition, much of it of a unique character.

Scholars, even, are viewed with particular suspicion, and those who dare challenge the conventional Zionist narrative are treated with disfavour. The disfavour invariably takes the form of attempts to undermine their scholarship in the simplest fashion available, namely by vilifying their persons and questioning their integrity. A scholar who dissents from the canonical narrative is never—not even once—honoured by having the substantive issues addressed in the fashion that is normal in academic discourse. Instead, in a manner reminiscent of the McCarthy era in the US, campuses are watched systematically.[5] Zionist cadres, instructed to press the equiparation of anti-Zionism with antisemitism and racism, and recently called 'to arms' by the explicit directives of the World Zionist Congress of 2002 (see Khalidi 2002), monitor the lectures of those suspected of deviating from the hegemonic Zionist narrative, and report back to their masters. The masters, in turn, who have long since sacrificed academic integrity to Zionist imperatives, deploy their literary skills in composing unflattering dossiers of academics, to be added to the catalogue of dissenters being compiled in a desperate effort to thwart any discussion. Relevant sections of this Portfolio of Dissenters are dutifully sent to universities and other institutes, where pressure is applied by zealots on the ground to withhold, or even withdraw platforms from any of the dissenting scholars on the list of the Campus Watchers. Where relevant, hints are dropped that badly-needed philanthropic—if ideologically-tied—funding might be withdrawn.[6] In their own institutions, pressure is applied to impede the

---

[5] See, e.g., the vigilance of 'CAMPUS WATCH', http://www.campus-watch.org/ accessed on 7 February 2004. Among the other services it renders the academic community is a list of 'Recommended Professors', which contains a number of distinguished '*Nakba*-deniers'.

[6] This is how the system worked in my case. The invitation to me to give a lecture in the Jesuit-run College of the Holy Cross, Worcester, Massachusetts (19 November 2002) was withdrawn. During the course of my US lecture tour I spoke at sixteen academic and Church institutions, including the universities of Notre Dame, Boston, Harvard, and Chicago. Each chose from thirteen lecture topics I proposed (giving an abstract in each case). Holy Cross chose 'The Christian Churches, Zionism and the State of Israel'. The first signs of trouble came on 4 November. My host, Professor David O'Brien requested me 'not to emphasize Zionism in the title', since his 'Jewish colleagues are justifiably concerned

academic tenure of the non-conformists, or to inhibit their promotion. Since integrity is seldom the guiding principle of much of successful academia much of the pressure works, particularly, but not exclusively, in the US.

So sensitive are Zionists to preserving their meganarrative unchallenged that their fury is turned on even those scholars who challenge the naive Zionist reading concerning even 'Ancient Israel'. The invective one detects in that debate assures one that more is at stake than customary objective scholarship in search of an elusive past. The academic transgression, of course, consists in trespassing on a carefully protected

---

... [at any lectures] leaning against Israel.' 'Most of our Jewish faculty', he assured me, 'are among the strongest supporters of the college and its Jesuit mission.' In thanking me 'for coming', he asked if I would approve the change of title. I readily agreed (5 November)! The following day O'Brien asked if I would 'object if I invited a friendly local rabbi to join us and offer an initial comment after your talk?' After consulting the hosts of my lecture tour, I replied (7 November) that I would be delighted if any rabbi were to come, but that I would not think it appropriate to invite any individual member of the audience to make an initial comment. Nevertheless, on that same day, O'Brien wrote that 'Politically it would be helpful if I could state that Rabbi David Coyne, Director of Hillel at nearby Clark University, would serve as a respondent. I replied (10 November) that I would find it very odd indeed for an overseas speaker to be invited to give a public lecture, which would be followed by a response from any invited respondent, from whatever interest group (Jewish Zionist, Jewish anti-Zionist, Christian Zionist, Christian anti-Zionist, Palestinian Christian, Palestinian Muslim, etc., and if one, why not the lot?). Such a procedure, I added, would be normal in a debate. I would, of course, be pleased to deal with questions or comments from any member of the audience. O'Brien thanked me (10 November), assuring me 'I look forward to meeting you November 19'. Nevertheless, on 12 November, the eve of my departure for the US, I received notification from Professor O'Brien that he was withdrawing the invitation to speak 'to save Holy Cross some further unnecessary division'. On receipt of protest letters, O'Brien attempted to explain his decision, ('To Interested Parties' 13 November). It appears that the Kraft-Hiatt Committee of the college would not accept O'Brien's invitation to me: 'local Jewish leaders ... had been informed that the College had invited an anti-Zionist, perhaps anti-Semitic, speaker', and to prevent 'a campus and community media event that would bring further division to the College and faculty', he yielded to the pressure. After I got back to London I wrote to the president of the college regretting that 'Rather than provide a forum for the dissemination of my perspectives, Holy Cross has chosen to be swayed by the charges of what appears to be a certain pro-Israeli lobby which has earned a not-undeserved reputation in the university sector for chronic mendacity and altogether disedifying behaviour.' I requested that the college send me and my hosts in the USA an apology. Father McFarland later 'regretted the inconvenience' caused me, but 'stood by his man'. The text of my lecture is available in *New Blackfriars* 83 (no. 980, October 2002): 471-89. The text of my letter to the president is available at http://www.al-bushra.org/hedchrch/jesuit.html, accessed on 7 February 2004. Other letters of protest can be found by searching 'Michael Prior' + 'Holy Cross' on the internet.

discourse on 'Ancient Israel' that has implications for the legitimacy of developments in Palestine in our own time. Those who violate the sanctuary of the canonical discourse which carefully nurtures anachronisms concerning the ethnic identity of 'Israelites', 'Canaanites', etc. and highlight the discrepancies between the biblical narrative and other evidence, much of it archaeological, are sure to be sidelined as 'ideologically motivated' and are vilified, with respect to both their scholarship and their persons.[7] One such scholar of 'Ancient Israel', at least, has had to suffer death threats. Publishers, too, are intimidated, in the desperate hope that the lid can be kept on the pot, lest some uncomfortable truth escape. Sometimes the pressure is subtle, at other times brash and arrogant. Not infrequently, with commercial imperatives prevailing over that of the dissemination of truth, publishers conform.[8]

Challenging the Canonical Zionist Narrative

Nevertheless, despite all attempts to stifle it the truth emerges, however slowly. Recent scholarship has produced evidence from a range of disciplines—history, political science, theology, biblical studies, archaeology, ethnology, etc.—that, cumulatively, is fatal to the canonical Zionist narrative. In my *The Bible and Colonialism. A Moral Critique* (1997),

---

[7] See the discussion on History and Narrative in Prior 1999a: 176-80. See also the *apologia* of Niels Peter Lemche, one of the 'minimalists' (Lemche 2000).

[8] In November 1995, I went by arrangement to discuss with Sheffield Academic Press my draft MS on 'The Bible and Zionism'. The press had already published two of my monographs. Before even looking at the MS, the editor said, 'We simply could not publish a book with such a title.' He suggested that I extend the discussion to include the uses of the Bible with respect to Latin America, South Africa, as well as Israel. Thus was born my *The Bible and Colonialism. A Moral Critique* (1997). Therein I promised (note 2, p. 259) that I would discuss elsewhere the more theological aspects of Zionism. In conformity with the terms of my contract with Sheffield Academic Press I submitted a draft MS of my *Zionism and the State of Israel: A Moral Inquiry* in November 1997. Even though the anonymous reader found it to be 'a brilliant book which must be published', the press declined, because, I was informed orally—none of this was in writing, of course—it had 'a very strong Jewish list', and could not offend that constituency. They would boycott its publications and refuse to submit their own MSS, as a result of which 'our specialised press would go under.' An American publishing company judged the MS to be 'a prodigious achievement of historical and theological investigation', and 'a very important work' it deemed that it would not suit its publishing program. Routledge, finally, 'bit the bullet' (Prior 1999a).

Zionism and the State of Israel. A Moral Inquiry (1999a), and other articles, I present a range of evidence from recent scholarship that challenges conventional 'truths' and contradicts the ingredients of the canonical Zionist historical narrative, rendering it unsustainable not only ethically but in academic terms. It is not possible in this essay to do more than indicate the substance of the new scholarship, and point interested readers to seek out more details elsewhere. The new evidence demands a thorough reassessment of the Zionist-Arab conflict and much else besides, and points to some of the ethical and theological implications of such a reassessment.

The Challenge of the New Historiography on 1948

The elements of the canonical Zionist narrative on 1948—that Zionists intended no ill to the Arabs of Palestine, who left their homes and villages at the orders of the Palestinian leadership who had malicious intent; the few unsavoury Zionist actions were the result of the stresses of war; etc.— stood unchallenged not only in the West but in Israel itself. One might have expected the victims of the Zionist triumph, the Palestinians, to have challenged the hegemonic Zionist narrative of lies and half-truths, and produced their own narrative. As late as 1995, however, the late Edward Said lamented their failure in not having done so.[9] Even by then, the story of the loss, both in 1948 and 1967, had not been told by the Palestinians themselves, but, in so far as it had been told at all, it had been partially reconstructed either by Israelis or foreigners. Said attributed that neglect not only to Palestinian powerlessness but also to its collective incompetence. It was no longer acceptable, he pleaded, to repose in the customary comfort of lamentation.

Meanwhile, in Israeli society there were the beginnings of a questioning of the direction of Israeli policies and of the society itself. Some of the impetus for this development came by way of reaction to what its proponents judged to be the immoral occupation of the West Bank and the Gaza Strip. The events of 1948, of course, remained above reproach. There was no appetite to compromise on the question of the 'right of return' of the 1948 refugees, for example, or to abandon the

---

[9] Keynote Lecture at the *International Conference on Jerusalem* in London in 1995.

basic principles of Labour Zionism. For the Israeli 'Left', the moral rot had set in only in the wake of the 1967 war. Whereas one might have expected a labour movement to embrace the concerns of the Israeli Jews from Arab lands, in fact the opposition championed their cause, leading to the election victory of 1977, after which Menachem Begin became Prime Minister. That election was an earthquake in Israeli politics, when the pariahs of Zionism had replaced the party that built the nation. Begin, an erstwhile terrorist (leader of the *Irgun*, 1943-48), had come in from the political cold.

The disenchanted followers of the Labour Party and of parties further to the Left, projecting themselves and their brand of Zionism as being in line with Western liberal thinking, railed against the occupation, and gave birth to the 'Peace Now' movement (1978). It later became a focus of significant opposition to the Lebanon war (1978-82), in which Israel 'for the first time' had embarked on an aggressive war. While it remained active throughout the first *Intifada* (1987-93) 'Peace Now' was dormant during Yitzhak Rabin's Labour-led government (1993-95). The moral criterion according to which the occupation was judged to be unacceptable was that it was bad, not so much for the damage it was doing to its victims, but, rather, because it was corrupting its perpetrators. The occupation was 'bad for the Jews', i.e., it was corrupting the otherwise high moral character of Israel. But if it was 1967 and its corrupting aftermath that caused moral perturbation to the Peace Camp who had no problem with 1948 or the comportment of the state since its foundation, towards the end of the 1980s, a number of Israeli scholars were beginning to write about the past, especially 1948 itself, in a way which contradicted the canonical Zionist-Israeli historical narrative. Some of the most sacred 'historical truths' of that narrative were being debunked. Moreover, in the overall international context the Zionist conquest of Palestine was appearing rather eccentric.

In an age when indigenous peoples throughout the world were throwing off the shackles of colonialism and imperialism—Jordan, the Philippines, India, Pakistan, Ceylon, etc. already from the mid 1940s— and the West itself was becoming increasingly embarrassed by its history of colonialism, the very nature of the Zionist conquest was beginning to appear anomalous. While a 'pigmentocracy' would manage to survive for another generation in apartheid South Africa the prospect of a Jewish 'ethnocracy' in Palestine rested less than comfortably on Western liberal

shoulders. Already by 1945 the European nations in particular were embarking on a programme of decolonisation which was to last right up to the end of the century. 'Colonialism' was a bad word.

Zionists, too, were becoming embarrassed by any association of Zionism with colonialism, preferring the language of 'liberation'. The early Zionists, of course, had no such scruples, as the names of some of their associations illustrate: the Jewish Colonisation Association, the Society for the Colonisation of the Land of Israel, the Palestine Jewish Colonisation Association, the Jewish Colonial Trust, etc. Moreover, Herzl looked to the support of Bismarck, 'the greatest living empire builder' (1960: 120), and of Cecil Rhodes, a role model in matters colonial (1960: 1193-94). Furthermore, the Twelfth Zionist Congress set up a 'Colonisation Department'. Likewise, Chaim Weizmann compared the Zionist movement with the French colonisation of Tunisia (1949: 191). Zionism also deployed the full battery of colonialist attitudes, not least a disdain for the indigenous population. A core element of the stereotypical colonialist rhetoric is that adventurous Europeans pioneered in a savage wilderness and brought civilisation to it. Such language, however, would be less than convincing to liberal ears. As elsewhere, in rationalising the subjugation of the indigenes, moral scruples would have to be stifled and embarrassing facts suppressed. These, however, would eventually force themselves to the surface, not least in Israel itself.

The 'post-Zionist' authors[10]—the general term given them by the Israeli press—while not acting in unison, offered a formidable inner-Israeli criticism of Zionism, and showed how the Jewish state had been built on the ruins of the indigenous Arabs of Palestine.[11] The disjuncture between what actually happened to the indigenous Arab population of Palestine in 1947-49 and the official Israeli version was striking.

The Israeli government pamphlet on the refugee question, first published in 1953, proclaimed that the Palestinian Arabs were induced or incited to leave temporarily by express instructions broadcast by the president of the Arab Higher Executive. The absence of corroborating evidence, and the presence of abundant proof to expose it as false were straining the myth. Even the report of the intelligence branch of the

---

[10] The group included Simha Flapan (1979 and 1987), Baruch Kimmerling (1983), Benny Morris (1987, 1990, 1993 and 1999), Ilan Pappé (1988 and 1992), Tom Segev (1986), Israel Shahak (1975), and Avi Shlaim (1988).

[11] See the description and analysis of the post-Zionist tendency in Pappé 2002.

Israel Defence Force ('Emigration of the Arabs of Palestine in the Period 1.12.1947–1.6.1948') ascribes the flight of 72 percent of the Palestinian refugees (some 391,000 people during that critical period) to Israeli military force. In other words, the ethnic cleansing was well underway before the declaration of the state, and the invasion by 'the Arab armies'. Moreover, the available evidence stresses that the exodus was *contrary* to the desires of the Arab Higher Committee and the neighbouring Arab states. In fact, Arab broadcasts encouraged the population to stay put, to the extent of issuing threats to stave off the exodus (see Hitchens 1988: 75). The myth is still repeated, despite the fact that already in 1961 Erskine Childers revealed that as a guest of the Israeli Foreign Office in 1958 he requested to see the primary evidence for the charge that the Palestinians had been urged to flee by the Arab leadership. Despite claims of 'a mountain of evidence' and a 'wealth of evidence', no evidence, though promised, was produced then, or since (London's *Spectator* 12 May 1961). Moreover, there was abundant evidence for systematic 'horror recordings' and a 'psychological blitz' on the part of the Yishuv to clear the area of Arabs (see Childers 1987: 183–202).

The new evidence was showing how even the grandees of Labour Zionism played their part in the ethnic cleansing. In addition to the general overseeing role of David Ben-Gurion, Yitzhak Rabin presided over some of the most ruthless expulsions of the 1948 war. On 12 July, after the slaughter of more than 250 Arabs in Lydda, Head of Operations Rabin ordered: 'The inhabitants of Lydda must be expelled quickly without attention to age … Yiftah (Brigade HQ) must determine the method.' Although a similar order was issued for the expulsion of the inhabitants of neighbouring Ramle, Israeli historians during the 1950s, 1960s and 1970s insisted that the inhabitants had violated the terms of surrender, and 'were happy at the possibility given them of evacuating' (Morris 1990: 2–3). Rabin's admission that what happened in Lydda and Ramle had been 'expulsions' was excised from his text by Israeli government censors, but to his embarrassment *The New York Times* later published the offending passage (23 October 1979—see Kidron 1988: 90–94). Already in 1990, Benny Morris, one of the most prominent of the 'New Historians' confessed that, if pressed to evaluate morally the Yishuv's policies and behaviour in 1948, he would be loath to condemn, and opined that 'any sane, pragmatic leader' would have done the same (Morris 1990: 20–21). Later, in January 2004 as we shall see, the same

Morris would lament that the war crimes were not sufficiently robust.

Ben-Gurion's ultimate intention was to evacuate as many Arabs as possible from the Jewish state, using a range of methods: an economic war to destroy Arab transport, commerce and the supply of foods and raw materials; psychological warfare, ranging from 'friendly warnings' to intimidation and exploitation of panic caused by underground terrorism; and the destruction of whole villages and the eviction of their inhabitants by the army (Flapan 1987: 92). Plan Gimmel, and Plan Dalet of April 1948, before the declaration of independence, show the determination to rid the land of Arabs in 1948. Moreover, Israel's real, but publicly undeclared intentions are confirmed by its ongoing insistence up to the present day on not allowing the Palestinians to return: 'Israelis like to argue whether the Arabs escaped voluntarily or were expelled by us. As if this made any difference. We could always have let them return after the war'.[12]

'Self-defence' can be applied only in an Orwellian sense to the conquest of 1947-49, and later the aggression against Egypt in 1956, the invasion of Lebanon in 1978 and 1982, and the frequent bombardments of Lebanon since. The myth of Israel's self-perception as morally superior in its 'purity of arms'—the slogan of the Haganah in 1948—also has had to be abandoned in the face of the evidence. That Jews, too, were capable of committing atrocities has been comprehensively unmasked, not least by Benny Morris.

Thus, the perspective of the Palestinian victims of the Zionist project was beginning to surface and force its way into the Zionist narrative. For its part, the academic community was being forced to come face to face with not only some of the sordid reality of 1948 and since, but also how the academy had hitherto steadfastly advanced the canonical narrative of history. The research of the 'New Historians'—based largely on recently declassified archival sources, and ongoing inquiry into the lives of the ordinary people in the conflict—however divergent in details of interpretation, manifestly delegitimised many of the foundational claims of the Zionist historical narrative. It gave more credence than hitherto to Palestinian historiography, and demanded a considerable reassessment of the Arab-Israeli conflict. The interdisciplinary methodology of the 'New Historiography' viewed with a certain

---

[12] 'The 1948 Refugees are the Original Sin of Israeli Society', *Ha'aretz* 5 December 1993.

scepticism all historical narratives which are the product of nationalist elites and ideologies, and was critical of how the establishment Israeli academy had covered up what was unsavoury. Worse was to come.

The challenge of the Zionist Population Transfer Imperative

It was one thing to have to face the facts concerning 1948—that to the accompaniment of massacres, threats, rapes, etc., 80 percent of the Arabs in what became the State of Israel were expelled, and more than 400 of their villages were destroyed to ensure they could not return—it was quite another to acknowledge that the ethnic cleansing was not merely due to the strains of war, but was an integral part of the Zionist programme from the beginning. Yet, this discovery should not have been altogether shattering for Zionists. The population-transfer imperative was well recognised by the founder of Political Zionism himself, although, of course, he did not publish the fact. Herzl cared little, if at all, for the rights of the Arab inhabitants of Palestine, who constituted 95 percent of the population, and who would have to be got out of the 'state for Jews' (*Der Judenstaat*). He was careful in his public pronouncements, of course, to pretend that his project would not have any deleterious effect on the Arab population. On the contrary, he pretended, it would be to their benefit.

A close study of Herzl's *ipsissima verba*—particularly as reflected in his private diaries—published in seven volumes in the period 1983-96, lays bare his attitudes to the indigenous non-Jewish population of Palestine. Among the issues he discusses in his diary entries for 12 June 1895 was his proposal for a transition from a Jewish *society* in the land to forming a *state* for Jews. This would require occupation, the expropriation of the private property, and the ethnic cleansing of the land:

> We shall endeavour to expel the poor population across the border unnoticed, procuring employment for it in the transit countries, but denying it any employment in our own country.[13]

---

[13] My translation of Herzl's, 'Die arme Bevölkerung trachten wir unbemerkt über die Grenze zu schaffen, indem wir in den Durchzugsländern Arbeit verschaffen aber in unserem eigenen Lande jederlei Arbeit verweigern' (Herzl 1983: 117-18, in Prior 1999a: 9).

Herzl added that both 'the process of expropriation and the removal of the poor must be carried out discreetly and circumspectly.'

In seeking support for his project, Herzl reflected typical nineteenth-century European colonialist-imperialist attitudes. His proposed state for Jews would be 'a portion of the rampart of Europe against Asia, an outpost of civilisation [Herzl's term was *Kultur*] opposed to barbarism'.[14] Elsewhere he reflects the world-view of European racist superiority. He assured the Grand Duke of Baden that Jews returning to their 'historic fatherland' would do so as representatives of Western civilisation, bringing 'cleanliness, order and the well-established customs of the Occident to this plague-ridden, blighted corner of the Orient'.[15] In Joseph Conrad's terms, Herzl's state for Jews would be an 'outpost of progress' in 'the heart of darkness'.

Such attitudes can be detected also in Herzl's novel *Altneuland* ('Old New Land'), completed in 1902 but set in 1923 and for European consumption. The modern, secular Jewish commonwealth was a haven of the liberal spirit and a blessing for the natives.[16] Not only did it bring its hero, David Littwak, from rags in Vienna to riches in Haifa—from being a 'Jewboy beggar' to having a gatekeeper, two footmen, servants, magnificent works of art, and chandeliers of silver and gold crystal, etc., and finally, to his being President of the New Society—it was a haven of philanthropy and voluntary service. Before the advent of the New Society. in Jaffa 'The alleys were dirty, neglected, full of vile odors. Everywhere misery in bright Oriental rags. Poor Turks, dirty Arabs, timid Jews lounged about—indolent, beggarly, hopeless. A peculiar, tomblike odor of mold caught one's breath' (p. 42). 'The once royal city of Jerusalem could have sunk no lower' (p. 44). The only bright light were the Jewish colonies (Rishon-le-Zion, Rehobot, and others) which 'lay like oases in the desolate countryside' (p. 47). In the Valley of Jezreel of 1923, one no longer saw 'the filthy nests that used to be called villages in Palestine,' but innumerable Jewish settlements (p.120). To the visiting Christian, Mr Kingscourt, who had asked, 'Were not the older inhabitants of Palestine ruined by the Jewish immigration? And didn't they have to leave the country?', the Palestinian Rashid Bey, himself also a member of the New Society, replied, 'What a question! It was a great blessing for all of us' (pp. 121-22). The

---

[14] Herzl 1896, in the Pordes edition 1993: 30.
[15] *The Complete Diaries*, Vol. I: 343, in the Patai edition.
[16] *Old New Land* (Herzl 2000), to which the page indicators refer.

Arabs were better off than at anytime in the past (p. 124). To the further question, 'Don't you regard these Jews as intruders?', Rashid Bey insisted, 'Would you call a man a robber who takes nothing from you, but brings you something instead? 'The Jews have enriched us, why should we be angry with them. They dwell among us like brothers. Why should we not love them?' (p. 124).

The real Herzl, of course, was in no doubt about what was necessary to establish a state for Jews in a land already inhabited. He was not alone in his determination to rid the land of its indigenous Arabs. The Zionist archives confirm the consistency of the transfer imperative within the Yishuv leadership. Those dissenting from it did so on grounds of impracticality rather than morality.

While the subsequent Zionist leaders also were determined to keep their plans secret they did, however, leave behind not only the physical outcome in 1948 of their transfer enterprise, but also a considerable body of written material which indicates clearly their intentions. There is a 'mountain' of evidence in the Zionist and Israeli archives tracing the consistency of the 'population transfer' line of thinking within the Jewish leadership in Palestine. This evidence has been systematically examined by Nur Masalha, and has been brought to public attention since the early 1990s.

From the Zionist archives we learn in detail how prominent was the theme of the necessity of 'transfer' in the thinking of the Zionist leadership from the middle 1930s, at least. We read of the establishment and comportment of the two 'Population Transfer Committees' (1937 to 1944), and of the third 'Population Transfer Committee' established by the government of the State of Israel in August 1948. The damage done to the indigenous population in 1948, then, was neither accidental nor due to the unique pressures of war, but was at the heart of the Zionist enterprise from the beginning. The Palestinian *Nakba* ('Catastrophe') was foreseen as necessary, was systematically planned and was executed at the first opportunity, in 1948, both before and after the declaration of the State of Israel.[17]

---

[17] See Masalha 1992 for a comprehensive treatment of the expulsion imperative in Zionist ideology from the beginning to the establishment of the state, and Masalha 1997 which illustrates the transfer programme 1949-96. Masalha 2000 is a comprehensive treatment of the imperial imperative within Herzlian Zionism. His *The Politics of Denial: Israel and the Palestinian Refugee Problem* (2003) exposes Israel's pretence to innocence on the question of the Palestinian expulsees.

Masalha's studies, based on primary research in various Zionist archives, fundamentally undermine the hegemonic Zionist narrative that its intentions were altogether innocent, if not indeed altruistic. By uncovering such evidence Masalha demonstrates that the imperative to 'transfer' the indigenous Arab population was at the core of the Zionist enterprise from the beginning, and was pursued with determination at the levels of both planning and execution. His contribution to the discourse on 1948 is more complete than that of the Israeli 'New Historians', for he not only lets the Zionist evidence concerning 1948 speak for itself, but also shows how prominent was the necessity of 'transfer' in the thinking of the Zionist leadership right from the beginning.

On coping with the new historiography: the new Benny Morris

Benny Morris' books describe some of the atrocities of the *Nakba*, and he, too, drew attention to how the incriminating Zionist documents were falsified, and published version of diaries (e.g., of Yosef Weitz and Ben-Gurion) intentionally 'doctored'. The fabricators of propagandistic Zionist history were, he had concluded, among the most accomplished practitioners of the strange craft of source-doctoring, rewriting not only their history, but the documents upon which such a history was based. The propagandistic intent was evident, particularly in removing references to the 'transfer' intentions of the Yishuv, and all references to massacres, rapes and expulsions (Morris 1995: 44, 56-57). The aim was to hide things said and done, and to bequeath to posterity only a sanitised version of the past. Morris suggested that the IDF's behaviour at least down to 1953 reflected a pervasive attitude that Arab life was cheap and that only Jewish life was sacred. Killing, torturing, beating and raping Arab infiltrators was not particularly reprehensible and might well go unpunished (Morris 1993: 166).

Morris confirmed that in the months of April-May 1948, units of the Haganah were given operational orders to uproot the villagers, expel them and destroy the villages. Altogether, he documents about a dozen rapes—some of them gang-soldier ones—which usually ended with murder.[18] He concedes that the number (a dozen) is merely the tip of the

---

[18] The quotations which follow are taken from Morris' interview with Ari Shavit, published in *Ha'aretz* (8 January 2004): 'Survival of the fittest', www. haaretzdaily.com, accessed on 9 January 2004.

iceberg. He documents some twenty-four cases of Israeli massacres in 1948. Moreover, he argues that, from April 1948, Ben-Gurion created a consensus in favour of transfer:

> Ben-Gurion was a transferist. He understood that there could be no Jewish state with a large and hostile Arab minority in its midst ... Ben-Gurion was right. If he had not done what he did, a state would not have come into being. That has to be clear. It is impossible to evade it. Without the uprooting of the Palestinians, a Jewish state would not have arisen here ... In certain conditions, expulsion is not a war crime. I don't think that the expulsions of 1948 were war crimes. You can't make an omelet without breaking eggs. You have to dirty your hands.

Morris 'understands' the perpetrators and their motives. In their place he, too, would not have felt pangs of conscience. On the contrary, 'Without that act [*Operation Dani*, whereby 50,000 were expelled from Lod], they would not have won the war and the state would not have come into being.' 'Moreover, in the choice between ethnic cleansing and genocide—the annihilation of your [sic!] people— I prefer ethnic cleansing.' Although 'it doesn't sound nice' Morris adopted the term 'cleanse' (to 'cleanse' the hinterland, the border areas, the main roads, the villages, etc.) 'from all the 1948 documents in which I am immersed.'

Moreover, the need to establish the state for Jews overrode the injustice that was done to the Palestinians by uprooting them. Even the great American democracy, he claims, could not have been created without the annihilation of the Indians. There are cases, Morris assures us, 'in which the overall, final good justifies harsh and cruel acts that are committed in the course of history. And in our case it effectively justifies a population transfer.' In Morris' moral universe, 'small war crimes' are acceptable. In comparison to massacres perpetrated in Bosnia, the some 800 Palestinians who were massacred or executed is 'peanuts', and is 'chicken feed' compared to the numbers the Russians massacred at Stalingrad. In all, 'taking account that there was a bloody civil war here and that we lost an entire 1 percent of the population, you find that we behaved very well.'

For Morris, then, the only moral objection to Ben-Gurion's ethnic cleansing policy was that it was not sufficiently thorough:

> I think he [Ben-Gurion] made a serious historical mistake in 1948. Even though he understood the demographic issue and the need to establish a Jewish state without a large Arab minority, he got cold feet during the war. In the end, he faltered ... If he was already engaged in expulsion, maybe he should have done a complete job. I know that this stuns the Arabs and the liberals and the politically correct types. But my feeling is that this place would be quieter and know less suffering if the matter had been resolved once and for all. If Ben-Gurion had carried out a large expulsion and cleansed the whole country—the whole Land of Israel, as far as the Jordan River. It may yet turn out that this was his fatal mistake. If he had carried out a full expulsion—rather than a partial one—he would have stabilized the State of Israel for generations ... If the end of the story turns out to be a gloomy one for the Jews, it will be because Ben-Gurion did not complete the transfer in 1948... As an historian, I assert that a mistake was made here. Yes. The non-completion of the transfer was a mistake.

Morris, however, would not 'at this moment' support the transfer and expulsion of the Arabs from the West Bank, Gaza and perhaps even from Galilee and the Triangle. Such would be neither moral nor realistic. Not realistic, apparently, because the Arab world would not allow it, and not moral, echoing the 'not-good-for-the-Jews' criterion of morality, because 'it would destroy the Jewish society from within.' But in other, apocalyptic, circumstances, which are liable to be realized in five or ten years, in the context of a war, 'acts of expulsion will be entirely reasonable. They may even be essential.' It will, of course, include the Israeli Arabs, who, he says, 'are a time bomb', 'an emissary of the enemy that is among us,' 'a potential fifth column'. 'If the threat to Israel is existential, expulsion will be justified.' Meanwhile, 'Something like a cage has to be built for them [the Palestinian Arabs, or at least the Muslim ones, since he does not mention the Christians throughout] ...There is no choice. There is a wild animal there that has to be locked up in one way or another.'

Thus we see the metamorphosis of Labour/Meretz supporter Benny Morris, 'the great documenter of the sins of Zionism'—and once reviled for doing so—into a supporter of those sins, and a critic of them only insofar as they were not sufficiently grievous. Far from condemning the 'small war crimes' of 1948, Professor Morris now laments that they were not bigger, and carried out with greater effect. If anyone reading Morris's books in the 1990s—however much one lamented that his conclusions fell far short of the evidence he had produced—presumed that, being human, he would be ashamed that all of that was done in the name of the collective of Jews, his interview with Ari Shavit is sufficient to disavow him.

Without suggesting that Morris acts as a barometer of the Israeli Left—he still insists on proclaiming his Left credentials—indicating a profound shift of the movement towards the Right, his moral mutation does reflect a development in thinking which may pave the way for a new attitude to the past. Rather than being embarrassed by the revelation of the atrocities associated with the Zionist project—the details of which were studiously hidden from public scrutiny, and formally denied in the canonical Zionist narrative—the new ideologues may well lament the incompleteness of the moral turpitude, and long for the day when amends can be made for the incompleteness of the ravages of 1948. Translated into the terms of the canonical Zionist narrative, this would read that, since the Zionists committed atrocities before in the higher goal of establishing a state for Jews, history has bequeathed the State of Israel the licence to complete the job.

The Biblical Narrative: Canonical 'Ancient Israel'

The injustice done by Zionists to the indigenous population of Palestine has, until recently, been passed over in much Western discourse. Indeed, in some religious circles the Zionist enterprise is even clothed in the garment of piety. This is obviously the case in the Christian Zionist constituency, but adulation for the Zionist project is apparent also in the mainstream. People involved in Jewish-Christian dialogue, in particular, deploy a unique vocabulary of favour, not least in describing its culmination as 'The Miracle of Israel's Rebirth'.[19] Characteristically, also,

---

[19] 'The living reality of the State of Israel should evoke the respect and admiration of the Christian theologian. How could the renewal of the land be anything to the theologian

they repeat the whole range of the canonical Zionist narrative. Herzl the Zionist visionary, we learn, pursued his 'messianic pilgrimage' with a zeal 'infused with a compelling humanitarianism combined with traces of Jewish mysticism'. And now that Herzl has died, the 'mystery' and 'majesty' of Zionism appears in its glory from his tomb (Drinan 1977: 32, 39); the Zionists never intended any disadvantage to the Palestinians; the Arabs 'emigrated' from Israel in 1947 and 1948, despite 'the objective evidence that Israelis in many instances urged Arab residents to remain'; etc. Typically there is no mention of the destruction of the Palestinian villages, and no reference to natural justice or the imperatives of international law—even from Jesuit Father Robert F Drinan, former Dean of Boston College Law School, who was a member of the US House of Representatives (Democrat-Massachusetts) for a ten-year period (Drinan 1977). I have shown elsewhere how the Jewish-Christian dialogue as we know it is altogether subservient to the programme of Political Zionism (Prior 2003a).

Western support for the Zionist enterprise is particularly striking from a moral perspective. Whereas elsewhere the perpetrators of colonial plunder are objects of opprobrium, the Zionist conquest is widely judged to be a just and appropriate accomplishment, with even unique religious significance. How was this possible? The answer lies in the Bible, and its religious authority.

Colonisers invariably seek out some ideological principle to justify their actions, and when these involve dubious deeds of exploitation the search is all the more intense. Awaiting the turn of the tide on the Thames as he embarked on another colonial expedition, Joseph Conrad's Marlow, musing on the whole enterprise of imperial conquest, noted that 'the conquest of the earth is not a pretty thing when you look into it too much'. Indeed, it was 'just robbery with violence, aggravated murder on a great scale, and men going at it blind—as is very proper for those who tackle a darkness'. Conquerors needed only brute force, and a justifying ideology. 'What redeems it is

---

but a wonder of love and vitality, and the reborn state be anything but a sign of God's concern for his people? (Monsignor John Oesterreicher, in Fisher, Rudin and Tanenbaum 1986: 35), and Christians should 'rejoice in the return of the Jewish people to a small sliver of their ancient homeland—if not from compassion and a sense of justice at least from a sense of guilt and repentance' (Father Edward Flannery, in Fisher, Rudin and Tanenbaum 1986: 76).

the idea only. An idea at the back of it ... and an unselfish belief in the idea—something you can set up, and bow down before, and offer a sacrifice to ...' (*Heart of Darkness*, pp. 31-32).

A perusal of the emerging nationalisms which burgeoned throughout Europe in the second half of the 19th century quickly reveals the attempt to root each one in a glorious past of heroes and even demigods. In addition to fabricating continuity with whatever glories one could detect in the nation's real history, the domain of folklore was mined assiduously in the attempt to link up the ordinariness of contemporary life with a putatively eminent national past. National groups invariably constructed a foundational nationalist narrative consisting of not only historical memories, but of *myths of origins*. Where possible and desirable, religion was mobilised to sacralise national sentiment. In the case of Zionism, however, there was a problem, beyond that posed by the fact that its ideologues were stridently anti-religious. Judaism's holiest collection of books, the Talmud, which was accorded precedence over even the *Torah*,[20] since its deliberations constituted the ultimate source on all matters of Jewish comportment (*Halakha*), was next to useless.[21] Despite its prominence in Jewish life, it was worse than useless in promoting Political Zionism.

Although the Talmud had been central to Jewish identity since medieval times, it did not offer anything like the support necessary to advance the Zionist project. It had no glorious story of a nation, few heroic figures, and little narrative of a glorious past. And, most critically, it did not promote any particular relationship to an ancient homeland, nor advance the sentiment of longing to return. It could scarcely promote the ideal of Political Zionism, since it had no 'geography which arouses longing in the reader or a sense of connection to an ancient home' (Halbertal 1997: 131). Rather than lamenting exile, and longing to return home, the perspective of the Talmud accepted the exile as determined by God, and any attempt to end it before the coming of the Messiah would be an abomination. Instead, the Talmud concentrated

---

[20] The first five books of the Hebrew Bible, named, in English, Genesis, Exodus, Leviticus, Numbers and Deuteronomy, and their divine provenance is encapsulated in the phrase *Torah min haShamayim* (the Torah is from heaven).

[21] The two extant forms of the Talmud, the Palestinian and the Babylonian, were compiled during the 5th century AD, using much earlier material. They embody the *Mishnah* (oral teaching) and the *Gemara* (discussion on the *Mishnah*).

on living out the details of the Jewish law in any and every experience of daily life, wherever a Jew found her/himself. Rather than reflecting sentiments of longing and return, its overall thrust was antipathetic to Political Zionism.

The Bible, on the other hand, provided many of the ingredients of a 'master narrative', in particular, those relating to the promised land, exile from, and return to it, elements that easily fed into the Zionist project of establishing a state for Jews in the ancient homeland of Palestine. In the biblical narrative there was a first 'exile' in Egypt, a second in Babylon, from each of which there was a homecoming. Now, close on 2,000 years after the Romans 'exiled Jews in their entirety from Palestine'—which they did not, of course—Zionism would gather them in. The Bible's 'exile-return' motif, then, provided the necessary 'foundation myth' or 'master commemorative narrative' for Zionism. To this day, as David Gunn has shown, quotations from the Bible are presented on the top of pages on the website of the Israeli Ministry of Foreign Affairs, like religious proof-texts, lending (divine) authority to the achievements of Zionism.[22] That the Bible read in its totality implies that exile invariably follows settlement because of the injustice of the leaders—'Exile is potentially only an injustice away' (Gunn 2003: 260)—however, is conveniently ignored.

The link between the Bible and Zionism is firmly established in the popular mind also.[23] Zionism's claims to exclusive Jewish title to the 'land of Israel' (*Eretz Yisrael*) are constantly predicated on the basis of the Bible, particularly of the narratives of the promise of land to Abraham and his descendants (Genesis 12-50), the preparation for entry into the land (Exodus, Leviticus, Numbers and Deuteronomy) and the execution of the promise in the narrative of Joshua's conquest (Joshua). Even for secular or atheist nationalists, uninterested in it as the repository of a theological claim, the biblical narrative can be invoked to function as the 'historical account' of Jews' title to the land. Thus, for Ben-Gurion, Israel's first prime minister, the Bible was the 'Jews' sacrosanct title-deed to

---

[22] 'Facts About Israel (1996)', at www.mfa.gov.il/mfa/go.asp?MFAH00080.

[23] The Google search engine has some 44,800 entries for the combination 'Bible' + 'Zionism' (accessed on 3 February 2004), many, of course, representing the view that there is no essential connection between the two.

Palestine ... with a genealogy of 3,500 years.'[24] Although it was a secular ideology and enterprise from the beginning, and was bitterly opposed by the Jewish religious establishment, when it suited their purposes the proponents of Zionism—including Herzl himself—however non-religious, atheistic or agnostic, could look to the Bible for support. Such is the case, even though the predominantly secular Zionist movement was a rebellion against, and a conscious repudiation of classical Judaism and its theological tenets. For many political Zionists, religion was irrational, non-empirical, imperialistic, and an altogether repressive and regressive force, from which no anthropological validity, social bonding, psychological insight, or existential illumination could be expected. Indeed, for many of its supporters one's way to salvation was to escape from the prison of the sacred.

Nevertheless, according to the late Chief Rabbi of the British Commonwealth, Lord Sir Immanuel Jakobivits,

> The origins of the Zionist idea are of course entirely religious. The slogan, 'The Bible is our mandate' is a credo hardly less insistently pleaded by many secularists than by religious believers as the principal basis of our legal and historical claim to the Land of Israel ... Modern Political Zionism itself could never have struck root if it had not planted its seeds in soil ploughed up and fertilised by the millennial conditioning of religious memories, hopes, prayers and visions of our eventual return to Zion ... No rabbinical authority disputes that our claim to a Divine mandate (and we have no other which cannot be invalidated) extends over the entire Holy Land within its historic borders and that halachically we have no right to surrender this claim (Jakobivits 1982: 19-20).

---

[24] Ben-Gurion 1954: 100. Ben-Gurion regularly convened the 'Prime Minster's Bible Study Circle', which included President Zalman Shazar. His lecture, 'The Bible and the Jewish People' (Nahalal, 20 July 1964) makes abundant use of biblical texts, especially those dealing with the promise of restoration. While he alludes to the Hebrew prophets and their concern for justice, Ben-Gurion does not deal with the injunctions to disinherit the Canaanites, the Joshua legend, nor with the biblical traditions that reflect racist, ethnicist, xenophobic and militaristic tendencies. His sole, oblique reference to the indigenous Palestinians, is that while the whole world regarded Israel with respect and admiration, 'Our Arab neighbours have as yet not made peace with our existence, and their leaders are declaring their desire to destroy us' (Ben-Gurion 1972: 294). See also Dayan 1978.

His successor, current Chief Rabbi Jonathan Sacks, considers that the State of Israel is for many religious Jews 'the most powerful collective expression' of Jewry, and 'the most significant development in Jewish life since the Holocaust'.[25] In the course of his speech at the service for Israel's fiftieth anniversary, Sacks portrayed the birth of the state as a coming to the promised land in line with the biblical stories of Abraham and Sarah, Moses and the Exodus, Ezra and Nehemiah. His speech reflected also the core elements of the canonical Zionist reading of Jewish history.[26] Within a few generations of chief rabbis, then, Political Zionism had been metamorphosed from being an anathema, and a repudiation of Judaism and the Scriptures (Hermann Adler), to becoming a core ingredient of Jewish religious life (Immanuel Jakobivits and Jonathan Sachs): it had moved from the secular to the sacred.

The role of the biblical narrative within the Zionist ideology increased significantly in the wake of the 1967 War and the rise of *Gush Emunim*. The biblical paradigm was the backdrop for the Zionist self-portrayal as the (sole) 'descendants of the biblical children of Israel', while the natives [Arabs] were 'Canaanites'. This introduced into the secular discourse a religious authority justifying the new conquest of the land and the maltreatment of its population. Measured against the divine right of the colonisers, appeal to the human rights of the local population, considered to be 'interlopers', 'sojourners' and obstacles to the divine plan, carried no conviction.

More recently, the otherwise forward-looking and ecumenically eirenic statement *Dabru Emet* ('Speak the Truth'), signed by 150 prominent Jews in the USA (12 September 2000, and by more since), promotes exclusively Jewish claims to Palestine, clothing the Zionist enterprise in the garment of piety, even though its determination to create a state for Jews would require the 'ethnic-cleansing' of the indigenous Arab population. Acceptance of these claims and its contemporary implications is a requirement of the conventional Jewish-Christian dialogue:

> Christians can respect the claim of the Jewish people upon
> the land of Israel. The most important event for Jews since

---

[25] *The Daily Telegraph*, 31 December, 1993: 21.

[26] Speech at the Service for Israel's Fiftieth Anniversary in the presence of HRH The Prince of Wales, at St John's Wood Synagogue, London, 29 April 1998.

the Holocaust has been the reestablishment of a Jewish state in the Promised Land. As members of a biblically-based religion, Christians appreciate that Israel was promised—and given—to Jews as the physical centre of the covenant between them and God. Many Christians support the State of Israel for reasons far more profound than mere politics. As Jews, we applaud this support.

Virtually everything, then, rests on the authority of the Bible. While other factors, such as 'endemic', 'irredentist' antisemitism in 19th-century Europe, the barbarism of the *Shoah* in the 20th, etc., could be invoked as justifications for establishing a state, they might not be considered adequate to warrant ethnically cleansing Palestine of its indigenous non-Jewish population. The Zionist conquest would need an even bigger 'idea' to redeem it, and the Bible was to hand (see Prior 1999b).

Whatever pangs of conscience one might have in the modern period about the expulsion of a million Palestinian Arabs, and the destruction of their villages to ensure they would not return—if one could bring oneself to acknowledge that such was the reality, and indeed the intention of Zionism—the Bible could be appealed to, to salve it. It could provide the most authoritative legitimisation for the Zionist conquest, claiming that it was merely restoring the land to the Jews in accordance with the clear intentions of God as recorded in its narrative. The divine provenance of the Bible and the authority that springs from such origins would supply the moral authority that was otherwise lacking. Thus, the normal rules of morality could be suspended, and ethnic cleansing could be applauded, even by the religious spirit.

The Moral Challenge to the Biblical Narrative

The land traditions of the Bible, however, pose fundamental moral questions, at two levels. At the level of content, the divine promise of land in the biblical narrative is integrally linked with the *mandate*—not merely the permission—to exterminate the indigenous peoples of Canaan. Even the Exodus narrative is problematic on moral grounds. While it portrays Yahweh as having compassion on the misery of his people, and as willing to deliver them from the Egyptians, and bring them to a land flowing

with milk and honey (Exodus 3.7-8), that was only part of the picture. Although the reading of Exodus 3, both in the Christian liturgy and in the classical texts of liberation theologies, halts abruptly in the middle of v. 8 at the description of the land as one 'flowing with milk and honey', the biblical text itself continues, 'to the country of the Canaanites, the Hittites, the Amorites, the Perizzites, the Hivites, and the Jebusites'. Manifestly, the promised land, flowing with milk and honey, had no lack of indigenous peoples, and, according to the narrative, would soon flow with their blood.[27] At the level of the use to which these morally problematic texts have been put—what scholars call the Reception History of the text—there is a further moral problem. These biblical land traditions have been deployed in favour of various colonial enterprises, including Zionism. Far from being charters for liberation, then, they have been deployed as instruments of oppression (see Prior 1997).

Altogether, then, in the light of the double problematic of the land traditions of the Bible—their projection of genocide as being divinely *mandated*, and their deleterious use in favour of oppressive colonialism— perhaps every copy of the Bible should contain a health warning:'Reading this Book may Damage Somebody Else's Health.' It is possible, of course, to insist that the relevant land traditions are historical in the sense that they approximate to what actually happened—and many evangelical do so. To do so, however, leaves one with a god who is a xenophobic nationalist and a militaristic ethnic-cleanser. Reliance on the authority of the gift of land from such a god, then, should be problematic for any reader who might presume that the divinity would entertain the values of the Fourth Geneva Convention and the Universal Declaration of Human Rights, at least. On moral grounds, therefore, one is forced to question whether the *Torah* in fact provides divine legitimacy for the occupation of other people's land, and the virtual annihilation of the indigenous peoples.

By modern standards of international law and human rights the land narratives of Exodus-Joshua *mandate* 'war-crimes' and 'crimes against humanity'. To dismiss their contemporary moral implications by pleading that such texts ought not to be judged by the standards obtaining today is not sufficient. Nor is it acceptable either to seek refuge in the claim that the problem lies with the predispositions of the modern reader,

---

[27] For an exposition of the offending biblical texts and a fuller commentary on them, see my moral critique (Prior 1997).

rather than with the text itself. One must acknowledge that much of the *Torah*, and the Book of Deuteronomy in particular, contains menacing ideologies, and racist, xenophobic and militaristic tendencies. Manifestly, the Book of Joshua is a morally scandalous component in a collection of religious writings. The implications of the existence of such dubious moral dispositions and actions, presented as *mandated* by the divinity, within a book which is canonised as Sacred Scripture invites the most serious investigation.

The Challenge to the Historical Value of the Land Traditions of the Bible

Much of biblical studies, as Keith Whitelam has demonstrated (1996), has been propelled by the search for 'Ancient Israel' as the taproot of Western civilisation, and the antecedent of Christianity. What might otherwise be considered reasonably to be a highly problematic moral precedent—the biblical narrative's presentation of the genocide attendant upon the establishment of biblical Israel—required no apologia. God, according to the biblical narrative, had ordained it so, and the times were 'primitive'. Moreover, with the 19th-century European assurance that human culture was evolving in an inexorable rise from savagery to civilisation—reaching its evolutionary zenith in the form of Western Christendom, preferably of the Reformed type, and best of all American—divine breaches of modern human rights protocols could be easily tolerated. Thus, even William Foxwell Albright, the doyen of US biblical archaeologists, had no qualms about the plunder attendant upon Joshua's enterprise, which he understood in a largely historically reliable way.[28] An analogous indulgence obtains in the modern period also in the benign Western assessment of the Zionist enterprise, which cleanses the land of its indigenous defilers, and so Albright himself also judged that through Zionism Jews would bring to the Near East all the benefits of European civilisation (1942: 12-13).

---

[28] 'From the impartial standpoint of a philosopher of history, it often seems necessary that a people of markedly inferior type should vanish before a people of superior potentialities, since there is a point beyond which racial mixture cannot go without disaster ... Thus the Canaanites, with their orgiastic nature worship, their cult of fertility in the form of serpent symbols and sensuous nudity, and their gross mythology, were replaced by Israel, with its pastoral simplicity and purity of life, its lofty monotheism, and its severe code of ethics' (Albright 1957: 280-81).

Even for people not revolted at the portrayal of God as the Great Ethnic Cleanser two lines of thought converge to challenge a naive reading of the land traditions. Rather than reading ancient texts from within the context of contemporary categories of race, ethnicity, nation, etc., the first task of the biblical scholar is to establish the literary forms of the texts one is studying. In simple terms, does every occurrence of verbs in the past tense imply that the narrative is essentially history, as we broadly understand that term as giving insight into the period described in the narrative? And, is every use of the future tense in the biblical narrative indicative of prophetic texts which will be fulfilled in a literalist way in our present, or in some future? Christian Zionists, and many evangelical Christians, would answer both questions affirmatively. As well as presenting moral problems, such predispositions in reading the biblical text conflict with general principles of literary criticism, and ignore critical evidence. Space allows only an indication of current developments in biblical scholarship.[29]

Recent biblical scholarship, aided by increasing archaeological evidence, makes it impossible to evaluate the biblical narratives of land as pointers to what actually happened in the period portrayed in the text. In the wake of the seminal works of Thomas L Thompson (1974) and John Van Seters (1975) it is now part of the scholarly consensus that the patriarchal narratives of Genesis do not record events of an alleged patriarchal period, but are retrojections into a past about which the writers knew little, reflecting the author's intentions at the later period of composition, perhaps that of the attempt to reconstitute national and religious identity in the wake of the Babylonian exile, or even later (see further Prior 1997: 216-23). In such circumstances it is naïve to cleave to the view that God made the promise of progeny and land to Abraham after the fashion indicated in Genesis 15.

Neither do the Exodus-Settlement accounts present empirical facts of history. The archaeology of Palestine shows a picture quite different from that of the religiously motivated writings of the Bible. The evidence from archaeology and extra-biblical literature, supplemented by insights

---

[29] For further discussion on reinterpreting the biblical evidence, and on the relevant literary and historical questions concerning the Patriarchal Narratives, the Pentateuchal Narratives, and the Israelite Conquest-Settlement Narratives, see Prior 1997: 216-52. See also my comments on Towards a Moral Reading of the Bible in Prior 1997: 253-86 and Prior 2003b.

from the independent methodologies of geography, sociology, anthropology, historical linguistics, Egyptology, Assyriology, etc., points in a direction altogether different from that implied by Joshua 1-12. This extra-biblical material suggests a sequence of periods marked by a gradual and peaceful coalescence of disparate peoples into a group of highland dwellers whose achievement of a new sense of unity culminated only with the entry of the Assyrian administration. The Iron I Age settlements on the central hills of Palestine, from which the later kingdom of Israel developed, reflect continuity with Canaanite culture, and repudiate any ethnic distinction between 'Canaanites' and 'Israelites' (see further Prior 1997: 228-47; 1999a: 159-83). The biblical narrative, then, unless read in a naïve, literalist fashion, offers little succour to ethnic-cleansers.

But even if the Patriarchal narratives of Genesis and the narratives of Exodus-Leviticus-Numbers-Deuteronomy-Joshua portrayed the past approximately as it happened, one would still have to contend with their ethical stance in portraying Yahweh as the great ethnic-cleanser. Were these narratives acknowledged to belong to the genre of legend rather than history, or to be confined to the realm of mere rhetorical discussion of ancient literature in its various genres, few would object. But when they have vital significance for people's lives even in one's own generation problems arise. As we have seen, much of the legitimacy associated with the establishment of the State of Israel, and the esteem it enjoys in religious circles, derives its major moral legitimisation from a particular reading of the 'Hebrew Bible'. And the matter is not merely rhetorical.

Important conclusions follow from the claim of exclusive Israelite/Jewish rights to Palestine. 'Jews' hailing from any part of the globe, who themselves were never displaced from Palestine, have the 'right of return'. Without the Bible, such a claim to legitimacy would have no currency in the wider world wherein, for one, a communal right of return operates only when a defined community has been subjected to recent expulsion—a *sine qua non* for orderly international behaviour. From a moral perspective there is a more problematic implication. The Jewish 'right of return' easily translates into the 'right to expel' the indigenous population, an aspiration which, as we have seen, was at the core of the Zionist enterprise from the beginning. And, since Jews have sole tenure, a claim deriving from a naïve reading of the biblical narrative, the recently expelled Palestinian Arabs have no right of return (see Prior 2001).

Facing Hard Truths

Any discussion of the enterprise of Political Zionism and its climax in the creation of the State of Israel must come to terms with a number of embarrassing truths—exposed by the New Historiography—the denial of which only adds to one's self-delusion and self-righteousness. There is a fundamental moral problem at the core of the Zionist programme which no amount of special pleading, or pretence to innocence, can side-step. This relates to the Zionist determination to establish a state for Jews at the expense of the indigenous Arabs. Theodor Herzl knew what was needed to establish such a state in a land already inhabited. Moreover, there is a 'mountain' of evidence in the Zionist archives tracing the consistency of this line of thinking within the Zionist leadership in Palestine and outside. It demonstrates that the expulsion of the indigenous Arabs was foreseen as necessary, was systematically planned—not least through establishing three successive 'Population Transfer Committees'— and was executed at the first opportunity, in 1948. The damage done to the indigenous population in 1948, then, was neither accidental nor due to the unique pressures of war, but was at the heart of the Zionist enterprise from the beginning. To accord legitimacy to such activity is highly problematic. To criticise the Zionist ethnic cleansing of Palestine in 1948 on the basis that it did not complete the job—the current position of Benny Morris—is even worse.

The espousal of Zionism by a majority of Jews world-wide marks the nadir of Jewish morality, and the degree to which a thoroughly Zionised Judaism debases Jewish-Christian dialogue, and even Christianity itself is a matter of concern. In such a scenario, the planned and systematically executed dislocation of the indigenous population of Palestine, far from incurring the wrath of post-colonial liberal thought, becomes an object of honour, and even of religious significance. It is in the unique case of Zionism that ethnic cleansing is applauded. It would be a pity if mutually respectful Jewish-Christian relations demanded the suspension of the normal rules of a universalist morality.

We have seen that the core ingredients of the canonical Zionist narrative, in its secular, in its religious, and in its biblical categories are strained under the weight of ongoing modern scholarship from disparate disciplines. Rather than being generated by religious idealism, the Zionist aspiration was prompted by a host of nationalist movements within the

turbulent politics of post-French Revolution, 19th-century Europe (Prior 1999a: 51-66). Political Zionism was rejected by both Orthodox and Reform wings of Judaism from the start: it was heretical, in the case of the former, and contrary to the mission of Judaism for the latter. Only gradually, but dramatically in the wake of the 1967 Israeli-Arab War, 'Religious Jewry' (with notable exceptions) rowed in with the achievement of secular Zionism, and in some circles 'sacralised' it (Prior 1999a: 67-102).

With respect to the history of ancient Jewry, the authoritative studies of such as Betsy Halpern-Amaru, John Barclay, Isaiah Gafni, *et alii*, undermine the 'Myth of the Ubiquitous and Perennial Jewish Longing for Palestine'. Rather than reflecting historical realities that myth has been imposed by Zionists, with no regard for the diversity of Jewish history and experience (see Prior 1999a: 212-18). In addition to suffering in various places at different times, Jews in several countries acquired positions for themselves which they have found eminently satisfying. Indeed, the majority of international Jewry chooses to live other than in Israel.

The claim in our own age that the biblical narrative, however repulsive its deployment as part of the ideological support for colonialism in the past, legitimises the 'ethnic cleansing' of the Palestinian Arabs should not remain unchallenged. Biblical scholars, at least, might be expected to protest against outrages perpetrated in the name of fidelity to the biblical covenant. Their performance up to now has not been impressive (see Prior 2003c). Biblical research should be conducted with an 'ethics of accountability', i.e., with a concern for exposing 'the ethical consequences of the biblical text and its meanings', especially when these have promoted various forms of oppression, not least through 'colonial dehumanisation', and for making their findings known to a wider public (Schüssler Fiorenza 1999: 28-29). Biblical exegesis, in addition to probing into the circumstances of the composition of the biblical narratives, should concern itself also with the real conditions of people's lives, and not satisfy itself with comfortable survival in an academic or religious ghetto, stimulating only its own 'in-house' constituency.

It is a particularly important task to identify the different literary forms of the Bible, and to distinguish, on literary grounds alone, between tracts that are historical, mythological, or legendary, etc. In the attempts to reconstruct the conditions of 'Early Israel' it would be unwise to be

circumscribed by the late and theologically-oriented accounts we find in the Bible. Nor should the perspectives of the biblical narratives determine the 'ethnic identities' that obtained hundreds of years earlier. It appears now that the 'Israel' of the period depicted by the biblical narrative represented a multiplicity of ethnic identities, reflecting the variety of provenances in the Late Bronze-Iron Age transition, added to subsequently by that brought about by three waves of systematic, imperial population transfer and admixture (Assyrian, Babylonian and Persian). The predication of Israelite *ethnic distinctiveness* prior to the Persian period is illusory, and the unity of the biblical *benei Israel* (children of Israel) is a predilection of the biblical authors, rather than the reality reflecting a commonality of ethnic identity or communal experience.

The needs of the much later final redactors of the biblical narrative dominated their ideological stance, which we may wish to call religious or pastoral, and issued in an ideal model for the future which they justified on the basis of its retrojection into the past of Israelite origins, the details of which only the surviving conflicting folkloric traditions provided. If we excuse the biblical writers for their misrepresentation of the past on the basis of their exhortatory motives for their own circumstances, we ought not to be equally indulgent with theologians and Church-Synagogue people for whom the evidence of what happened in the past is more reliable. The legendary account of Joshua 1-12 offers no legitimising paradigm for land plunder in the name of God, or by anyone arrogating to himself His authority. Indeed, the extra-biblical evidence promotes a respect for the evolution of human culture, rather than for a process that can deal with change only by way of violent destruction.

Much of my own biblical research into the hermeneutical and moral problems of the employment of the Hebrew Bible in favour of Zionism counters the 'canonical' Zionist narrative that the Bible provides the legitimisation for the State of Israel. It exposes the pretence that Zionism was a religious enterprise by pointing to its secular, and mostly anti-religious, origins. Its findings contradict the core ingredients of the established Zionist historical narrative and render it unsustainable academically. Since the hegemonic Zionist narrative provides the lens through which most of the Western world views the recent history of the region, any undermining of its truth-claims has significant implications. Such findings are not matters on which there are inevitably merely

different opinions and viewpoints. Many of them belong to the realm of historical fact, attested to by a mountain of archival and other documentary evidence, much of it in Zionist sources, the ongoing publication of samples of which is an irritant to those hitherto embracing the conventional Zionist fabrication of the recent past. Exposing the untruths of fabricated nationalist ideologies is a step in the direction of establishing dialogue on a foundation of truths, however unpalatable.

While generations of religious people have derived both profit and pleasure from the retelling of the biblical stories, the victims of the colonialist plunder which has been justified on the basis of them are likely to be less sanguine in their attitude to the texts, and would welcome any attempt to distinguish between the apparent ethnocentricity of the God of biblical books stretching from Genesis to 2 Kings, and the paranaetic (or exhortatory) and political intentions of authors writing much later. A major epistemological question arises. Do texts which belong to the genre of folkloric epic or legend, rather than of a history which describes what actually happened, confer legitimacy on the 'Israelite' possession of the land, and on subsequent forms of colonialism which looked to the biblical paradigm, understood as factual history, for legitimisation later? Does a judgement which is based on the premise that the genre of the justifying text is history in that sense not dissolve when it is realized that the text belongs to the genre of *myths of origin*, which are encountered in virtually every society, and which were deployed in the service of particular ideologies?

References

Abu Lughod, Ibrahim (ed.). 1987 (second ed.). *The Transformation of Palestine. Essays on the Origin and Development of the Arab-Israeli Conflict*. Evanston: Northwestern University Press

Albright, William Foxwell. 1942. 'Why the Near East needs the Jews', *New Palestine* 32: 12-13

Albright, William Foxwell. 1957. *From the Stone Age to Christianity: Monotheism and the Historical Process*. New York: Doubleday

Aruri, Naseer (ed.), *Palestinian Refugees and their Right of Return*, London and Sterling VA: Pluto Press

Barclay, John M.G. 1996. *Jews in the Mediterranean Diaspora from Alexander to Trajan (323 BCE-117 CE)*. Edinburgh: T&T Clark

Ben-Gurion, David. 1954. *The Rebirth and Destiny of Israel*. New York: Philosophical
    Library
Ben-Gurion, David. 1971-72. *Zichronot* (Memoirs),Vol. 1-4,Tel Aviv:'Am 'Oved
Childers, Erskine B. 1987. 'The Wordless Wish: From Citizens to Refugees', in Abu-
    Lughod 1987: 165-202
Conrad, Joseph. 1989. *Heart of Darkness*. Penguin, Harmondsworth
Dayan, Moshe. 1978. *Living with the Bible*. Philadelphia: Jewish Publication Society/
    New York: William Morrow
Drinan, Robert F. 1977. *Honor the Promise: America's Commitment to Israel*. Cape
    Town, NY: Doubleday
Ernst, Morris L. 1964. *So Far so Good*. New York: Harper
Fisher, Eugene J., A. James Rudin and Marc H. Tanenbaum. 1986. *Twenty Years of
    Jewish-Catholic Relations*. Maywah, NY: Paulist
Flapan, Simha. 1979. *Zionism and the Palestinians 1917-1947*. London: Croom Helm
Flapan, Simha. 1987. *The Birth of Israel: Myths and Realities*. London and Sydney:
    Croom Helm
Gafni, Isaiah M. 1997. *Land, Center and Diaspora. Jewish Constructs in Late Antiquity*.
    Sheffield: Sheffield Academic Press
Gunn, David M. 2003. '"Next Year in Jerusalem": Bible, Identity, and Myth on the
    Web', in Thompson 2003: 258-71
Halbertal, Moshe. 1997. *People of the Book: Canon, Meaning, and Authority*.
    Cambridge, MA, and London: Harvard University Press
Halpern-Amaru, Betsy. 1994. *Rewriting the Bible: Land and Covenant in Post-Biblical
    Jewish Literature*,Valley Forge: Trinity Press
Herzl, Theodor. 1896. *Der Judenstaat. Versuch einer Modernen Lösung der Judenfrage*.
    Leipzig und Wien: M. Breitenstein's Verlags-Buchhandlung, *The Jewish
    State. An Attempt at a Modern Solution of the Jewish Question*, the seventh
    edition, revised with a foreword by Israel Cohen. London: Henry Pordes,
    1993
Herzl, Theodor. 1960. *The Complete Diaries of Theodore Herzl*. 5 vols. (ed.) Raphael
    Patai, trans. by Harry Zohn. New York: Herzl Press
Herzl, Theodor. 1983-96.Vol. I (1983) *Briefe und Autobiographische Notizen. 1886-1895*.
    Vol II (1983) *Zionistiches Tagebuch 1895-1899*.Vol. III (1985) *Zionistiches
    Tagebuch 1899-1904* (Vols. I-III, ed. by Johannes Wachten *et al.*).Vol. IV
    (1900) *Briefe 1895-1898*.VolV (1993) *Briefe 1898-1900*. VolVI (1993) *Briefe
    Ende August 1900-ende Dezember 1902*. VolVII (1996) *Briefe 1903-1904*
    (Vols. IV-VII, ed. by Barbara Schäfer *et al.*) Berlin: Propylaen Verlag
Herzl, Theodor. 2000 (third printing). *Altneuland. Old New Land*, translated from
    the German by Lotta Levensohn, republished by Markus Wiener
    Publishers, Princeton
Hitchens, Christopher. 1988. 'Broadcasts', in Said and Hitchens (eds) 1988: 73-83
Jakobivits, Immanuel (Chief Rabbi). 1982. *The Attitude to Zionism of Britain's Chief
    Rabbis as Reflected in their Writings*. London: The Jewish Historical Society
    of England: Lecture delivered to The Jewish Historical Society of England
    in London, 9 May 1979

Khalidi, Walid. 2002. 'The Resolutions of the Thirty-Fourth World Zionist Congress, 17-21 June 2002', *Journal of Palestine Studies* 32(Issue 125, Autumn): 59-77

Kidron, Peretz. 1988. 'Truth Whereby Nations Live', in Said and Hitchens 1988: 85-96

Kimmerling, Baruch. 1983. *Zionism and Territory. The Socio-Territorial Dimensions of Zionist Politics*. Berkeley: University of California, Institute of International Studies (Research Series, No. 51)

Lemche, Niels Peter. 2000. 'Ideology and the History of Ancient Israel', *Scandinavian Journal of the Old Testament* 14(no. 2): 165-93

Masalha, Nur. 1992. *Expulsion of the Palestinians: the Concept of 'Transfer' in Zionist Political Thought, 1882-1948*. Washington, D.C.: Institute for Palestine Studies

Masalha, Nur. 1997. *A Land without a People. Israel, Transfer and the Palestinians 1949-96*. London: Faber and Faber

Masalha, Nur. 2000. *Imperial Israel and the Palestinians: The Politics of Expansion, 1967-2000*. London: Pluto

Masalha, Nur. 2003. *The Politics of Denial: Israel and the Palestinian Refugee Problem*. London and Sterling VA: Pluto Press

Morris, Benny. 1987. *The Birth of the Palestinian Refugee Problem, 1947-1949*. Cambridge: Cambridge University Press

Morris, Benny. 1990. *1948 and After: Israel and the Palestinians*. Oxford: Oxford University Press

Morris, Benny. 1993. *Israel's Border Wars*. Oxford: Oxford University Press

Morris, Benny. 1995. 'Falsifying the Record. A Fresh Look at Zionist Documentation of 1948', in *Journal of Palestine Studies* 24: 44-62

Morris, Benny. 1999. *Righteous Victims. A History of the Zionist-Arab Conflict 1881-1999*. New York: Alfred A. Knopf

Pappé, Ilan. 1988. *Britain and the Arab-Israeli Conflict 1948-1951*. London: Macmillan

Pappé, Ilan. 1992. *The Making of the Arab-Israeli Conflict, 1948-1951*. London and New York: I. B. Tauris

Pappé, Ilan. 2002. The Post-Zionist Discourse in Israel: 1990-2001', *Holy Land Studies. A Multidisciplinary Journal* 1: 9-35.

Prior, Michael. 1997. *The Bible and Colonialism. A Moral Critique*. Sheffield: Sheffield Academic Press

Prior, Michael. 1998. 'The Moral Problem of the Land Traditions of the Bible', in Prior, Michael (ed.). *Western Scholarship and the History of Palestine*, pp. 141-81.

Prior, Michael. 1999a. *Zionism and the State of Israel: A Moral Inquiry*. London and New York: Routledge

Prior, Michael. 1999b. 'The Bible and the Redeeming Idea of Colonialism'. *Studies in World Christianity* 5: 129-55

Prior, Michael. 2000. 'Zionist Ethnic Cleansing: the Fulfilment of Biblical Prophecy?' *Epworth Review* 27: 49-60

Prior, Michael. 2001 'The Right to Expel: the Bible and Ethnic Cleansing', in Aruri

2001: 9-35

Prior, Michael. 2002. 'Ethnic Cleansing and the Bible: A Moral Critique', *Holy Land Studies. A Multidisciplinary Journal* 1: 37-59

Prior, Michael. 2003a 'Speaking Truth in the Jewish-Christian Dialogue', in *A Faithful Presence. Essays for Kenneth Cragg*, ed. David Thomas and Clare Amos (London: Melisende), pp. 329-49

Prior, Michael. 2003b. 'A Moral Reading of the Bible in Jerusalem', in Thompson 2003: 16-45

Prior, Michael. 2003c. 'The State of the Art: Biblical Scholarship and the Holy Land', *Holy Land Studies. A Multidisciplinary Journal* 1 (no. 2): 65-92

Said, Edward W, and Christopher Hitchens (eds). 1988. *Blaming the Victims. Spurious Scholarship and the Palestinian Question*. London/New York: Verso

Schüssler Fiorenza, Elizabeth. 1999. *Rhetoric and Ethic. The Politics of Biblical Studies*. Minneapolis: Fortress

Segev, Tom. 1986. *The First Israelis*. New York: The Free Press/London: Collier Macmillan

Segev, Tom. 1993. *The Seventh Million. The Israelis and the Holocaust. (trans. by Haim Watzan)*. New York: Hill and Wang

Shahak, Israel. 1975 (2nd ed.). *Report: Arab Villages destroyed in Israel*. Jerusalem: Shahak

Shapira, Anita. 1992. *Land and Power. The Zionist Resort to Force*. Oxford: Oxford University Press

Shlaim, Avi. 1988. *Collusion across the Jordan. King Abdullah, the Zionist Movement, and the Partition of Palestine*. New York: Columbia University Press

Thompson, Thomas L. 1974. *The Historicity of the Pentateuchal Narratives: The Quest for the Historical Abraham*. Berlin/New York: de Gruyter

Thompson, Thomas L. (ed. with the collaboration of Salma Khadra Jayyusi). 2003. *Jerusalem in Ancient History and Tradition*. London: T & T Clark International

Van Seters, John. 1975. *Abraham in History and Tradition*. New Haven/London: Yale University Press

Weizmann, Chaim. 1949. *Trial and Error: The Autobiography of Chaim Weizmann*. New York: Harper and Row

Whitelam, Keith W. 1996. *The Invention of Ancient Israel: The Silencing of Palestinian History*. London and New York: Routledge

ZIONISM, CHRISTIANITY AND THE
ISRAELI-PALESTINIAN CONFLICT
Herman Ruether and Rosemary Radford Ruether

The Israeli-Palestinian conflict, and the relations of Christians in Palestine and Christians in the West to it, must first be seen in its historical context. A great deal of misunderstanding of this situation in the West stems from not only not knowing this history, but from being deliberately misinformed about this history by partisans of Israel. In this essay we will lay out the basic historical development of this conflict. We will then discuss some of the religious-ideological patterns that have obscured understanding it among Western Christians and Jews.

1. The historical background to the modern conflict.
The clash of three histories

The Israeli-Palestinian conflict can be seen as the product of the clash of three histories. These are: 1) the history of Zionism as a movement of Western and Eastern European Jews seeking to escape from an antisemitic environment in Europe, to return to what they saw as their historic homeland in Palestine and to found a Jewish state. Zionists began planting small colonies of immigrants in Palestine in the late 19th and early 20th centuries; 2) Arab nationalism that emerged from the disintegrating Ottoman empire in the Eastern Mediterranean and Near East and that sought to found an Arab state that would include the whole of the Arab-speaking world from Syria to Saudi Arabia; and 3) European colonialism, especially that of Britain and France, who were seeking to divide up the Arab world among themselves, having already taken control of much of Africa and Asia.

During the First World War the British entered into three conflicting agreements with these three different forces. They promised the symbolically important leader of the Arab world, the Sharif of Mecca, that they would support Arab independence from Ottoman rule, if the Arabs sided with them against the Germans and their allies, including a

newly emergent Turkish state. They also made a secret agreement with the French (the Sykes–Picot agreement, 1916) to divide up the Arab world into five areas. Two areas, which became defined as Syria and Lebanon, would become French mandate regions, and two that became defined as Iraq and Jordan, as British mandate areas, with Palestine as an international zone under the French, British and Russians. In the San Remo agreement of 1920 that confirmed these British and French mandate areas, Palestine was ceded to the British. The undeveloped Arab peninsula was left to Arab rule. The third agreement was the Balfour Declaration of 1917 that promised a 'homeland for the Jewish people' in Palestine under the sponsorship of the British.

The Arab world was outraged by the second and third agreements which were seen as betrayal of the promise of an Arab state, creating instead a Western colonisation of the area. Protests took place throughout the Arab world, leading eventually to independent Arab states: Iraq, Jordan, Syria and Lebanon. It is important to see that these Arab states had not existed before the First World War, but their borders were defined by this process of European colonisation. Palestinians also vehemently protested what they saw as a double colonisation, by the British occupying forces and their sponsorship of Zionist colonies intended to lead to a Jewish 'homeland'. Palestinian protests during the British mandate period led to open rebellion, which was violently suppressed by the British, using laws of collective punishment which are still employed by the Israelis to control Palestinian uprisings.

During the Second World War the British again feared the possibility of an Arab alliance with the Germans. They sought to pacify Palestinian protests by issuing a White Paper forbidding further Jewish settlement in the region. The British and Americans also limited Jewish migration to the British territories and to the United States. This meant the European Jews, seeking to escape from Hitler, found themselves blocked from areas of migration outside Europe. In general American Jewish leaders did not protest against this ban on Jewish immigration to the United States, since they envisioned a European Jewish population of six-eight million that would be uprooted by Hitler into concentration camps and could be moved as a block to Palestine after the war as the demographic base for a Jewish state. They envisioned this state to be made up of European, not Sephardic, Jews.

However, when the clouds of war dispersed in 1945, the horrible

reality of Nazi mass extermination of Jews was revealed, a reality that had been known, but not publicly acknowledged by the Allies during the war. The remaining European Jews now became beneficiaries of European guilt. A widespread sympathy for the Zionist cause emerged internationally as a kind of compensation for the mass extermination of Jews in Europe. It was in this atmosphere of compensatory guilt for the sins of Europeans against Jews that the United States, under President Harry Truman, a staunch ally of American Jews, pushed for the partition of Palestine. In 1947 the United Nations voted to partition Palestine into two states, giving 55 percent of the land to the Jewish settlers, who at that point were only 600,000 and had occupied some 7 percent of the land, and to give 44 percent to the Palestinian Arabs, who were at that time about 1.5 million people, more than half of whom were living in Galilee and the coastal regions that had been designated for the Jewish state.

The Palestinians, and Arabs generally, rejected the partition, while the Zionists accepted it. The Palestinians saw the partition as a violation of Palestinian Arab national sovereignty as the historical people of the region, a partition in which they had not been consulted, but which was imposed on them by Western powers as a continuation of Western colonialism. The Zionists accepted it in terms of the legal basis that it gave them for a Jewish state, but they did not accept the presence of so many Palestinians within this state, nor the existence of a Palestinian state alongside it. Key Zionist leaders, such as David Ben-Gurion, were determined to change these realities by war.

The Palestinian Nakba (Catastrophe)

During the war that broke out between the Arab states and the new Jewish state in 1948-9, the Israelis, with a better organised army, and in a covert alliance with the Jordanians, whose army was British-led, managed to accomplish their goals in three ways. They were able to expand their territory by another 20 percent, taking additional territory around Jerusalem, Western Galilee, the southern coastal area and the Negev. Secondly, they expelled the majority of Palestinian Arabs from this expanded region, about 750,000 refugees in all. These fled into the West Bank, Gaza, Lebanon and Jordan. Thirdly, the remaining territories of the Palestinian state were occupied by Jordan and Egypt.

The territory for the Palestinian state disappeared. Yet the basis for a Palestinian state remains in the 1947 partition vote, a fact ignored by Israel and the United States when they act as though the demand for a Palestinian state is a 'new thing'. The majority of the Palestinians became refugees, or found themselves living under occupying powers. Only a remnant of 160,000 Palestinians remained in the expanded territory of the Jewish state, many uprooted from their land. The new Jewish state declared the land of the refugees, including that of many Palestinians uprooted within Israel, to be forfeited, thereby expanding the land controlled by Jews from 10 percent to 90 percent. All this land was declared to be a permanent patrimony of the Jewish people. Palestinian Arabs in Israel were given nominal citizenship, but were kept under martial law until 1966, and still today are legally second class persons in a state defined as a Jewish state.

This first effort of expulsion, clearing the land for Jewish settlement, seemed to be a resounding success. However, the problem of the Palestinian presence for the Zionist project has continued. The Palestinian remnant in Israel has grown to 1.25 million today, more than 20 percent of the population of Israel. In 1967, Israel conquered the remaining Palestinian areas of the Gaza Strip and West Bank. Palestinians in those regions today number more than three million. Thus Israeli Jews face a Palestinian population of more than 4 million, while Jews, despite enormous efforts to import settlers, especially from Russia, are about 5 million. So the 'demographic problem' (i.e. a large Palestinian population that challenges the effort to create a Jewish majority) has not been 'solved'. This fact plays a major role in the calculations of successive Israeli governments about the terms for a 'final settlement'.

June 1967

While expulsion was covered up and denied in 1947-9 and was carried out without significant Western protest, this could not happen under the greater glare of visibility in 1967. In 1967 Israel made a pre-emptive strike on Egypt and Syria, claiming that these two nations were about to invade them. They destroyed their airforces on the ground and quickly occupied the West Bank, Gaza, the Golan Heights and the Sinai. The Sinai was later given back to Egypt under the Camp David Accords in

1978. Another 500,000 Palestinians were displaced by this war, many of them out of the country at the time for school or work and denied re-entry. The million and a half Palestinians under occupation were placed under military rule that has denied them basic civil and human rights.

Shortly after the 1967 conquest and occupation of the West Bank and Gaza, Israeli military and Labour party leaders conceived of a new plan to render this Arab population insignificant by a process of 'encirclement'. This was the Allon Plan of 1960s (named after its proposor, General Yigal Allon). This plan called for the building of a ring of settlements around Jerusalem and the annexation of this area into Israel. In addition a line of settlements would be placed along the Jordan valley. Land around these settlements would be expanded, while the Palestinian population would be reduced to largely landless enclaves in major population centres. The plan envisioned that this would eventually lead to a new partition of the West Bank and Gaza Strip, with the confiscated land taken into Israel, while the Palestinian enclaves would be placed under the government of Jordan.

Other military leaders, such as Moshe Dayan, as well as the militant outlook of the settlement movement and the Likud Party, disagreed with even this partial allocation of land to the Palestinians. They hoped to continue to effect, even if by slow but steady measures, the expulsion or forced migration of Palestinians. The Palestinians should become steadily fewer and more landless, and those remaining were kept under control by military occupation. They would neither be given Israeli citizenship nor autonomous control over any part of the land.

The policies of Israel toward the Palestinians in the Occupied Territories over the last thirty years have actually proceeded on a combination of these two 'plans'. There has been a continual building of settlements around East Jerusalem, first an inner ring and then an outer ring. A gerrymandered territory has been drawn around Arab East Jerusalem that avoids Palestinian population enclaves, while confiscating the agricultural land around them. This settlement ring has now grown to ten times the size of the former East Jerusalem, reaching beyond Ramallah to the north, almost to Jericho on the east and beyond Bethlehem to the south, with the first ring annexed into Israel.

In addition, settlements have been expanded in the West Bank and Gaza, as well as land taken for 'public purposes' (e.g., for roads or military use). The result is that Israel has confiscated about 70 percent of

the West Bank and 40 percent of Gaza. The Palestinians within these regions have been denied the right to expand their houses or build new ones, and are subject to a continual effort to revoke their residency permits in Jerusalem. A network of bypass roads (which Palestinians cannot use) has been and continues to be built, confiscating more Palestinian land, linking Jewish settlements with each other, but, through continual closures and denial of travel permits, cutting Palestinians in the enclaves off from each other and from Jerusalem. Thus, Palestinians have been ever more ghettoised in separate enclaves with few economic or cultural resources.

From the Intifada to Oslo

In 1987, Palestinians rose in protest against these repressive policies and organised a combination of street protests, boycotts and committees of economic and cultural survival and development. Despite violent repression in which some 2,000 people died and 150,000 were injured, many permanently, and hundreds of thousands detained (and tortured) in prison, this uprising (*Intifada*) continued until 1993. Sympathy and concern for a just settlement grew among Western nations. This was usually defined in terms of a two-state solution according to which Palestinians would be granted an independent state in the West Bank and Gaza (now less than 25 percent of historic Palestine, not the 45 percent given them by the United Nations in 1947).

Despite protests by militant Palestinian groups who continued to hope for a return of 'all' of historic Palestine, or at least a right of return to towns now in Israel from which they had been expelled, in 1989 the PLO, led by Yasir Arafat, accepted a 'historic compromise'. The PLO declared that they would recognize the state of Israel in its pre- June 1967 borders. This acceptance was contingent upon a return of the land taken in 1967 for an independent Palestinian state, with its capital in East Jerusalem.

Recognizing the growing international pressure for a settlement that would concede some kind of Palestinian 'entity'. Labour leaders Yitzhak Rabin and Shimon Peres, hit on a 'brilliant' plan. They would accede to a 'peace process' that would give some autonomous regions to Palestinian control, but in a way that would actually consolidate and legalise the settlements around East Jerusalem, the West Bank and Gaza. This would amount to a new partition of the remnant of Palestine, along

the lines conceived twenty-five years earlier in the Allon plan. The enclaves of Palestinian population would be given local self-government, but not real sovereignty, separated from the territories of Israeli settlement, which would be annexed to Israel.

What was needed for this Israeli plan was the existence of a Palestinian national leadership that could be entrusted with local Palestinian self-government as 'native police' under Israel, to enforce Palestinian compliance on a day-to-day basis. The idea of creating a puppet Palestinian police, billed as Palestinian 'self-government', had been tried in 1975 in the form of the 'village leagues'. But these failed due to the refusal of Palestinians in the towns and villages to accord the 'collaborators' the status of legitimate representatives. It was here that Rabin and Peres hit on their most ingenious solution. This was to co-opt a corrupt and declining PLO leadership under Yasir Arafat to play the role of leader of a collaborator 'local police'.

Arafat and the PLO had been vehemently demonised by Israel. All dialogue of Israelis with their representatives was made illegal. But Rabin and Peres were well aware that Arafat had not only declared that he would accept the 'historic compromise' of a mini-Palestinian state in the West Bank and Gaza, but said he would be willing to begin with any territory, no matter how small, that was conceded by Israel as a base for this state. Only Arafat and the PLO under him had the status of legitimate national leadership for Palestinians as a whole. A dramatic turnabout to dialogue and negotiation with the PLO under Arafat, allowing him and his guerrilla fighters to return to be the recipients of territory turned over to a Palestinian local administration, appeared to be a startling concession by Israel.

In the Oslo plan it was agreed that the densely populated Palestinians areas, the Gaza Strip, Jericho, Ramallah, Bethlehem, Nablus, Tulkarm and Hebron, would be turned over to a Palestinian 'National Authority'. Arafat and his PLO fighters would be transformed into this Authority. The hope was held out of a larger process in which the final status of East Jerusalem, additional land and the return of refugees would be resolved, leading to an eventual Palestinian sovereign state in all or most of the West Bank and Gaza.

The world was amazed and rejoiced at what was billed as a historic turn about and 'conversion' of these old enemies to 'peace'. In 1993 President Bill Clinton staged the historic handshake of Rabin and

Arafat on the White House lawn. But it soon became clear to Palestinians (but not to Westerners committed to a rosy view of this 'peace process') that what the Labour leaders really had in mind was not a process that would eventually lead to an independent Palestinian state in all or even most of the West Bank and Gaza, with Jerusalem as its capital, but rather a version of the old Allon and Village League plans in new disguise.

The 'peace process' turned out to be based on a division of the West Bank and Gaza into three zones. Area A, the densely-populated Palestinian enclaves, would be turned over to the Palestinian Authority. These together are less than 10 percent of historic Palestine. Area C (Israeli settlements) would remain under Israeli control. Intermediate areas (Palestinian agricultural land that was disputed and not yet settled by Israelis, including water resources) would be negotiated between the two authorities. The Wye agreement was to hand over about of this to the Palestinian Authority, but it was never fully implemented.

However, in the period between the first stage and the final stage of the 'peace process', Israel, far from refraining from further settlements, engaged in a rush to consolidate as much land in the West Bank and Gaza under exclusively Jewish control as possible. There has been stepped-up settlement around Jerusalem; feverish road building, linking Jewish areas, by-passing and cutting off Palestinian areas; intensified efforts to clear Palestinians from East Jerusalem and its expanded areas through denial of residency permits and destruction of houses deemed to have been constructed 'illegally'.

It became even more difficult for Palestinians to get permits to travel into and through Jerusalem, cutting off both employment in Israel and communication between Palestinian regions. Continual closures sealed these Palestinians off totally from one another and Israel. Soon militant Palestinians responded with new protests, and suicide bombings in the streets of West Jerusalem, killing dozens of Israelis. But each such incident became a new rationale for total closures and sealing of the Palestinian areas, new land confiscation and settlements, new demolition of Palestinian homes.

Moreover, although the Israeli armies had withdrawn from the centres of Palestinian population, they remained as the enforcers of the walls of enclosure around them. Each incident was used to pressure the Palestinian Authority to be the police agents of repression of dissent (especially of members of the militant Hamas movement), even though there was little evidence that most of the local Hamas members and

PLO critics arrested had direct links to the bombers. If Arafat did not do a good enough job at repression of his own people, money for the Palestinian Authority from international donors was to be withdrawn, with the final threat being a re-incursion of the Israeli army into the Palestinian enclaves to enforce this repression directly.

Little of the money given to Arafat or the Palestinian Authority has been used for development that gave new jobs or cultural institutions to Palestinians. It has become clear that this money was to be used primarily for police and security repression. During a visit by Al Gore to the region in 1999, it was reported that he made clear that the United States supported the Palestinian Authority primarily for this role of police repression of Palestinian protest. In the five years from the beginning of the 'peace process' to 1997, Palestinians grew rapidly even more impoverished, losing 36 percent of their already miserable income (the equivalent of $6 billion dollars), while a corrupt PLO leadership flaunted large houses and cars and was surrounded by bodyguards.

Thus it appears that the real meaning of the 'peace process' was a process of entrapment in an apartheid system that encloses Palestinians in their ghettos, denying them the possibility of real autonomous development. Yet there seemed to be no way to legitimately regain a voice to protest against this trap or to define an alternative that could be heard by the international community. The ultimate 'genius' of the Israeli 'peace process' was to deny Palestinians not only their land, but their voice as well.

From Rabin to Sharon

In November 1995, Yitzhak Rabin was gunned down by a militant Jewish fundamentalist who saw him as having betrayed the absolute claims of Jews to all the land, by 'giving away' land to the Palestinians and making peace with Israel's enemies. Thereafter the Labour party, led by Peres, was defeated and Benyamin Netanyahu of the Likud party became prime minister. These dramatic events made it easy for many people to cast Rabin as the hero-martyr for 'peace' who sought a just co-existence with the Palestinians, while Netanyahu was seen as representing an intransigent effort to scuttle the 'peace process'. The new Labour party government under Barak was portrayed in the American press as a return to an appropriate implementation of the 'peace process'.

In the closing months of the Clinton presidency there was a rush to close a deal between the Palestinians and Barak so Clinton could 'go down in history' as having solved this conflict. But the July 2000 talks ended without agreement. Arafat was then vehemently denounced by Israelis and Americans as having foolishly turned down Barak's 'generous offer' of 95 percent of the West Bank and Gaza. But this much repeated claim is misleading. What the Palestinians were offered was 95 percent of areas A and B, leaving the basic system of fragmentation and control by Israel intact. Moreover the Palestinians were to permanently give up any claim to East Jerusalem, or of the right of return, and/or compensation of refugees. Such a deal, which would have made a dependent apartheid situation final, was totally unacceptable to the Palestinians.

On 28 September 2000, Ariel Sharon, the Israeli ex-general responsible for many brutalities, most notably the 1982 massacre of Palestinian refugees in the Sabra and Shatila camps in Lebanon, made a visit to the Muslim holy site, the Haram al-Sharif or Dome of the Rock in the old city of Jerusalem, accompanied by many soldiers. Palestinians erupted in protest against this intentionally provocative gesture of claiming the area for Israel. Protestors at the Dome of the Rock were fired on by Israeli snipers, killing four and wounding a hundred. More protests erupted all over the West Bank and Gaza. This precipitated what came to be called the Second *Intifada*.

The Israeli Defense Forces responded with escalated aggression. A cycle of violence and counter violence ensued. By 26 June 2003, some 2,398 Palestinians had been killed and 23,150 injured, many of them permanently. Israelis have also suffered significant deaths and injuries, 704 deaths and 4,849 injuries. Unlike the first *Intifada*, which was carried out without arms on the Palestinians side, now some Palestinians formed sniper and suicide bomber groups and carried the struggle into Israel. In March 2001, Ariel Sharon was elected prime minister of Israel. The struggle with the Palestinians was by then defined as a quasi-war, with Israelis using tanks and missiles mounted on helicopters to bombard Palestinians areas.

Sharon seized the opportunity to virtually dismantle the Palestinian Authority, invading Ramallah to sack and destroy most of the budding Palestinian ministries that had begun to be developed. Arafat was confined to Ramallah, his headquarters reduced to rubble except for

a building where he resides. A new policy, called 'Operation Bronze', subdivided the West Bank and Gaza into 64 mini-regions, each surrounded by deep trenches and walls to prevent travel between them. Palestinians were confined to their homes for several days each week, prevented even from going into their yards to cultivate gardens. These continual curfews cut off Palestinians from access to jobs, schools and hospitals and further precipitated their descent into dire poverty.

The Republican administration of George W Bush that came to power in January 2001 was much more explicitly an ally of the hard-line Likud party and of Sharon in particular, in contrast to earlier American administrations that had favoured what was seen as the more flexible Labour party. Particularly after the 11 September 2001 bombings of the World Trade Center and the Pentagon, the Bush administration seemed disposed to give Sharon a totally free hand to repress the Palestinians. There was even talk by right-wing Israelis of mass expulsions of Palestinians, to 'complete the job' of the 1948-9 expulsions. Sharon seized on the 9/11 bombings and the subsequent American declaration of a world-wide 'war on terrorism' to seek to define the Palestinians in general and Arafat in particular as terrorists in the same vein as al-Qu'ida. Sharon even referred to Arafat as 'our Bin Laden'. The American government declared that they would not talk to the Palestinians until Arafat was replaced as prime minister. It appeared than any negotiations between Palestinians, Israelis and Americans was permanently stalled.

The US quickly took its war on terrorism into an invasion of Afghanistan, and soon after was talking of an invasion of Iraq, even though no links could be established between the Iraqi regime of Saddam Hussein and al Qaa'ida. The claims of both Bush and British Prime Minister Blair that Hussein had weapons of mass destruction poised for attack on the West has proven vacuous. But the invasion and quick victory of the American and British troops in Iraq in the spring of 2003 did bring the US to feel the need for some new effort to 'solve' the Israeli-Palestinian conflict, since this was seen as a major source of animus against the US in the Arab and Muslim world. Thus the Bush administration unveiled its 'road map' for new negotiations between the Palestinians and Israelis under US sponsorship, with the promise that this should lead to an independent Palestinian state.

The Palestinians, meanwhile, had accepted the replacement of their elected president, Yasir Arafat, by a titular Prime Minister, Mahmoud

Abbas (although Arafat remained in control behind the scenes). This allowed at least talks to begin between the two sides, since Arafat had been declared *persona non grata* by the Israelis and Americans. Some modest gains were made in the summer of 2003 with Israeli troops withdrawing from direct occupation of Gaza and Bethlehem, although still surrounding the areas, preventing Palestinians from free travel between Palestinian areas. The Bush 'road map' was extremely vague, with no concrete plans for crucial matters, such as stopping, much less dismantling the still expanding settlements in the West Bank and Gaza without which no contiguous territory for a Palestinian state would be possible. Bush has even been unwilling to condemn clearly the wall that the Israelis are building on Palestinian land to divide the West Bank from Israel. With the US almost totally on the side of Sharon, it seems there is little American will to force any real concessions from Israel, thus perpetuating the impasse.

2. What role for Western Christians?

The Christian community, both the Palestinian Christians and Western Christians in communication with them, could play a vital role in helping regain a Palestinian voice of protest and a quest for genuine alternatives. But this mediating role has been largely blocked by the gullibility of most Western Christians toward the chimeras of the 'peace process,' and the 'road map' fuelled by a desire to think the best of Israeli 'good will', and a readiness to stereotype Palestinians as terrorists, now made even worse as 'Islamic terrorists'.

Christians of Western Europe and North America fall into two major lines of thought toward Israeli-Palestinian relations, or more appropriately, toward Israel, since Palestinians are seldom thought about at all in either view. A small but militant and influential group, associated with more fundamentalist forms of Protestant Christianity, are Christian Zionists. A larger but more diffuse group of Western Christians share some Christian Zionist views, but their main perspective is shaped by a desire to compensate for past Christian antisemitism by affirming positive ecumenical relations with Jews.

While these sentiments that Christians should repent of past antisemitism and cultivate a positive relation with Jews and Judaism are

appropriate in themselves, unfortunately they have been construed primarily as a Christian duty of uncritical adulation for the State of Israel. This means that mention of the Palestinian plight is ignored altogether. Most such Christians avoid learning anything about the Palestinians. It is implicitly assumed that any concern for injustice to Palestinians, indeed any discussion of Palestinians at all, is to be construed as antisemitic. So, such Christians evade knowing and hence having to speak about them, in order not to be denounced as antisemitic by those Jews with whom they wish to cultivate 'ecumenical relations'.

Christian repentance for the Holocaust and antisemitism has been effectively distorted into a silencing of Western Christians in regard to Palestinian human and civil rights, a view carefully nurtured and reinforced by the Jewish establishment, especially in North America. Any effort to break through this wall of self-censorship of Western Christians in regard to injustices to Palestinians by those seeking to communicate an alternative reality encounters built-in walls of ignorance and self-silencing among Christians. It is difficult to communicate to such Christians that there might be some way of being concerned about justice for Palestinians that would also be an expression of positive regard for Jews as well. The notion that Christians can only have good relations with Jews by turning a blind eye to the plight of Palestinians seems unshakeable. Palestinians are made to pay for the sins of Western Christians against the Jews.

Western Christians need to understand what is happening to Palestinians in Israel and the Occupied Territories, but we also need to understand our own role as well, in the promotion of the ethnocide of the Palestinian people. In effect it is Western Christians, especially British and American, who created and continue to create the historical framework in which this process of ethnocide goes on. We have done it and continue to do it in the name of reconciliation with 'the Jews'. It is Americans particularly who provide the money and arms through our government that allow this to happen. But it is Western Christians who have created the historical ideology that legitimises this process. We legitimise it as something that is 'due' to the Jews, both from biblical land claims, and also as compensation for our past guilt. This legitimisation is then reinforced by the wall of silence around the resulting injustice to the Palestinians that prevents this from being seen, heard and understood. By doing this, we seek to salve our bad conscience for our past genocide of European Jews.

Christians in the West need to examine critically four theological themes that have been used effectively to silence Western Christians in regard to justice for the Palestinians:

1. that the belief that Jewish election by God includes a promise of the land of Palestine (Israel) to the Jews in a total, exclusive and permanent sense.
2. that Jewish restoration to Palestine is part of a messianic, redemptive process in which God is bringing redemption to the world.
3. that Zionism is identical with Judaism, and so any critique of Zionism or of the Sstate of Israel is anti-Jewish (antisemitic), and
4. that uncritical support of Israel is due from Christians as payment of their guilt for the Holocaust.

1. *God's promise of the land of Israel to the Jews*

Western Christians are often led to a one-sided assumption that Jews have an exclusive 'right' to Palestine by an ignorance of the actual history of the area. This land has never been a land of one people, but a land of many peoples. Many peoples lived there before the period of Hebrew political hegemony in antiquity. Many peoples continued to live side by side with the Hebrews during that period of Hebrew hegemony. Many peoples have come to this area, in migrations and amalgamations of peoples and cultures, for the last 2,500 years. These people became predominantly Christian in the 4th century, and became predominantly Muslim after the 7th century, with a significant Christian minority and a small Jewish minority. All three communities became arabized in language and culture.

The descendants of all those people are Palestinians. As the residents these people had the primary right to the land of Palestine in the mid-20th century. They were still the majority, some 70 percent of the population, when the land was partitioned in 1947. Thus, whatever rights must now be given to the Israeli Jewish population, largely descended from people who immigrated to this land in the 20th century, can only be on the basis of a recent construction of a national community in the

region, not on the basis of ancient religious claims. This national community has shaped its occupation of the land through a continual process of conquest and displacement of the earlier people that is fundamentally unjust. These unjust 'facts' of history must be adjusted to make place for at least an equal claim to the land of those who were present as the majority population until their forced and cruel displacement over the last fifty-six years.

What, then, of the claim that God gave this land to the Jews in ancient times and thus they have a prior claim to it? This claim makes essentially ethnocentric assumptions about God which are unacceptable to Christian theology. However much Christians need to honour the Jewish people and Judaism as our religious ancestors, Christians cannot accept an ethnocentric notion of God and of God's election of one people at the expense of others. Fundamental to Christian theology is a belief that God is a God of all nations, all peoples. In Christ, as Paul wrote to the Galatians, there is no more Jew or Greek (Gal. 3.28). No one people is especially favoured by God over others.

There is no doubt that Jews have a deep emotional symbolic identification with the land, that is rooted in ancient experience and has been carried through their religious tradition. But Palestinians also have a deep identification with the land rooted in their family and communal memories. Many Palestinians who have been refugees for more than fifty years still keep a vivid identification with their ancestral village and home. Ancient memories from two thousand years ago cannot be used to expel people from their homes who have been resident continually up to recent times.

Christians have often misconstrued their own universalism to deny Jewish particularity and to turn Christian universalism into imperialism. Authentic universalism must reject both a reversion to tribal ethnocentrism and also to universalist imperialism. This means that Christians should affirm a multi-particularist vision of co-humanity of many peoples and cultures. One should not use Jewish particularity to deny the rights of Palestinians, nor the reverse. One should affirm a co-humanity of Jews and Palestinians, actualised, as far as possible, in a just coexistence of both national communities in the land of Israel/Palestine.

2. The founding of Israel as the fulfilment of prophecy and the beginning of redemption

In the Jewish Scriptures and traditions the idea of a messianic return to the land as part of redemption was premised on an ethical vision of what redemption means. For both Jewish and Christian traditions the future fulfilment of redemptive hope includes the healing of enmity between nations. Swords are beaten into ploughshares. The weapons of destruction and death are transformed into the tools of cultivation of new life. Justice and peace flourish between nations. But Christian and Jewish militant fundamentalists ignore these ethical criteria in what is redemptive. They ignore the obvious fact that the foundation of the state of Israel has not been a means of healing between nations, but the source of an enormous outbreak of new enmity between nations in the Middle East and across the Christian and Muslim worlds.

The foundation of the state of Israel has been for Palestinians what they call the *Nakba* ('the catastrophe'), destroying their old way of life and continually evicting them from their land, destroying their society, killing or exiling their people. In no way is this redemptive history. Rather, it expresses utterly unredeemed modes of behaviour between peoples. To call such history 'redemptive' and the beginning of messianic times is a blasphemy toward what should be meant by those terms. This is false messianism, clothing evil-producing political projects with divine blessing.

This does not mean that the State of Israel is any worse than any number of other conquest and colonising projects which bring disaster upon other people and often upon one's own people. It means that these evil realities cannot be covered up by the trapping of special divinely ordained sanctity. Zionism, like many other political projects, is still operating with the ethics of competition and the negation of others. It may become redemptive, like any other human project, if it can overcome the ethics of domination of others and reshape itself by an ethics of mutuality that seeks to affirm one's neighbour as oneself.

3. Zionism as integral to Judaism

In fact, when Zionism first arose in the 19th and the first half of the 20th century, it was generally rejected by both Orthodox and Reform Judaism.

For Orthodox Jews the return to the land of Israel could be carried out only by the Messiah. For them Zionism was an unholy project carried out by non-observant Jews, and thus fundamentally contradicted their understanding of the conditions for restoring Israel to the land. Reform Jews also rejected Zionism because it denied their political universalism. Reform Judaism sought to detach Judaism as a religion from secular political identity and make Jews a religious community that could exist in any land as full and equal citizens.

It is not correct to claim that Judaism is unique in having a communal identity that unites religious and collective political identity. In their classical forms, Judaism, Christianity, Islam, even Buddhism and Confucianism, had collective forms that sought to create religio-political states. Today fundamentalist movements within all these religions are seeking to re-establish religious states. But such religious states are by nature exclusivist. They claim that only those of the established religion can be full citizens. The unjust treatment of the Palestinians is rooted in the effort to create an ethnically and religiously exclusive state or 'Jewish state' where, ideally, Jews are the absolute majority.

In Israel as a Jewish state only those defined as Jews in an ethno-religious sense can enjoy full citizen benefits. Palestinians are denied equal citizenship within Israel. This also makes it unacceptable to give the Palestinians in the Occupied Territories citizenship in Israel since this would mean that Jews would become a bare majority and perhaps eventually a minority. This is seen as a 'demographic problem'. But continued numbers of Palestinians are a demographic problem only if one continues to define Israel as a Jewish state, rather than accepting the reality that there are already in fact two national communities and three religions in the land. For justice and peace to be possible in Israel/Palestine any state or states in this land will have to accommodate and give equal citizenship to all people across this ethnic and religious diversity.

4. Christian guilt for the Holocaust demands uncritical support for Israel

Christians surely bear a burden of guilt because of the way their long-standing traditions of antisemitism were used to persecute Jews. These traditions were used by the Nazis to gain passive and active support of Christians for their project of genocide. But what is appropriate

repentance among Christians for this guilt? It would seem that Christians must seek to purge antisemitism from Christian teachings, and work to see that Jews are no longer burdened by this heritage in areas where Christians predominate. It is not appropriate to construe such repentance as collaboration with another injustice toward another people who are victims of the State of Israel.

On both the Jewish and the Christian sides there must be a distinction between the question of the Holocaust and its theological and ethical consequences for each religion and the questions about the State of Israel and its ethical deficiencies. One must stop using the Holocaust as if it mandated a 'compensation' that includes the right to create a state based on the expulsion of another people from their homeland. Although there are certainly emotional connections between these two events, they need to be delinked symbolically. Quite simply, one evil does not justify another.

One cannot continue to argue that the state of Israel is necessary because it provides a secure haven for Jews against the possibility of another antisemitic outbreak by Christians. In fact in the last fifty years there is no place more insecure for Jews than Israel. This is not because there is some 'cosmic hate' against Jews by gentiles, but because Israel has been built on an antagonistic relationship to the Palestinians in particular and the Arab world in general that generates a cycle of violence. There is certainly a desire of many on all sides, Jewish Israelis, Palestinian Arabs, both Muslims and Christians, and the Arab world, to end this cycle of violence. But this can only happen if there is real movement on the part of Israel and the West to recognize the historical injustice to the Palestinians and to grant some sharing of land and political self-rule that would enable the Palestinians to live normal human lives, able to cultivate their land, go to school, work and get medical care without threat of injury and death.

Our experience suggests that Western Christians cannot break out of the myopias created by these arguments against justice for the Palestinians by themselves, because its contradictions are too invisible to them. It is only through corrective experiences, especially personal contact with Palestinian people in their own homeland, that Western Christians can come face-to-face with the realities that can shatter their self-enclosed framework and open them up to a different approach. Palestinian Christians are key mediators here to both introduce Western Christians

to the Palestinian reality, but also to correct the misuse of Christian symbols, such as repentance, the promised land and Jewish-Christian ecumenical relations that have been misconstrued in Western Christian perspective.

It is here that Palestinian liberation and contextual theologies, as these are being developed by Palestinian Christian theologians, such as Naim Ateek and Mitri Raheb, can play a key role to shatter this distorted use of Christianity that justifies Israeli colonialism, and also to enunciate a positive theology of just coexistence of Jewish and Palestinian people in the homeland they both love. Central to these theologies is an affirmation of a God of justice for all people who calls us into mutually affirming co-existence. This is incompatible with exclusivist views that identify the oneness of God with the unique election of one religious group over others. Only a vision of God that loves and commands justice for all peoples equally can create the framework for just coexistence of the two people, Israelis and Palestinians, and the three religions, Judaism, Christianity and Islam, calling them to be equal partners, brothers and sisters, in sharing the land together in justice and peace. This is authentic ecumenism.

References and recommended reading

Ateek, Naim. 1991. *Justice and Only Justice: A Palestinian Theology of Liberation*. Maryknoll, NY: Orbis

Ateek, Naim, Marc Ellis and Rosemary Ruether. 1992. *Faith and the Intifada: Palestinian Christian Voices*. Maryknoll, NY: Orbis

Ellis, Marc H. 1990. *Beyond Innocence and Redemption: Confronting the Holocaust and Israeli Power*. San Francisco: Harper and Row

Flapan, Simha. 1987. *The Birth of Israel: Myths and Realities*. New York: Pantheon

Prior, Michael. 1997. *The Bible and Colonialism. A Moral Critique*. Sheffield: Sheffield Academic Press

Raheb, Mitri. 1995. *I am a Palestinian Christian*. Minneapolis: Fortress

Reinhart, Tanya. 2002. *Israel/Palestine. How to End the War of 1948*. New York: Seven Stories Press

Ruether, Herman J. and Rosemary Radford Ruether. 2002. *The Wrath of Jonah: The Crisis of Religious Nationalism in the Israeli-Palestinian Conflict*. Minneapolis: Fortress

Shlaim, Avi. 2000. *The Iron Wall: Israel and the Arab World*. New York and London: WW Norton

Websites

Between the Lines, Box 681 Jerusalem, joint Israeli–Palestinian newsletter.
www.between.lines.org

B'tselem. Israeli Human Rights Organization. www.Btselem.org

Electronic Intifada, critical information and news on Palestine and the Middle East,
founded by Ali Abu-Nimah, Palestinian human rights journalist, Chicago,
www.electronicintifada.net

Law and Society. Palestinian Law and Justice Organization, West Bank, Palestine,
www.lawsociety.org

Not in my Name. American Jewish Human Rights and Justice group.
www.NIMN.org

Salem. Israeli group working with Palestinians on preventing house demolitions.
www.salem.org

STATE OF DENIAL:
THE *NAKBA* IN ISRAELI HISTORY
AND TODAY
Ilan Pappé

For Israelis, 1948 is a year in which two things happened which contradict each other: on the one hand, Zionism, the Jewish national movement, claimed it fulfilled an ancient dream of returning to a homeland after 2,000 years of exile. From this perspective, 1948 was 'a miraculous event' in the collective Israeli Jewish memory. It constitutes a chapter in history that not only proclaims triumph and the realisation of dreams but also carries associations with moral purity and absolute justice. This is why anything that happened in that year is wedded to the most basic values of present Israeli society. Hence, the military conduct of the Jewish soldiers on the battlefield in 1948 became a model for generations to come, and the leadership's statesmanship in those years is still a paragon for future political elites. The leaders are described as people devoted to the Zionist ideals and as men who disregarded their private interests and good for the sake of the common cause. 1948, then, is a sacred year, revered in more than one way as the formative source of all that is good in the Jewish society of Israel.

On the other hand, 1948 marked also the worst chapter in Jewish history. In that year, Jews did in Palestine what Jews had not done anywhere else in the previous 2,000 years. Even if one puts aside the historical debate about why what happened in 1948 in fact transpired, no one seems to question the enormity of the tragedy that befell the indigenous population of Palestine as a result of the emergence and success of the Zionist movement. Jews expelled, massacred, destroyed and raped in that year, and generally behaved like all the other colonialist movements operating in the Middle East and Africa ever since the beginning of the 19th century.

In normal circumstances, as Edward Said recommended in his seminal *Culture and Imperialism* (1993), painful dialogue with the past should enable a given society to digest both the most evil and the most glorious moments of its nation's history. But this could not work in a case where a moral self-image is considered to be the principal asset in the

71

battle for public opinion, and thus the best means of surviving in a hostile environment. The way out for the Jewish society in the newly-founded state was to erase in the collective memory the unpleasant chapters of the past, and leave intact the gratifying ones. It was a conscious mechanism put in place and motion in order to solve the impossible tension arising from the two contradictory messages of the past.

Moreover, the fact that so many of the people living in Israel today lived through the1948 period has made the task all the more difficult. 1948 is not a distant memory, and the crimes committed then are still visible in the landscape around for the present generation of Israelis to behold and comprehend. And on the Palestinian side, of course, there are still victims living, who can tell their story; and when they are gone, their descendants—who have heard the tales of the 1948 horrors over and over again—are likely to represent their point of view for generations to come. And, of course, there are people in Israel who know exactly what they did, and there are even more who know what others have done.

Nevertheless, the Israeli authorities continue to succeed in eliminating these deeds totally from the society's collective memory, while struggling vigorously against anyone trying to shed light on the repulsive chapters of the 1948 history, whether inside or outside Israel. When one examines Israeli textbooks, curricula, media, and political discourse one notices that this chapter in Jewish history—the chapter of expulsion, colonisation, massacres, rape, and the burning of villages—is totally absent. In its stead one finds chapters of heroism, glorious campaigns and amazing tales of moral courage and military competence, unheard of in any other history of a people's liberation in the 20th century.

Let us, then, begin with a brief overview of the denied chapters of the history of 1948. Some of these chapters are also missing so far from the Palestinian collective memory. The two forms of amnesia stem, of course, from two very different ways of dealing with the past: Jewish Israelis are unwilling to acknowledge, or be accountable for what happened in 1948, whereas the Palestinians, as a community of victims, have little appetite to revisit the traumas of the past. For such distinct reasons, popular memory on both sides, and the failure, or unwillingness of professional historians to provide a true representation of the past have left us without a clear picture of the 1948 events.

The erased chapters of evil

The 1948 war's diplomatic manoeuvres and military campaigns are well engraved in Israeli Jewish historiography. What is missing is the chapter on the ethnic cleansing carried out by the Jews in 1948. As a result of that campaign, 500 Palestinian villages and 11 urban neighbourhoods were destroyed, 700,000 Palestinians were expelled and several thousands were massacred.[1] Even today, it is hard to find a succinct summary of the planning, execution and repercussions of these tragic results.

In November 1947, the UN proposed to partition Palestine into a Jewish and an Arab state as the best solution to the conflict. That scheme was very problematic from its inception, for three major reasons. Firstly, it was presented to the two contending parties, not as a basis for negotiation but as a *fait accompli*, even though the total Palestinian rejection of the principles underpinning the plan was well known to the UN. The alternative course, as proposed by a number of UN member states, and later recognised by the American State Department as the best option, was to begin, in 1948, negotiations under the auspices of the UN that would last for several years. The scheme proposed by the UN, on the other hand, faithfully represented the Zionist strategy and policy. Imposing the will of one side, through the agencies of the UN, could not have been a recipe for peace, but rather, for war. The Palestinian side viewed the Zionist movement as the Algerians did the French colonialists. Just as it was unthinkable for the Algerians to agree to share their land with the French settlers, so it was unacceptable for the Palestinians to divide Palestine with the Zionist movement. Even the Palestinians recognised, of course, that the cases were different, and consequently a longer period of negotiations was needed, but was not granted.

Secondly, the Jewish minority (660,000 out of two million) was offered the larger part of the land (56 percent). The imposed partition, then, would begin with an unjust proposal. Thirdly, because of the demographic distributions of the two communities—the Palestinians and the Jews—the 56 percent of the land offered to the Jews as a state included an equal number of Jews and Palestinians. All the Zionist leaders, from left to right concurred on the need to maintain a considerable Jewish

---

[1] The scope of the tragedy is well described in a collection of articles in Karmi and Cortran 1999.

majority in Palestine; in fact, the absence of such a solid majority was regarded as heralding the demise of Zionism. Even a cursory knowledge of Zionist ideology and strategy, should have clarified to the UN peace architects that such a demographic reality would lead to the virtually total cleansing of the local population from the future Jewish state.

On 10 March 1948, the *Hagana*, the main Jewish underground in Palestine, issued a military blueprint preparing the community for the expected British evacuation of Palestine, scheduled for 15 May 1948. The total Arab and Palestinian rejection led the Jewish leadership to declare the UN resolution dead to all intents and purposes. Already in May 1947, the Jewish Agency had drawn a map which included most of Palestine as a Jewish state, apart from the West Bank of today which was granted to the Transjordanians. Thus, a plan was devised on 10 March 1948, to take over these parts, which together constituted 80 percent of Palestine. The plan was called Plan D (plans A, B and C had been similar blueprints in the past formulating Zionist strategy *vis-à-vis* an unfolding and changing reality). Plan D (or *Dalet* in Hebrew) instructed the Jewish forces to cleanse the Palestinian areas falling under their control. The *Hagana* had several brigades at its disposal, and each one of them received a list of villages it had to occupy and destroy. Most of the villages were destined to be destroyed and only in very exceptional cases were the forces ordered to leave them intact (see Pappé 1992: 124-43).

The ethnic cleansing operation, beginning in December 1947, continued well into the 1950s. Villages were surrounded on three flanks, and the fourth one was left open for flight and evacuation. In some cases the tactic did not work, and many villagers remained in their houses—it was in such cases that the massacres took place. This was the principal strategy of the Judaization of Palestine.

The ethnic cleansing took place in three stages. The first one was from December 1947 until the end of the summer of 1948, when the coastal and inner plains were destroyed, and their population evicted by force. The second one took place in the autumn and winter of 1948-49 and included Galilee and the Naqab (Negev).

By the winter of 1949, the guns in the land of Palestine were silent. The second phase of the war had ended, and with it the second stage of the cleansing had terminated. Nevertheless, the expulsion continued long after the noise of war had subsided. The third phase of

the ethnic cleansing would extend beyond the war, up until 1954 in fact, when dozens of additional villages were destroyed, and their inhabitants were expelled. Of the approximately 900,000 Palestinians living in the territories designated by the UN as a Jewish state only 100,000 remained on, or near their lands and houses. Those who remained became the Palestinian minority in Israel. The rest were expelled, or fled under the threat of expulsion, and a few thousand died in massacres.

The landscape of the countryside, the rural heartland of Palestine, with its 1,000 colourful and picturesque villages was ruined. Half of the villages were erased from the face of the earth, run over by Israeli bulldozers which set to work in August 1948 when the government decided either to convert them into cultivated land, or to build new Jewish settlements on their ruins. A special committee was established to give hebraised versions of the original Arab names to the new settlements—thus, e.g., Lubya became Lavi, and Safuria was turned into Zipori. David Ben-Gurion, the first prime minister of Israel, explained that this was done as part of an attempt to prevent future claims to these villages. This process was supported also by the Israeli archaeologists who authorised the names, not so much as a take-over of a title, but rather as a form of poetic justice which restored to 'ancient Israel' its ancestral map (see Benvenisti 2000: 1-50). Placenames were taken from the Bible and attached to the destroyed villages.

Urban Palestine was torn apart and crushed in a similar way. The Palestinian neighbourhoods in mixed towns were wrecked, apart from a few quarters which were left empty, waiting to be populated later by incoming Jewish immigrants from Arab countries.

The Palestinian refugees spent the winter of 1948 in tent camps provided by voluntary agencies. Most of these locations were to become their permanent residences. The tents were replaced by clay huts that became the familiar feature of Palestinian existence in the Middle East. The only hope for these refugees, at the time, was the one offered by UN resolution 194 (11 December 1948), promising them a speedy return to their homes. This is one of many pledges made by the international community to the Palestinians that remains unfulfilled until to-day.

The catastrophe that befell the Palestinians would be remembered in the collective national memory as the *Nakba* ('the disaster'), kindling the fire that would restore the Palestinians as a national movement. The self-image of this national movement would be that of an indigenous

population led by a guerrilla movement striving to turn the clock back, with, as it transpired, very little success.

The Israelis' collective memory, on the other hand, would depict the war as an act of a national liberation movement, fighting both British colonialism and Arab hostility, and ultimately triumphing against all the odds. The loss of one percent of the Jewish population, of course, would cast a cloud over the joy of having achieved independence, but would not deter the will and determination of the Zionists to judaize Palestine and turn it into the future haven for world Jewry. In the event, Israel has turned out to be the most dangerous place for Jews to live in in the second half of the 20th century. Moreover, most Jews have preferred to live outside Israel, and quite a few did not identify in general with the Jewish project in Palestine, and did not wish to be associated with its dire consequences in Palestine. Nevertheless, a vociferous minority of Jews in the United States continues to give the impression that world Jewry in general condones the uprooting of the Palestinians and the other events of 1948. The illusion that the majority of Jews have legitimised whatever Israel had done in 1948, and thereafter, has dangerously compromised the relationship between Jewish minorities and the rest of society in the Western world particularly in places where public opinion since 1987 has become increasingly hostile to Israel's policies towards the Palestinians.

Professional remembering and the Nakba

Until very recently, the Israeli-Zionist representation of the 1948 war has dominated the academic world, and probably because of that also, the more general public's perception of the *Nakba*. A consequence of this is that the events of 1948 have been consistently portrayed as primarily a war between two armies. Such an assumption calls on the expertise of military historians, who can analyse the military strategy and tactics of both sides. In such a manner, all activities, including even atrocities, are portrayed as part of the theatre of war, wherein things are judged on a moral basis in a manner very different from the way they would be treated in a non-combat situation. For instance, it is within this context that the death of civilians during a battle is accepted as an integral part of the battle, and condoned as an action deemed necessary as part of the

overall attempt to win a war—although even within a war, of course, there are exceptional atrocities which are not accepted, but are treated as illegitimate in military historiography.

Portraying a conflict as a 'war' entails also the presumption of parity in questions of moral responsibility for the unfolding events on the ground, including in our case the massive expulsion of an indigenous population. In such a fashion, the paradigm of balancing between the two sides was deemed to be 'academic' and 'objective', while any Palestinian narrative claiming that there were in 1948, not two equally equipped armies, but, rather, an expeller and an expelled, an offender and its victims, was dismissed as sheer propaganda.

I suggest, however, that the events that unfolded after May 1948 in Israel and Palestine should be reviewed from within the paradigm of ethnic cleansing, rather than as part of military history. Historiographically, this would mean that the deeds perpetrated then were part of the domestic policies implemented by a regime *vis-à-vis* civilians—in many cases, given the fact that the ethnic cleansing took place within the designated UN Jewish state, these were operations conducted by a regime against its own citizens.

A Palestinian resident of the village of Tantura has described this new reality better than any historian. His village, situated 30 kilometres south of Haifa, on the coast, became, on 15 May 1948, part of the Jewish state, in virtue of UN partition resolution 181 (29 November 1947). On the 23 May [1948] this person, like many others, found himself in a prison camp in Umm Khaled (30 kilometres to the south of his village), and after being there for a year and half, was expelled to the West Bank. 'A few days after my new state occupied my village, I became a prisoner of war rather than a citizen.' He was a young boy—not an 'enemy soldier'—at the time. He was, however, luckier than others of his age who were massacred in his village. Indeed his village Tantura was not a battlefield between two armies, but, rather, a civilian space invaded by military troops. Ethnic ideology, settlement policy and demographic strategy were the decisive factors here, not the military plans. Massacres, whether premeditated or not, were an integral, and not an exceptional part of the ethnic cleansing act, even though history has taught us that, in most cases, expulsion was preferred to killing.

The evidence for historians in the archives of the regime committing the ethnic cleansing prevents a clear picture emerging, since

the aim of the regime from the beginning was to obscure its intentions, and this is manifested in the language of the orders and that of the post-event reports. This is why evidence of victims and victimisers—even if with hindsight—is so vital. In the case of the Tantura venture, for example, it was possible to reconstruct what happened mainly through the 'bridging' of the evidence provided by the collective and individual memories of victim and victimiser alike.

The ethnic cleansing paradigm also explains why expulsions, rather than massacres were of the essence of such crimes. As emerges from the evidence of the Balkan wars of the 1990s, within the general pattern of ethnic cleansing the sporadic massacres that were perpetrated were motivated more by revenge rather than by the acting out of a clear-cut plan. However, the scheme to create new ethnic realities was facilitated by these massacres, no less than if they had been the result of a policy of systematic expulsion.

The Jewish operation in 1948 fits into the definitions of ethnic cleansing contained in the UN reports on the Balkan wars of the 1990s. The UN council for human rights linked the wish to impose ethnic rule on a mixed area—the making of Greater Serbia—with acts of expulsion and with other violent mechanisms. The report defines acts of ethnic cleansing as including the separation of men from women, the detention of men, the blowing-up of houses and their re-population by another ethnic group later on. This was precisely the repertoire of the Jewish soldiers in the 1948 war.

Nakba *memory in the public eye*

That ethnic cleansing was perpetrated in 1948 and later is altogether denied both in and by Israel. The mechanism of denial is so forceful in Israel, and among its ardent supporters in the United States, that the perspective in this essay exposes much deeper questions. The most important question is the relevance of the Zionist ideology in general to the crimes committed in 1948. Others have shown already that the massive expulsion was the inevitable outcome of a strategy dating back to the late 19th century.[2]

---

[2] See, in particular, Nur Masalha's *Expulsion of the Palestinians: the Concept of 'Transfer' in Zionist Political Thought, 1882-1948* (1992), and his *A Land without a People. Israel,*

The ideology of 'transfer' emerged the moment the leaders of the Zionist movement realised that the making of a Jewish state in Palestine could not be achieved as long as the indigenous people of Palestine remained on the land. The presence of a local society and culture had been known to the founding fathers of Zionism even before the first settlers set foot on the land. Theodor Herzl, the founding father of Zionism, already predicted that his dream of a Jewish homeland in Palestine would necessitate expulsion of the indigenous population, as evidenced in one of his diary entries for 12 June 1895. Moving on from his comments on constituting a Jewish *society* in the land he got down to the question of forming a *state* for Jews. He wrote that, having occupied the land and expropriated the private property, 'We shall endeavour to expel the poor population across the border unnoticed, procuring employment for it in the transit countries, but denying it any employment in our own country.' Herzl added that both 'the process of expropriation and the removal of the poor must be carried out discreetly and circumspectly.'[3] Ethnic cleansing was also in the minds of the leaders of the Second Aliya, a kind of Zionist Mayflower generation (Masalha 1992: 93-141).

Two means were used to alter the demographic and 'ethnic' reality of Palestine, and impose the Zionist programme on the local reality: the dispossession of the indigenous population from the land, and its re-populating with newcomers—i.e., expulsion and settlement. The colonisation effort was pushed forward by a movement that had not yet won regional or international legitimacy, and, therefore, that had to buy land, and create enclaves within the indigenous population. The British empire was very helpful in making this scheme into a reality. Yet, from the very beginning of the Zionist strategy, the leaders of Zionism knew that settlement was a very long and measured process, which might not be sufficient to realise the revolutionary dreams of the movement, and its desire to alter the realties on the ground, and impose its own interpretation

---

Transfer and the Palestinians 1949-96 (1997). Masalha's later book, *Imperial Israel and the Palestinians: The Politics of Expansion, 1967-2000* (2000) is a comprehensive treatment of the imperial imperative within Herzlian Zionism. His most recent book, *The Politics of Denial: Israel and the Palestinian Refugee Problem* (2003) exposes Israel's pretence to innocence on the question of the Palestinian expulsees.

[3]   This is Michael Prior's translation of 'Die arme Bevölkerung trachten wir unbemerkt über die Grenze zu schaffen, indem wir in den Durchzugsländern Arbeit verschaffen aber in unserem eigenen Lande jederlei Arbeit verweigern' (Prior 1999: 9) .

on the land's past, present and future. To achieve that, the movement needed to resort to more telling means, such as ethnic cleansing and transfer.

As means of judaizing Palestine transfer and ethnic cleansing—which would be possible to achieve as suitable 'historical opportunities' presented themselves—had been closely associated in Zionist thought and practice. Appropriate circumstances could include the indifference of the international community, or the presence of such 'revolutionary conditions' as war would provide. The link between purpose and timing had been elucidated very clearly in a letter David Ben-Gurion had written to his son Amos on 5 October 1937:

> We must expel Arabs and take their places ... and if we have to use force—not to dispossess the Arabs of the Negev and Transjordan, but to guarantee our own right to settle in those places—then we have force at our disposal (in Teveth 1985: 189).

This notion re-appeared ever after in Ben-Gurion's addresses to his MAPAI party members throughout the Mandatory period (see, e.g., Masalha 1992), right up to the time when such an opportune moment arose—in 1948.

It is not surprising to read in the Israeli press today, then, that Ariel Sharon considers himself to be the new Ben-Gurion, who is about to settle the Palestine question once and for all. While the media in the West may be misled to believe that this is part of a newly adopted discourse of peace on the part of a past warmonger, it is, in fact, an ever-loyal contemporary representation of a Ben-Gurionist's search for yet another revolutionary moment, that would enable to further, if not to complete, the process of de-arabizing Palestine and judaizing it, which had begun already in 1882.

The struggle against Nakba denial

Nakba denial in Israel and the West was helped by the overall negation of the Palestinians as a people—the notorious statement of Israeli Prime Minister Golda Meir in 1970 epitomised this attitude. Towards the end

of the 1980s, as a result of the first *Intifada*, the situation improved somewhat, with the humanisation of the Palestinians in the Western media, with the result that they could be introduced into the field of Middle Eastern studies as a legitimate subject matter. In Israel itself, even in those years, Palestinian affairs, academically or publicly, were discussed only by academics who in the past had been intelligence experts on the subject, and who still had close ties with the security services and the IDF (Israeli Defense Force). This Israeli academic perspective effectively erased the *Nakba* as a historical event, and prevented local scholars and academics from challenging the overall denial and suppression of the catastrophe in the world outside the ivory towers of the universities.

The mechanisms of denial in Israel are very effective, because it is a comprehensive means of indoctrination, covering the whole of a citizen's life from the cradle to the grave. It ensures the state that its people do not get confused by facts and reality, or, at least, that they view reality in such a way that it does not create any moral problems.

Nevertheless, already in the 1980s, cracks were beginning to appear in the wall of denial. Even in Israel and the West, the wide exposure in the world media of Israeli war crimes ever since 1982 raised troubling questions about Israel's self-image of being 'the only democracy in the Middle East', or as a community belonging to the world of human and civil rights and universal values. But it was the emergence of critical historiography in Israel in the early 1990s—the so-called 'new history'—which relocated the *Nakba* at the centre of the academic and public debate about the conflict. This 'new history' in effect legitimised the Palestinian narrative, after it had been portrayed for years as sheer propaganda by even Western journalists, politicians and academics.

The challenge to the hitherto hegemonic Zionist presentation of the 1948 war appeared in various areas of cultural expression—in the media, academia and popular arts. It affected the discourse both in the US and Israel; but it never entered the political arena. The celebrated 'new history', in fact, was no more than a few books on 1948 written by professionals in English—e.g., Flapan 1979 and 1987; Kimmerling 1983; Masalha 1992; Morris 1987, 1990, and 1993; Pappé 1988 and 1992; Segev 1986 and 1993; Shahak 1975; Shapira 1992; Shlaim 1988—only some of which were translated into Hebrew. These, nevertheless, made it possible, for anyone wishing to do so, to learn how the Jewish state had

been built on the ruins of the indigenous people of Palestine, whose livelihood, houses, culture and land had been systematically destroyed.

Public response in Israel at the time moved between indifference and the total rejection of the findings of the 'new historians'. It was only through elements of the media and the educational system that people were stimulated, somewhat hesitantly, to take a new look at the past. Meanwhile, however, from above, the establishment did everything it could to quash these early buds of Israeli self-awareness, and the recognition of Israel's role in the Palestinian catastrophe, a recognition that would, in the event, have helped Israelis considerably to understand better the continued deadlock in the peace process.

Outside the academic world, in the West in general, and in the US and Israel in particular, this shift in the academic perception had very little impact on the mainstream media and the political scene. In both America and in Jewish Israel, terms such as 'ethnic cleansing' and 'expulsion' are still today totally alien to politicians, journalists and common people alike. The relevant chapters of the past that would justify categorically the application of such terms to Israeli origins are either distorted in the recollection of people, or are totally absent.

A brief look at Western public opinion is illuminating. One notes that new initiatives were taken in several European countries in the course of the 1990s to relocate the history and future refugees. It is too early yet to judge how much such efforts—undertaken in the main by pro-Palestinian NGOs—would affect the policies of the various governments. Even in the United States there were signs of movement in a similar direction, when, in April 2000, the first ever American 'Right of Return' conference was convened, with some 1,000 representatives from all over the country in attendance.[4] But, so far, such efforts have failed to impinge upon Capitol Hill, the *New York Times*, or the White House, irrespective of who was in office over the last fifteen years. However, the events of 11 September 2001 have so far put an end to the new trend, and have promoted the revival of anti-Palestinianism in the US.

---

[4] The conference papers, with a number of additional invited papers, were published in Aruri 2001.

Nakba *denial and the Palestine-Israel peace process*

But even before the U-turn in American public opinion after 11 September 2001, the movement of academic critique in Israel and the West, with its fresh view on the 1948 ethnic cleansing, was not a particularly impressive player on the stage. It made no impact whatsoever on the Palestine/Israel peace agenda, even though Palestine was the focus of peace efforts precisely at the time when the fresh voices were being heard. At the centre of these peace efforts was the Oslo Accord that began to roll in September 1993. The concept behind this process, as in all previous peace endeavours in Palestine, was a Zionist one. Hence, the peace process of the 1990s, the Oslo Accord, was conducted according to the Israeli perception of peace, from which, of course, the *Nakba* was totally absent. The Oslo formula was architected by Israeli thinkers from the Jewish peace camp, people who ever since 1967 had played an important role in the Israeli public scene. They were institutionalised in an extra-parliamentary movement 'Peace Now', and had several parties on their side in the Israeli parliament. In all their previous discourses and plans these 'Peace Now' people had totally evaded the 1948 issue, and had sidelined the refugee question. They did the same in 1993, and this time with the dire consequences of raising hopes of peace, as they seemed to find a Palestinian partner which would embrace a concept of peace that altogether buried 1948 and its victims.

With the final stages approaching, the Palestinians realised that, in addition to not witnessing a genuine Israeli withdrawal from the occupied West Bank and Gaza Strip, there was no proposed solution to the refugee question on offer. In frustration they rebelled. The climax of the Oslo negotiations at Camp David—the summit meeting between the then Prime Minister of Israel, Ehud Barak, and Yasir Arafat in the summer of 2000—gave the false impression that nothing less than the end of the conflict was on offer. The somewhat naïve Palestinian negotiators put the *Nakba*, and Israel's responsibility for it, at the top of the Palestinian list of demands. This, of course, was totally rejected by the Israeli team which succeed in enforcing its point of view on the summit. But to the Palestinian side's credit, we can acknowledge that, at least for a while, the catastrophe of 1948 was brought to the attention of a local, regional, and, to a certain extent global, audience. Yet, it is clear that the continued denial of the *Nakba* in the peace process was the main explanation for

the failure of the Camp David summit, the consequence of which was the second uprising in the occupied territories.

Clearly, it was necessary to remind those concerned with the Palestine question, not only in Israel, but also in the US, and even in Europe, that the Palestine/Israel conflict involved more than the future of the occupied territories. It also had to contend with the fact of the Palestinian refugees, who had been forced from their homes in 1948. The Israelis had succeeded earlier in sidelining the issue of the refugees' rights from the Oslo Accords, an aim facilitated by ill-managed Palestinian diplomacy and strategy.

Indeed, the *Nakba* had been so efficiently kept off the agenda of the peace process that when it suddenly appeared on it, the Israelis felt as if a Pandora's box had been prised open in front of them. The worst fear of the Israeli negotiators was that there was a possibility that Israel's responsibility for the 1948 catastrophe would now become a negotiable issue, and this 'danger' was, accordingly, immediately confronted. In the Israeli media and parliament (Knesset), a consensual position was formulated: no Israeli negotiator would be allowed even to discuss the right of return of the Palestinian refugees to the homes they had occupied before 1948. The Knesset passed a law to this effect, and Barak made a public commitment to it on the stairs of the plane that was taking him to Camp David.

It can be seen, then, that a public debate on the issue of the *Nakba*, whether conducted in Israel itself or in the US, its imperial protector, could open up questions concerning the moral legitimacy of the Zionist project as a whole. The mechanism of denial, therefore, was crucial, not only for defeating the counter-claims made by Palestinians in the peace process, but, far more importantly, for disallowing any significant debate on the very essence and moral foundations of Zionism.

But after the horrid events of 11 September 2001 and the outbreak of the second *Intifada*, with its waves of suicide bombers, the cracks that had already appeared in academia and were beginning to break into public discourse began immediately to 'close-up'. Soon the practice of past denials re-emerged in Israel, with added strength and conviction.

In the US, an unholy coalition of neo-conservatives, Christian Zionists and AIPAC—the main pro-Israeli Jewish lobby in the States— has had, since 2001 in particular, a firm hold over the American media's

presentation of the conflict in Palestine. That coalition's portrayal of the conflict—an altogether innocent, civilised society under siege by terrorists—enables Israel to get away with both its past behaviour and its present policies, which, if perpetrated by any other state would surely merit for it the designation 'pariah state'.

Future prospective

As I review the attempts that I have made—I have been involved personally in the struggle against *Nakba* denial in Israel, and, together with others, have attempted to bring the *Nakba* onto the Israeli public agenda—a very mixed picture emerges. I detect serious cracks in the wall of denial and repression that surrounds the issue of the *Nakba* in Israel, that have come about as a result of the debate on the 'new history' in Israel, and of the new political agenda of the Palestinians in Israel. The new atmosphere has also been helped by a clarification of the Palestinian position on the refugees issue towards the end of the Oslo Peace Process. As a result, notwithstanding more than fifty years of systemic government suppression, it is becoming more and more difficult in Israel to deny the expulsion and destruction of the Palestinians in 1948. However, this relative success has also brought with it two negative reactions, which were formulated after the outbreak of the *Aqsa Intifada.*

The Israeli political establishment was the first to react. The Sharon government, through its minister of education, has undertaken the systematic removal of any textbook, or school syllabus, that refers to the *Nakba,* even marginally. Similar instructions have been given to the public broadcasting authorities. The second reaction has been even more disturbing, and has encompassed wider sections of the public. Although a very considerable number of Israeli politicians, journalists and academics have ceased to deny what happened in 1948, they have nonetheless also been willing to justify it publicly, not only in retrospect, but also as a prescription for the future. Thus, the idea of 'transfer' has entered Israeli political discourse openly for the first time, portraying 'population transfer' as legitimate, being the most effective means of dealing with the Palestinian 'problem'.

Indeed, if I were asked to nominate what best characterises the current Israeli response to the *Nakba,* I would stress the growing

popularity of the transfer option in the Israeli public mood and thought. The *Nakba*—the expulsion of the Palestinians from Palestine—now seems to many in the centre of the political map as an inevitable and justifiable consequence of the Zionist project in Palestine. If there is any lament, it is that the expulsion was not completed. The fact that even an Israeli 'new historian' such as Benny Morris now subscribes to the view that the expulsion was inevitable, and should have been more comprehensive in 1948, helps to legitimise future Israeli plans for further ethnic cleansing.

'Population Transfer' is now the official, moral option recommended by one of Israel's most prestigious academic centres, the Centre for Interdisciplinary Studies in Herzliya, which advises the government. It has appeared as a policy proposal in papers presented to their government by senior Labour Party ministers. It is openly advocated by university professors, media commentators, and very few now dare to condemn it. This is manifestly true of historians, Professor Benny Morris of Beer Sheba University and Professor Yoav Gelber of Haifa University, and of geographer Professor Arnon Sofer of Haifa University, and indirectly the case also with Professor Shlomo Aviner of Hebrew University, as well as of Ephraim Sneh of the Labour Party, who suggest the annexation of the Palestinian parts of Israel to a Palestinian state. And, lately, even the leader of the majority in the American House of Representatives, Dick Armey, has openly endorsed it (2 May 2002).

Thus, the circle is being closed, almost before our very eyes. When Israel took almost 80 percent of Palestine in 1948, it did so through settlement, and the ethnic cleansing of the original Palestinian population. The country now has a prime minister who enjoys wide public support, and who wants to determine by force the future of the remaining 20 percent. He has, as did all his predecessors, from Labour and Likud alike, resorted to settlement as the best means for doing this, adding, as his unique contribution, the destruction of an independent Palestinian infrastructure. He senses—and he may not be wrong in this—that the public mood in Israel would allow him to go even further, should he wish to do so. He could emulate the ethnic cleansing of 1948, this time not only by driving the Palestinians out of the occupied territories, but, if necessary, also the one million Palestinians living within the pre-1967 borders of Israel.

In such an atmosphere, then, the *Nakba* is not so much denied in Israel, as cherished. Nevertheless, the full story of 1948 needs to be told to the Israelis, as there may still be some among that state's population who are sensitive about their country's past and present conduct. This segment of the population should be alerted to the fact that horrific deeds were concealed from them about Israeli actions in 1948, and they should be told, too, that such deeds could easily now be repeated, if they, and others, do not act to stop them before it is too late.

The struggle against the denial of the *Nakba* in Israel is now very much the agenda of certain Palestinian groups, both inside and outside Israel, committed to the cause. Since the fortieth anniversary of the *Nakba* in 1988, the Palestinian minority in Israel has associated, in a way that it never did previously, its collective and individual memories of the catastrophe with the general Palestinian situation, and with their predicament in particular. This association has been manifested through an array of symbolic gestures, such as memorial services during *Nakba* commemoration day, organised tours to deserted or formerly Palestinian villages in Israel, seminars on the past, and extensive interviews with *Nakba* survivors in the press.

In Israel itself, through its political leaders, NGOs and the media, the Palestinian minority has been able to force the wider public to take notice of the *Nakba*. This re-emergence of the *Nakba* as a topic for public debate will also disable any future peace plans that will be built on *Nakba* denial, including, of course, the various plans and initiatives of 2003: the Road Map, the Ayalon-Nusseibeh initiative, and the Geneva Accords.

References

Aruri, Naseer (ed.). 2001. *Palestinian Refugees and their Right of Return*. London and Sterling VA: Pluto Press

Benvenisti, Meiron. 2000. *Sacred Landscape: The Buried History of the Holy Land since 1948*. Berkeley: University of California Press

Flapan, Simha. 1979. *Zionism and the Palestinians 1917-1947*. London: Croom Helm

Flapan, Simha. 1987. *The Birth of Israel: Myths and Realities*. London and Sydney: Croom Helm

Karmi, Ghada and Eugene Cortran (eds). 1999. *The Palestinian Exodus, 1948-1988*, London: Ithaca

Kimmerling, Baruch. 1983. *Zionism and Territory. The Socio-Territorial Dimensions of Zionist Politics.* Berkeley: University of California, Institute of International Studies (Research Series, No. 51)

Masalha, Nur. 1992. *Expulsion of the Palestinians: the Concept of 'Transfer' in Zionist Political Thought, 1882-1948.* Washington, DC: Institute for Palestine Studies

Masalha, Nur. 1997. *A Land without a People. Israel, Transfer and the Palestinians 1949-96.* London: Faber and Faber

Masalha, Nur. 2000. *Imperial Israel and the Palestinians: The Politics of Expansion, 1967-2000.* London: Pluto

Masalha, Nur. 2003. *The Politics of Denial: Israel and the Palestinian Refugee Problem.* London and Sterling VA: Pluto Press

Morris, Benny. 1987. *The Birth of the Palestinian Refugee Problem, 1947-1949.* Cambridge: Cambridge University Press

Morris, Benny. 1990. *1948 and After: Israel and the Palestinians.* Oxford: Oxford University Press

Morris, Benny. 1993. *Israel's Border Wars.* Oxford: Oxford University Press

Pappé, Ilan. 1988. *Britain and the Arab-Israeli Conflict 1948-1951.* London: Macmillan

Pappé, Ilan. 1992. *The Making of the Arab-Israeli Conflict, 1948-1951.* London and New York: I B Tauris

Prior, Michael. 1999. *Zionism and the State of Israel: A Moral Inquiry.* London and New York: Routledge

Segev, Tom. 1986. *The First Israelis* (English Language Editor, Arlen N. Weinstein). New York: The Free Press/London: Collier Macmillan

Segev, Tom. 1993. *The Seventh Million. The Israelis and the Holocaust. (trans. by Haim Watzan).* New York: Hill and Wang

Shahak, Israel. 1975 (2nd ed.). *Report: Arab Villages destroyed in Israel.* Jerusalem: Shahak

Shapira, Anita. 1992. *Land and Power. The Zionist Resort to Force.* Oxford: Oxford University Press

Shlaim, Avi. 1988. *Collusion across the Jordan. King Abdullah, the Zionist Movement, and the Partition of Palestine.* New York: Columbia University Press

Teveth, Shabtai. 1985. *Ben-Gurion and the Palestinian Arabs.* Oxford: Oxford University Press

WHY WE REMEMBER DEIR YASSIN[1]

Daniel McGowan

The Massacre

There are many different accounts and interpretations of what happened on 9 April 1948 at Deir Yassin, a small village on the west side of Jerusalem. For ardent Zionists it was a battle at the beginning of Israel's War of Independence. For most historians it was a massacre of Arabs committed by dissident Jewish factions of the Irgun and the Stern Gang. For Palestinians it was the beginning of the *Nakba* or the Catastrophe when they were stripped of 78 percent of historical Palestine.[2]

Despite these different interpretations, almost all will agree on the following:

◻ Deir Yassin was a village of about 750 Arabs located 3 km west of Jerusalem near the top of a hill accessible only by one road coming from the east.

◻ With about 120 men the Jewish terrorist gangs known as The Irgun and the Stern Gang attacked Deir Yassin at 4 a.m. on 9 April 1948 in their first joint 'military operation'.

◻ Alerted by guards, the villagers from within their stone homes and with few weapons (including two machine guns) were able to kill four of the terrorists and wound thirty-six, bringing the attack to a standstill by late morning.

◻ The gangs then sought the help of soldiers from the Palmach, the elite fighters of the Haganah or the main Jewish

---

[1] This is the text of the address given by Daniel McGowan, Director of *Deir Yassin Remembered*, www.deiryassin.org, on the occasion of the dedication of the First Deir Yassin Memorial in the United States, in Geneva, New York (24 September 2003).

[2] Matthew Hogan provides the best and most concise account of the Deir Yassin incident in *The Historian*, Winter 2001, http://www.findarticles.com/cf_0/m2082/2_63/72435149/print.jhtml

military force. These seventeen professional soldiers, using a 52-mm mortar, conquered the village within an hour.

□ After the Palmach soldiers had left, the gangs went from house to house killing women, children, and old men.

□ They paraded some of the Palestinian men through the streets of Jerusalem and then brought them back to the stone quarry on the south side of Deir Yassin. There they shot them all to death.

□ The Irgun and the Stern Gang then herded the villagers who were unable to flee (down the mountain to the southwest toward Ein Karem) into the school and threatened to blow up the building with all the people inside.

□ The bloodbath was finally ended when Jews from the neighbouring settlement of Givat Shaul intervened, forcing the gangs to let the Palestinians out and send them towards East Jerusalem.

□ In the following two days the bodies of over a hundred Palestinian villagers were either thrown into cisterns or burned in the quarry.

□ During the evening of 9 April at a tea and cookies party for the press, the leader of the Irgun bragged at having killed 254 Arabs. This number was recorded in the *New York Times* on 10 and 13 April.

□ Within a year, the homes of Palestinians at Deir Yassin were resettled by Jews, mostly from Romania. Sometime in the 1950s the Israeli government moved them and created a mental hospital among the buildings in the Center of Deir Yassin. It was called Gival Shaul Bet and later the Kfar Shaul Hospital.

'Remember Deir Yassin!' became the fear-provoking threat of Jews in their subsequent ethnic cleansing of over 800,000 inhabitants from 530 Arab villages. It also became the battle cry of Arabs in reprisal attacks, such as the massacre of the medical convoy at Mount Scopus on 13 April.

Today's battle over the memory of Deir Yassin

Zionists often resist and belittle the idea of memorialising the victims of Deir Yassin because the truth about the massacre drives a stake into the heart of so many of their myths. For example,

> ▢ If you know that Deir Yassin was a vibrant Arab village, hundreds of years old, with the ruins of a monastery, located not far from the birthplace of John the Baptist, then you would also know that Palestine was not 'a land without people', a myth born with Zionism and still taught in schools today.
>
> ▢ If you know that all the inhabitants of Deir Yassin were either killed or driven out, that their possessions were plundered, that their homes were given to immigrating Jews, then you would recognize these actions to be ethnic cleansing, no more, no less. The Arabs did not leave voluntarily, nor were they called out by the mufti, or some other such nonsense.
>
> ▢ If you know that Deir Yassin was a small village with no soldiers, standing fast against 120 armed terrorists and ultimately defeated by 17 professional soldiers, then you might understand that the 1948 war was won by Israel to a large extent because it had more soldiers in Palestine and more arms than the combined Arab forces. The story of little David surrounded by six mighty Arab armies is another myth that dissolves when the facts are revealed.
>
> ▢ If you know that most of the dead at Deir Yassin were shot point blank, then the myths of 'purity of arms' (Israeli soldiers only draw blood when necessary), 'Tikkun Olam' (Jews strive to heal the world), 'a light unto Nations', and 'the Chosen People' lose lustre and credibility.
>
> ▢ If you know the horror of Deir Yassin and the impact it had on the Palestinian people, you begin to recognize great hypocrisy. You begin to understand, for example, why Noam Chomsky refers to the Nobel Peace Prize laureate Elie Wiesel as a 'terrible fraud'. Wiesel, who is the icon of the Holocaust industry (a term coined by Norman Finkelstein), claims to

be proud to have worked for the Irgun and refuses to apologise for what they did at Deir Yassin. Even as Wiesel pontificates that 'the opposite of love is not hate; it is indifference' he shows complete indifference to the death, destruction, and dehumanisation of the Palestinians. Even as he demands that Poles, Romanians, Austrians, and Germans apologise for what they or their parents did to Jews in the Nazi genocide, he steadfastly refuses to even acknowledge the murders and ethnic cleansing committed by those for whom he was working.

When Wiesel and virtually every American politician visits the most famous Holocaust museum at Yad Vashem, they look over the valley to the north and ignore the fact that they are looking directly at Deir Yassin. Mouthing the words 'Never forget!' and 'Hope lives when people remember', they hypocritically ignore the single most memorable tragedy in 20th century Palestinian history. That Jews shot innocent Palestinian men, women, and children, mutilated their bodies, threw them into cisterns, heaped others in piles and burned them over several days following the massacre is horrible enough. To build a Holocaust museum within sight of this crime while totally brushing it off is unconscionable. To continue to show indifference towards Deir Yassin, while standing in front of it, is hateful.

◻ If you know that Zionists founded the neighbouring Jewish settlement of Givat Shaul in 1906, you would realise that the idea of building a purely Jewish state was born long before the Holocaust. Creating a Jewish state upon land where more than half of the population is not Jewish is wrong. It was wrong before the Holocaust and it is wrong today.

◻ If you know that most of the Jewish terrorists who attacked Deir Yassin were not Holocaust survivors, then you would understand that the Holocaust was not the *raison d'être* for the creation of a Jewish state, but rather the propellant for a movement that started in the 1880s. While the practice of 'pumping in' Jews to a new homeland may be questionable, 'pumping out' the indigenous population as was done at

Deir Yassin is both immoral and repugnant, even to many Zionists in whose name it was carried out. What Menachem Begin, leader of the Irgun and later Prime Minister of Israel and another Nobel Peace Prize laureate, called 'a splendid act of conquest' is in fact what Martin Buber rightly called 'a black stain on the honor of the Jewish nation.'

Out of darkness comes a ray of hope

Perhaps the most important lesson gained from the remembrance of Deir Yassin is one rarely mentioned by historians—Zionist, Palestinian, revisionist, or others. And that lesson lies in the fact that the imminent massacre of the remaining women, children, and old men of Deir Yassin, who had been herded into the village school, was prevented by their neighbours, the Jewish settlers of Givat Shaul. It was these unarmed Jews who faced down the murderers of the Irgun and the Stern Gang and demanded that the remaining Palestinian lives be spared. The true Judaism of these brave people finally outweighed the extreme Zionism witnessed earlier that fateful day.

Long before the Holocaust, the Jews of Givat Shaul immigrated to Palestine to build a state for Jews only. They worked the land and built houses next to Deir Yassin. They fought with their neighbours, but also respected them and had even signed a non-aggression pact to which both villages adhered. Certainly they must have preferred to live only among Jews, but there was a limit (*Yesh G'vul*). Murdering, plundering, terrorising, dehumanising, and expelling the indigenous population were not and are not in keeping with the true spirit of Judaism, the Judaism of the prophets.

Such strategies may well have worked in America in the 19th and 20th centuries, but they will not be allowed to work today, not in the Holy Land or historical Palestine between the Mediterranean Sea and the Jordan River. And who will oppose them? Many, and in the vanguard there will most certainly be Jews.

For every Zionist (Christian, Jewish, or otherwise) who ignores injustice against Palestinians, there will be Jews who courageously fight for it. For every Alan Dershowitz, there will be a Lea Tsemel and a Felicia Langer. For every Elie Wiesel, there will be a Norman Finkelstein

and a Marc Ellis. For every Meir Kahane, there will be a Rabbi Dovid Weiss and a Rabbi Dovid Feldman. For every Moshe Levinger, there will be a Rabbi John Rayner and a Rabbi Jeffrey Newman. For every Sidney Zion, there will be an Amy Goodman. For every Michael Bard there will be a Cheryl Rubenberg or an Ilan Pappé. For every Barbara Streisand, there will be a Yehudi Menuhin. For every Chuck Schumer and Joe Lieberman there will be Jewish politicians willing to represent the United States as honest and unbiased peacemakers. One day soon such politicians will no longer make the visit to Yad Vashem without also visiting Deir Yassin and reflecting on the tragedy it represents to all of the people in historical Palestine. To date, not a single American politician has done that.

Jews have always been leaders in the struggle for human rights. When Edmond Fleg (French poet, playwright, and essayist) says, 'I am a Jew because for Israel, humanity is not yet fully formed; humanity must perfect itself,' he does not mean perfection through murder, plunder, ethnic cleansing, apartheid walls, and targeted assassinations. Indeed, as many Jews already acknowledge, perfection is not achieved through the formation of a Jewish state on land where half the people are not Jews and where two-thirds will not be Jews by the year 2020.

Jewish people have been implicated in crimes against Palestinian humanity at least since the massacre at Deir Yassin. To ignore this, while exhorting the whole world to never forget man's inhumanity to man, cheapens the message so dramatically portrayed in every Holocaust memorial from Los Angeles to Berlin to Sydney and particularly in Jerusalem where the message is repeated in view of the remains of those Palestinians massacred at Deir Yassin.

Not only are Jews more likely to lead in the struggle for human rights for Palestinians, they are more capable of doing so. The antisemitic tarbrush, which is so often used to stifle legitimate criticism of Israel, does not stick well when applied to Jews. And the epithet 'self-hater' is far less offensive or punishable by academic tribunals. When Lenni Brenner, Alfred Lilienthal, and even Rabbi Michael Lerner criticise Israel, it is hard to dismiss them as being antisemitic.

Because it promotes peace

In size and scope the *Nakba* and the Holocaust cannot be compared; even though both ethnic cleansing and genocide are crimes against humanity, the latter is far worse than the former. Nevertheless, both are crimes and the ethnic cleansing, subjugation, depopulation, and dehumanisation of the Palestinian people for over 55 years cannot be ignored simply because the Nazi genocide killed six million Jews and maimed millions more.

Deir Yassin was not the only massacre, nor was it the largest. But it is the prime symbol of Palestinian suffering and displacement. Because there is no memorial at the scene, because Deir Yassin is not taught in Israeli schools, because Deir Yassin is deliberately flushed down the memory hole of Jews in Israel and in the diaspora, Deir Yassin has become a symbol of Jewish denial or *Nakba* denial, as Ilan Pappé would say. *Nakba* denial is no less painful to Palestinians than is Holocaust denial to Jews.

For Jews to recognize Deir Yassin and for Palestinians to recognize the victimisation of Jews in the Holocaust are steps toward recognising the humanity and suffering of both people. What better place for such mutual recognition than in Jerusalem and specifically at Yad Vashem and at Deir Yassin? What better place to share each other's pain and victimisation? What better place to come 'out of the ashes' as Marc Ellis says in his latest book, *Israel and Palestine: Out of the Ashes.*

In the words of Deborah Maccoby,

> In remembering Deir Yassin, we remember that we have displaced and in many cases driven out an entire people in order to establish ourselves upon their stolen land—that we made our gain as a people out of another people's loss. In remembering Deir Yassin we remember that we have been guilty of atrocity. In remembering Deir Yassin, we recognize that we are still committing atrocities and are at the moment in the process of denying all justice to the Palestinian people, of crushing them as a people and thus destroying our own meaning as a people. In remembering Deir Yassin we remember ourselves and what we ought to represent (Deir Yassin Commemoration, Chichester Cathedral, 9 April 2003)

The role of *Deir Yassin Remembered*

Deir Yassin Remembered grew out of four proposals to shake off the negative image of Palestinians fomented in the Western media; they were presented to Yasir Arafat in 1994 at a conference in Gaza. The Deir Yassin idea was simple and inexpensive: to work to build a memorial at Deir Yassin, and thereby resurrect what is arguably the single most important event in 20th century Palestinian history. It was seen as a 'single-bullet approach' to humanising a people and validating their history. The other three proposals were accepted and distributed to Arafat's advisers, but the Deir Yassin proposal was given back to me with the request, directly by President Arafat, 'Would you work on this for us?' followed by the disingenuous comment by one of his aides, 'We really have no one able to do this project.' In fact, that was the polite way of saying, 'Given all the strains of the *Intifada* and the general reluctance of Palestinians to support national causes, at least financially, you will soon become discouraged and give up. And that is fine with us, because we in the Palestinian Authority, in being allowed to return from Tunis, have made a deal with the Israelis to ask for nothing behind the Green Line, and a memorial at Deir Yassin would clearly be behind the Green Line.'

Eighteen months later my daughter, Sahar Ghosheh (wife of the Minister of Labour), and I travelled to Gaza and met with Suha Arafat and Ahmed Qurei, also known as Abu Ala. We described our progress and told them that *Deir Yassin Remembered* had been formed as a Program Service of the Middle East Cultural and Charitable Society and was developing quite nicely. Sahar and I had put together a twenty-person board, half Jews, half non-Jews; half men and half women. We were planning an international Deir Yassin conference to be held in El Bireh. We had developed an appropriate logo, the prickly sabre (that stubborn little cactus that is all that remains of many destroyed Palestinian villages), and we had secured tax-exempt status to encourage contributions from supporters in America. We asked if the Palestinian Authority was willing to give us a grant or support in some other form.

To our great surprise, Abu Ala was neither impressed nor pleased. He said this was the wrong time for such a project and asked that we stop all work immediately. We told him that that was not the impression given to us by Yasir Arafat, both face to face and in writing. He assured

us that he spoke for President Arafat and again asked us to desist. I told him that was no longer possible.

Since then we have held two international conferences. Marc Ellis, Saleh Abdel Jawad, Faisal Husseini, and I were the featured speakers at the first one, 9 April 1997, during a snowstorm in El Bireh. Both conferences were organised by our Jerusalem Director, Khairieh Abu Shusheh, a tireless Palestinian grade-school teacher who also has led a march to Deir Yassin every April for the past five years. (Although Sahar lives in Ramallah only 12 miles away, she has been unable to attend these because she does not have a permit to enter Jerusalem.) The marches themselves require lengthy permits, which have been secured for us by the well-known defence lawyer, Lea Tsemel, an early supporter and board member. We have also received active support from another Jerusalemite, Roni Ben Efrat, editor of *Challenge Magazine*.

Over the past six years we have held hundreds of lectures and scores of commemorations in Boston, Rochester, Burlington, Washington, San Francisco, Los Angeles, Atlanta, London, Glasgow, Edinburgh, Melbourne, and Kuala Lumpur. Our most polished have been four commemorations in London under the auspices of our UK Director, Paul Eisen, and a team of Palestinians, Jews, and others working with him.

Dr Alijah Gordon, whose institute contributed the beautiful painting used for the cover of our first book, hosted two commemorations in Kuala Lumpur, one featuring Israel Shamir and the other Adam Shapiro of the International Solidarity Movement. Bob Green, a distant relative of Ben-Gurion, has hosted several *Deir Yassin Remembered* events in Burlington. This past April Reverend Nicholas Frayling choreographed a beautiful Deir Yassin remembrance at the famous Chichester Cathedral. Brian Filling has led Deir Yassin commemorations every year in Glasgow. And the list goes on and on. But the most valuable and most generous member of *Deir Yassin Remembered* was a Palestinian friend of mine, Issam Nashashibi.

Issam Nashashibi

Born in Jerusalem, caught outside of the country in 1967 and not allowed to return, Issam was a staunch advocate of Palestinian human rights in many different ways. We met at an American-Arab Anti-Discrimination

Committee conference in Washington. We immediately bonded and worked together on *Deir Yassin Remembered* (DYR) virtually every day until his premature death on 28 August 2003.

When Issam took his father on a last visit to see Jerusalem, I was privileged to go with them. That trip opened many new contacts for *Deir Yassin Remembered* and paved the way for subsequent trips to the Israeli Defense Forces archives for information on Deir Yassin that had not yet been disclosed. Although by then rather old and frail, Issam's father, Mufid, was an activist at heart; he and his extensive collection of books meant that we now had a virtual reference librarian on board. A year before his death in 1999 Mufid Nashashibi insisted on being a part of the DYR vigil in front of the Museum of Tolerance in Los Angeles. Mufid held the placard to remember Deir Yassin, while Issam held him up. A Palestinian father and son, together in front of the Holocaust museum with a sign calling for people to remember Deir Yassin, would be the very definition of the Arabic word *sumud*, which in English might be called 'steadfastness and resilience.'

For this first Deir Yassin memorial in the United States, it was Issam Nashashibi who set the bar for major donors at $5,000 and it was Issam and his wife, Margaret, who made the first contribution. In his best street talk, Issam would say, 'This is America, man. Justice does not come from above. *You want justice? You got to be willing to pay for it.*'

Justice—Issam paid for it and he lobbied for it. He worked on congressional campaigns in several different states and frequently attended fundraisers for members of Congress. He never stopped urging people, especially Arab Americans, to register and to exercise their right to vote.

Issam worked with *Deir Yassin Remembered* and for other Palestinian human rights projects all over the world. He had lived in London, Chapel Hill, Washington, New York, Malaysia, Puerto Rico, San Diego, San Jose, and (finally) Dawsonville, Georgia. But in his heart he always was a Palestinian from Jerusalem. In many ways he is like the olive tree, torn from its roots by violence in the Holy Land, yet clinging to the earth and to the people from whence he came.

The first Deir Yassin Memorial in the United States

When Paul Eisen, Issam and I met in London in April 2003, it was like three brothers at a family reunion. It was Paul's third theatrical Deir

Yassin commemoration at the Peacock Theatre; each one had been a monumental effort prepared over several months by Paul, Janet St John-Austin, and a couple of others. Issam and I were there to help in any way possible. But while we were busy with the current event, we were also planning for the future.

Paul wanted to produce a CD of songs involving Deir Yassin, some of which we had collected and some of which had been created for us. Janet had used the poetry of Randa Hamwi Duwaji in the commemoration and now wanted to encourage Randa to expand this into a book of poetry solely on Deir Yassin. Issam wanted to approach foundations and make grant applications to fund our new projects and to prepare for a design competition for a large memorial and information centre at Deir Yassin.

I introduced the idea of a new website, RighteousJews.org, to tap into the political benefits generated by its counterpart, Righteous Gentiles (aka Righteous Among Nations) at Yad Vashem. At first Paul and Issam did not like this idea, but later they agreed to it after the hearty endorsement by Marc Ellis who had attended the London commemoration as a featured speaker. Salma Khadra Jayyusi was our other featured speaker and she too was very enthusiastic about the new website, but counselled us not to make it a part of *Deir Yassin Remembered*, not because it didn't 'fit', but because it would dilute our single-purpose objective of building a memorial at Deir Yassin. We agreed, and Bob Green and I became the moderators of the RighteousJews.org website and list.[3]

---

[3] The three criteria necessary for a person to be considered a 'Righteous Jew' are: (1) The candidate must consider himself or herself to be Jewish. He or she does not have to be religious. Non-practising Jews and even atheists can be considered. (2) The candidate must have demonstrated solidarity with Palestinians as human beings, deserving of being treated equally with all other people in the lands between the Mediterranean Sea and the Jordan River, one country with equal citizenship for all. (3) The candidate must have faced disparagement, discrimination, or even death as a consequence of his or her standing up for the rights of Palestinians. It is not important why a 'Righteous Jew' has defended Palestinian rights or whether his or her actions were based on friendship, altruism, religious belief, humanitarianism, or simple human decency. (Candidates may even be considered posthumously.) By these three simple criteria, Elie Wiesel and Alan Dershowitz would not be considered 'righteous' for they miserably fail (2) and (3). Nor would Israel Shamir, who would get an A+ for (2) and (3), but who fails the first criterion, because he no longer considers himself to be Jewish.

Back at the Methodist International Center, an adult hostel in London where Issam and I were staying, we lamented that none of us was likely to live long enough to see a suitable memorial built at Deir Yassin. After all, we had been working on this project for over eight years and had yet to see even a simple signpost at Deir Yassin indicating that it once was an Arab village. This was not just a question of Israeli intransigence; we had sent two missions to the Knesset to request a site at Deir Yassin. We had written countless letters, most of which went unanswered. It was also a question of Palestinian parsimony or a general reluctance (for a variety of reasons) to support national causes and nation-building projects such as this.

It was then that Issam asked rather hypothetically, 'There are only two memorials to the victims of Deir Yassin—a small plaque in Jerusalem at Dar al Tifl al Arabi and a small stone at Kelvingrove Museum in Glasgow; why don't we build one in the United States?' My first response was that we simply did not have the money, but Paul told us both to relax, 'If the project is right, and this one is, the money will come from somewhere.'

We talked about location and decided that Washington should be the preferred site. After all there is a huge Holocaust memorial on the National Mall and the United States certainly has had more to do with causing the Palestinian diaspora than it did with causing the Jewish diaspora. But this idea was soon abandoned given the current political climate, the influence of the neo-conservatives, and the overwhelming prejudice against Palestinians among the so-called Christian Right. In spite of the fact that there are 6 to 7 million Muslims in the United States (against 5.2 million Jews), it is as difficult to find a Muslim in Congress as it is to find one on National Public Radio. A proposal to build a monument to slain Palestinians on the National Mall would certainly open *Deir Yassin Remembered* up to ridicule. On the other hand it might have got the three of us one-way tickets to Kfar Shaul, the mental hospital now occupying the buildings of Deir Yassin. Most of the patients there suffer from the Jerusalem syndrome, which probably comes from too much religion; patients frequently believe they are John the Baptist, Jesus Christ, or some other biblical character.

We thought about Patterson, New Jersey or Dearborn, Michigan where there are large Arab-American populations. These are very reasonable locations for Deir Yassin memorials and we intend to foster

their being built there in the future. But for now and for expediency we chose Geneva, New York. But why Geneva? First, we already had a beautiful site, next to a four-star hotel (Geneva on the Lake) and adjacent to a fine liberal arts college (Hobart and William Smith). There would be no calls for 'balance' and no communal control over the form and message of the memorial. Second, the fact that there is only one Palestinian family in Geneva is no worse than in Glasgow, Scotland where only a handful of Palestinians reside. And it is no worse than the location of the plaque in Jerusalem, which is behind a wall and unknown by most Palestinians and virtually all tourists. Third, the site is quasi-public, so some control could be exercised over those who might wish to demonstrate or counter-demonstrate at the site. Fourth, I live close by and could provide the necessary supervision and tools for the footers and the physical construction of a memorial.

Ideally, we would have liked to organise a well-publicised competition for the design for the Geneva memorial; we would have liked to offer a substantial prize and thereby created considerable press coverage. After hosting thirty commemorations in April however, our coffers were empty. So in the name of expediency, we decided to approach Khalil Bendib, whom we knew had done the sculpture of Alex Odeh, the ADC director in Los Angeles slain in a 1985 terrorist attack believed to have been perpetrated by the Jewish Defense League (JDL). In addition to being a sculptor, Khalil is a widely published political cartoonist, some of whose work has recently appeared in a book called *It Became Necessary To Destroy the Planet in Order To Save It*. Khalil Bendib's bronze work can be seen at www.studiobendib.com and his cartoons are on view at www.bendib.com.

To our great surprise (and relief) this incredibly busy and prolific artist not only welcomed a Deir Yassin Memorial Project, but he was willing to put off other projects to begin this one right away. Our only disagreement was that he did not like Issam's idea to create a bronze statue of our logo, the sabre. Khalil said it would give the wrong message; the image was too combative and too stubborn. With input from Randa Hamwi Duwaji and Janet St John-Austin we decided instead to create a sculpture of an olive tree, uprooted, but still alive and still clinging to the earth.

The olive tree has always been a symbol of peace and enlightenment. This one shows that the peace has been violated by a

protracted struggle by one religion to control land owned and long-inhabited by people of three major religions and many other variants as well. The tree's tortured, angular lines illustrate the many decades of Palestinian dispossession and dehumanisation that began before 1948 and continue today. The extended branches add movement and drama; they appear dead and yet are still alive. The torn roots of the displaced olive tree are wrenched from the earth, root-remnants still entrenched, clinging to the motherland.

But where would we get the money for even such a modest project? As was often the case, Issam stepped up to the plate; he and his wife would contribute $5,000. Let others follow his example. And follow they did. The second donor was Nabil Qaddumi who lives in Kuwait and whose father was one of the founders of the PLO. The third donor, Israel Taub, whom we had never met and who was not even a member of *Deir Yassin Remembered*, sent us $6,000. This was exactly the type of 'righteous' gesture that highlights the coming together of Jews and Palestinians to tell the truth and acknowledge the tragic history of both sides.

The fourth donation came from Nabil's daughter, Yasmeen. This was especially heartening since it is the next generation to which the Deir Yassin memory and the duty of remembrance must be passed. The fifth donation was of particular historical significance; Yousef Asad, one of the few remaining Deir Yassin survivors, contributed $5,000 and also helped us to cover some of the expenses for our previous two Jerusalem commemorations.

The meaning of Deir Yassin to the future of Israel/Palestine

Regardless of those who wish to believe that Israel is a Jewish state, it is not. It is a state controlled by Jews in which half of the population that is non-Jewish has lesser rights or no rights at all. In spite of all the nuclear, biological, and chemical weapons possessed by Israel, in spite of all the helicopter gunships, tanks, fighter planes, and bulldozers, there will never be peace as long as the dehumanisation of the Palestinian population continues. No amount of American aid and intervention on behalf of the apartheid status that now prevails in Israel can break the will of the Palestinians to be treated with equal rights and equal respect.

The sabre is a symbol of that resistance. Remembering Deir Yassin is a symbol of that resistance. Songs, poems, and commemorations of Deir Yassin are symbols of that resistance. So are memorials like this uprooted-olive-tree sculpture and plaque in upstate New York. Such symbols explicitly and implicitly say,

> We Palestinians shall not be forgotten. Jews were victims throughout history; they suffered most under the Nazi genocide. But we are also victims of the Nazi genocide and we are victims of calculated and methodically planned ethnic cleansing and murder in the name of Zionism. For over 55 years Deir Yassin has been the poster child of that ethnic cleansing. If Auschwitz is hallowed ground to Jews, Deir Yassin is hallowed ground to us. Jews demand that the world recognize what was done to them. We demand that the world recognize what Zionists have done to us. That is the beginning of peace and reconciliation.

Remembering Deir Yassin is for Palestinians what remembering the massacre at Kelcie is for Jews. In the words of the director of the United States Holocaust Memorial Museum in Washington, memorials 'help us honor the dead, enlighten the living, and pave the way for a better future for everyone.' Remembering Deir Yassin helps us to preserve the memory of those who died there and of those who have been uprooted all over Palestine by a political movement to cleanse the land of Arabs. Remembering Deir Yassin resurrects Palestinian history, preserves it, and teaches the lessons of what happens when the values of civilisation and humanity break down.

Perhaps the opposite of love is indeed indifference. If so, indifference, like hate, is no basis for peace. Remembering Deir Yassin shows that we are not indifferent to the tragic history of the Palestinians, and that recognising their history, their humanity, their right to be treated equally, and their right to live between the Mediterranean and the Jordan River are requisites for peace in the Middle East.

THE INTERNATIONAL CHRISTIAN EMBASSY, JERUSALEM: A CASE STUDY IN POLITICAL CHRISTIAN ZIONISM

Stephen Sizer

> Biblical Christian Zionism includes the following basic tenets:
> Belief that the restoration of the modern State of Israel is
> no political accident, but rather a visible fulfilment of God's
> word and promise (ICEJ 1988).

This essay will use the International Christian Embassy in Jerusalem (ICEJ) as a representative case study of the wider Christian Zionist movement, tracing, in particular, its political agenda. Having outlined its historical roots, it will describe its theology and politics, and, finally, will offer a critique.

1. The historical roots of the ICEJ

Of all the Christian Zionist organisations, the International Christian Embassy Jerusalem (ICEJ) is probably the most influential and controversial. Its founding in 1980 by Jan Willem van der Hoeven, in West Jerusalem near the home of the Israeli Prime Minister, represented the coming of age of Christian Zionism as a high profile, politically astute, international movement.

Ironically, the embassy building had originally been the home of the family of the late Professor Edward W Said, the distinguished Palestinian-American academic, before being confiscated in 1948 when it was first given to the Jewish philosopher, Martin Buber. It then became the Chilean embassy before becoming the home of the ICEJ. This is itself a paradigm of the impact Christian Zionists such as the members of the ICEJ have had upon the indigenous Palestinian people and Christian community, in particular.

The timing was actually precipitated by the co-ordinated withdrawal of the last thirteen embassies still based in Jerusalem. From 1947, the majority of embassies had located in Tel Aviv in response to

the partition plan agreed by the United Nations. The Dutch embassy and twelve Latin American embassies finally vacated Jerusalem in 1980 following the passing of the Jerusalem Bill by the Knesset, in which Israel unilaterally declared Jerusalem to be its exclusive and undivided, eternal capital.

Jan Willem van der Hoeven describes how the ICEJ was 'birthed' on 30 September 1980, '… in a direct response to the world's cowardice and especially the cowardice of those nations which, unable to stand up to Arab blackmail, moved their embassies to Tel Aviv' (van der Hoeven 1993: 151-52).

In 1985 the ICEJ organised the first International Christian Zionist Congress in Basel, Switzerland, in the same hall used by Theodor Herzl to launch the Zionist movement in 1897. Claiming to have staff in over eighty countries, the ICEJ draws its support almost exclusively from charismatic, evangelical and fundamentalist Christians particularly in the USA, Canada and South Africa.

From its foundation the 'charter' of the ICEJ has been to 'comfort' Israel. This has been defined in terms of encouraging and facilitating the 'restoration' of the Jews to Eretz Yisrael, although the exact geographical extent of 'greater' Israel is usually left ambiguous. In 1993, the ICEJ declared itself to have nine objectives, many of which were overtly political.

- To show concern for the Jewish people and the reborn State of Israel, by being a focus of comfort.
- To be a centre where Christians can gain a biblical understanding of Israel, and learn to be rightly related to the nation.
- To present to Christians a true understanding of what is taking place in the Land today so that world events may be interpreted in the light of God's Word.
- To remind and encourage Christians to pray for Jerusalem and the Land of Israel.
- To stimulate Christian leaders, churches and organisations to become effective influences in their countries on behalf of the Jewish people.
- To encourage Jewish people to return to their homeland.
- To be a channel of fulfilment of God's promise that one day Israel and her Arab neighbours will live in peace under

the blessing of God, in the middle of the earth.
▫ To begin or assist projects in Israel, including economic ventures, for the well being of all who live here.
▫ To take part through these activities in preparing the way of the Lord and to anticipate His reign from Jerusalem. (ICEJ 1993: 5)

The main priorities of the ICEJ since its inception have been to 'bring comfort' to Israel through the encouragement of Soviet and Eastern European Jews to emigrate to Israel; a social assistance programme for integrating Jewish immigrants into Israeli life; the sponsoring of an annual Christian Zionist Feast of Tabernacles Celebration in Jerusalem; and Diplomatic Banquets and Receptions through which church leaders and government officials around the world are lobbied on behalf of the State of Israel. The ICEJ has also developed a sophisticated and professional news service which produces weekly radio and TV programmes, a *Middle East Intelligence Digest,* together with daily pro-Israeli press releases. These are aimed, according to Jan Willem van der Hoeven, at countering 'increasingly warped and twisted' coverage which apparently has a 'marked bias against Israel' (Corley 1997: 7).

The ICEJ has gained significant status within right-wing Jewish political circles for its sponsorship of an annual Feast of Tabernacles celebration at which the Prime Minister of Israel is invited to address Christian Zionists from around the world. Every Prime Minister since 1980 has addressed the celebration. ICEJ claim that this event, attended by up to five thousand pilgrims from over 100 nations, is the largest single annual tourist event in Israel. The ICEJ believes that the reintroduction of what it terms 'Davidic worship' through the Feast of Tabernacles is a 'prophetic foreshadowing' of the celebration to be held during the Millennium after the Messiah returns.

A significant part of the ministry of the ICEJ also involves fund-raising from Western evangelical donors, working closely with Israeli embassies and consulates as well as the Jewish Agency in channelling support and funds to Israel.

2. The theology of the ICEJ

ICEJ is a self-appointed and self-regulated 'Christian embassy'. Throughout its literature it insists, somewhat pretentiously, that they, '... represent Christians from all over the world who love Israel and the people of Israel ... and ... represent Israel and what the Bible says about its destiny to the Christian world' (ICEJ 1993: 22-23), being a channel for international Christian concern for Israel.

Dispensational Literalist Hermeneutic

At the Third International Christian Zionist Congress held in Jerusalem during February 1996, under the auspices of the ICEJ, some 1,500 delegates from over 40 countries unanimously affirmed a proclamation of Christian Zionism which included the following tenets,

> God the Father, Almighty, chose the ancient nation and people of Israel, the descendants of Abraham, Isaac and Jacob, to reveal His plan of redemption for the world. They remain elect of God, and without the Jewish nation His redemptive purposes for the world will not be complete ... Christian believers are instructed by Scripture to acknowledge the Hebraic roots of their faith and to actively assist and participate in the plan of God for the ingathering of the Jewish People and the restoration of the nation of Israel in our day ... The Lord in His zealous love for Israel and the Jewish People blesses and curses peoples and judges nations based upon their treatment of the Chosen People of Israel ... According to God's distribution of nations, the Land of Israel has been given to the Jewish People by God as an everlasting possession by an eternal covenant. The Jewish People have the absolute right to possess and dwell in the Land, including Judea, Samaria, Gaza and the Golan (ICEJ 1996).

This declaration indicates the dispensational presuppositions of the ICEJ leadership who believe that the restoration of the Jews to Israel

and the contemporary State of Israel are the fulfilment of biblical prophecy. For example, Johann Luckoff, the director of ICEJ wrote, 'The return to Zion from exile a second time (Isaiah 11.11) is a living testimony to God's faithfulness and his enduring covenant with the Jewish people' (Luckoff 1985). The ICEJ has consistently repudiated those who refuse to acknowledge the central place of Israel within God's continuing purposes,

> While Gentile believers have been grafted into that household of faith which is of Abraham (the commonwealth of Israel), replacement theology within the Christian faith, which does not recognise the ongoing biblical purposes for Israel and the Jewish People, is [a] doctrinal error (ICEJ 1996)

The ICEJ explicitly distinguishes the Church from Israel, speaking of 'the former and latter rains', and, 'His beloved people, both Jew and Gentile' (ICEJ 1993: 15). Whereas the New Testament emphasises that Jesus Christ has made the two one, so that in Christ there is now neither Jew nor Gentile, the ICEJ insists on maintaining a distinction, and accords superior status to those of Jewish ethnic descent, who remain, even apparently, apart from faith in Jesus Christ, the chosen people, 'His Jewish sons and daughters' (ICEJ 1993: 9). The ICEJ's preoccupation with a futurist dispensational emphasis on Judaism is also evident from its reinterpretation of Christian mission.

Christian mission and restorationism

The ICEJ has disavowed evangelism (preaching the Gospel) among Jews, in part for pragmatic reasons, since this ensures the continued favour of the Israeli establishment, itself keen to have a compliant Christian Zionist presence to diffuse criticism of her policy toward Palestinians. A further reason arises from its dispensational theology. Evangelism is essentially unnecessary as the ICEJ believes that the Jewish nation, once restored to the Land of Israel, will collectively acknowledge its Messiah when he returns. Following Cyrus Scofield, the author of the Scofield Reference Bible (OUP, 1918), the ICEJ believes the petition of the Lord's Prayer, 'Your kingdom come, your will be done on earth as it is in heaven' is

therefore essentially for the future not the present. When asked by a reporter from the *Jerusalem Post* whether the ICEJ was actually a 'covert' missionary organisation working in Israel, van der Hoeven replied,

> Not so. The Zionist Christians are different. Our objectives are not as you describe. We don't believe in conversion, we don't want to make the Jews into Christians ... The Jewish religion must modify itself in the course of time—but on one point only, the identity of the Messiah ... they must make the modification as a collective entity. Suborning individuals to secede would serve no purpose (Ross 1990: 17).

It is acknowledged that at times in history Christians have initiated and participated in antisemitic activities. This is in part why the ICEJ has disavowed traditional methods of evangelism among Jews. Messianic believers in Israel, who share many of the Zionist presuppositions of the ICEJ, nevertheless distance themselves from the ICEJ's apparently contradictory non-evangelistic form of evangelicalism.

> ... the Embassy's repeated hedging on this issue gives credence to the growing conviction by some that the Embassy believes political and economic support in the name of Christ are all that is needed, and that evangelism is, at best, peripheral. Such an opinion is further strengthened by the oft-repeated reports (never publicly denied by the Embassy) that participants in Embassy-related events in Israel are discouraged by Embassy staff from commending their faith to Jewish friends (Maoz 1990: 3).

John Ross, deputy director of *Christian Witness to Israel* and a minister of the Free Church of Scotland insists this failure to engage in evangelism is 'a form of religious anti-Semitism which is as basically evil as the philosophy of the Nazis' (Ross 1990: 24). The term 'International Outreach', though traditionally understood by Christians to describe world-wide evangelisation through the proclamation of the gospel of Jesus Christ, has been invested with new meaning by the ICEJ. Based on Old Testament prophecies in Jeremiah and Isaiah which were originally spoken to Jews in exile in Babylon, the ICEJ interpret

the promise of salvation as finding its fulfilment in the 'return' of Jews to Zion.

> The biblical mandate concerning the proclamation and the restoration of Israel is clear ... In the same sense that the first apostles were commissioned by the Lord to be his witnesses from Jerusalem to the uttermost parts of the earth, we also feel compelled to proclaim the word of Israel's restoration, and the Christian's response to it, to every country and in every place where there are believers (ICEJ 1993: 22).

The comparison of the 'restoration' ministry of the ICEJ with that of the apostolic commission to preach the gospel to the whole world is simply without precedent. Don Wagner points to the final saying of Jesus as recorded in the New Testament book of the Acts of the Apostles:

> So when they had come together, they asked him, 'Lord, will you at this time restore the kingdom to Israel?' He said to them, 'It is not for you to know times or seasons that the Father has fixed by his own authority. But you will receive power when the Holy Spirit has come upon you, and you will be my witnesses in Jerusalem and in all Judea and Samaria, and to the end of the earth' (Acts 1.6-8).

Wagner concludes that Jesus thereby rejected the 'futurist pro-Zionist state scenario'. Instead, Jesus 'challenges true disciples with the task of taking the gospel into the entire world, including Jerusalem and the most difficult places. That mission has not changed, despite the revision of Christianity by the ICEJ' (Wagner 1995: 112).

The ICEJ has also reinterpreted God's purpose for the Jewish people. It claims biblical justification for the belief that, '... the destiny of nations, of Christians, and of the Church' lies not in how individuals respond to the claims of Jesus Christ, but in terms of '... their role in the restoration of Israel' (ICEJ 1998). The ICEJ, therefore, has consistently and repeatedly compromised the biblical mandate to proclaim the gospel to all people, including the Jews, yet continues to insist on designating itself as an evangelical organisation.

Eschatology: signs of the times

The ICEJ holds to a traditional pre-millennial dispensational eschatology, believing the ingathering of the Jews to Palestine to be the fulfilment of Old Testament prophecies. So, for example, the immigration of Soviet Jews to Palestine is seen as evidence that these are the Last Days and a necessary precursor to the 'spiritual restoration' of the Jews. Before the return of the Messiah, however, van der Hoeven warns that there will be a final Battle of Armageddon, when the nations will come against Israel. 'Repeatedly the Bible states that the betrayal of Israel will be a major reason for the wrath of God being heaped upon the nations in the latter days' (Wagner 1995: 102). Wagner offers this astute assessment of the theology of the ICEJ.

> If the church is deemphasized and a modern secular/ethnic government assumes total authority, the Christian message is clearly undermined. The gospel of Jesus becomes secondary. The task of doing justice and proclaiming salvation in Jesus Christ is lost. The future survival of all nations, their prosperity and destiny, are made conditional on the degree to which they support the political state of Israel (Wagner 1995: 104).

The theology of the ICEJ is, therefore, consistent with traditional dispensationalism which has elevated a restored Israel to a superior role and position over the Church in the future purposes of God and in which the latter is downgraded and, as John Nelson Darby, the father of Dispensationalism who taught that God has two chosen people, the Jews his earthly people and the Church his heavenly people (Wagner 1995: 81, 88) taught, merely a 'parenthesis' to the former (Darby 1962: 222).

3. The politics of the ICEJ

In its promotional literature ICEJ ask the question, '*Is Standing With Israel a Political Act?*' Using an unusual quotation from Paul's letter to the Corinthians concerning the nature of the bodily resurrection, the ICEJ claims that political support for the State of Israel will lead to her spiritual renewal and, by implication, the return of Jesus Christ.

The fact of Israel's political existence evokes prejudice and hostility in world forums such as those in New York and Geneva. Christians must therefore take a stand against this and counter lies with truth. This is not primarily political but a part of the warfare to help protect the Lord's people … To stand with Israel politically and practically, therefore, has ultimate spiritual implications, even if Israel has to go through agonizing birthpangs to arrive at God's destiny for her (ICEJ n.d.).

Thus the ICEJ claims that its support for the State of Israel is not primarily political but spiritual. It does, however, justify political involvement because of the criticisms made of Israel and the need to engage in this 'warfare'. The ICEJ's ministry is, in fact, highly politicised in several significant ways.

Unconditional support for the State of Israel

From its inception, the ICEJ has carefully courted the favour of the Israeli right-wing Likud political establishment because of their common commitment to the realisation of *Eretz Yisrael*. ICEJ has also lobbied foreign governments on behalf of Israel through its Diplomatic Banquets, and makes wide use of testimonials by Jewish leaders such as Teddy Kollek, Yitzhak Rabin, Menachem Begin and Yitzhak Shamir.

In 1997, fighting to keep his coalition together and stalling the already delayed Oslo Peace Accord, Benyamin Netanyahu took the opportunity to seek support from Christian Zionists by attending the ICEJ's annual Feast of Tabernacles celebration, during which he said:

Now I don't have to tell you that the media isn't always scrupulously fair when it comes to Israel. You can counter those distortions. You can tell the story, our story in the world. All we need to triumph in this struggle, is for the truth to be told. You can do for us what no one else can do. I am counting on you. I am relying on you. I am relying on your friendship, on the constancy of your support, and I deeply appreciate it, in the name of my family, my wife, my children, but especially in the name of the Children of

Israel, all of the People of Israel. We respect and appreciate, and thank you for your continual love for the State of Israel. Thank you very much (ICEJ 1997a).

With such impressive endorsements from the Israeli political Right, ICEJ has increasingly become the semi-official voice of a broad coalition of Christian Zionist organisations, frequently cultivated, exploited and quoted by the Israeli Government whenever a sympathetic Christian view point is needed to enhance its own policies, and rebut Western political or indigenous Christian criticism. In an amplification of the resolutions passed at the ICEJ Third International Christian Zionist Congress (February 1996), the following declarations reveal ICEJ's explicit religio-political agenda:

> Further, we are persuaded by the clear unction of our God to express the sense of this Congress on the following concerns before us this day,

> Because of the sovereign purposes of God for the City, Jerusalem must remain undivided, under Israeli sovereignty, open to all peoples, the capital of Israel only, and all nations should so concur and place their embassies here.

> As a faith bound to love and forgiveness we are appreciative of the attempts by the Government of Israel to work tirelessly for peace. However, the truths of God are sovereign and it is written that the Land which He promised to His People is not to be partitioned ... It would be further error for the nations to recognise a Palestinian state in any part of Eretz Israel.

> The Golan is part of biblical Israel and is a vital strategic asset necessary for the security and defense of the entire country ...

> The Islamic claim to Jerusalem, including its exclusive claim to the Temple Mount, is in direct contradiction to the clear biblical and historical significance of the city and its holiest site ...

> Regarding Aliyah, we remain concerned for the fate of imperilled Jewish People in diverse places, and seek to

encourage and assist in the continuing process of Return of the Exiles to Eretz Israel. To this end we commit to work with Israel and to encourage the Diaspora to fulfil the vision and goal of gathering to Israel the greater majority of all Jewish People from throughout the world. (ICEJ 1996).

Moreover, the ICEJ consistently endorses and defends right wing members of Likud and the smaller religious parties which are resolute in their commitment to confiscate, annexe and build further settlements in the Occupied Territories including Gaza and the Golan Heights.

The territorial extent of Eretz Israel

Central to the ICEJ's political and theological position is the conviction that Eretz Yisrael belongs exclusively to the Jewish people by divine mandate. The fourth resolution of the 'Declaration of the First International Christian Zionist Leadership Conference' held under the auspices of the ICEJ in August 1985, was entitled, 'All Nations Should Recognise Judea and Samaria as Belonging to Israel'. The position of the ICEJ on the Occupied Territories is indistinguishable from that of the Likud Party: 'The Congress declares that Judea and Samaria (inaccurately termed 'the West Bank') are, and by biblical right as well as international law and practice ought to be, a part of Israel' (ICEJ 1985).

No country, of course, recognises Israel's claim to the Occupied Territories. On the basis of the Fourth Geneva Convention of 1949, the international community through the United Nations has repeatedly condemned Israel's continued occupation of territory gained by war, for example in resolutions 242 and 338. The ICEJ nevertheless uses biblical terms to invest this illegal occupation with an air of legitimacy, and thereby justify God's apparent favour toward one ethnic group at the expense of all others. Jan Willem van der Hoeven offers a theological interpretation of recent historical events. Speaking of the war in 1967 he speculates:

> God wanted to give His people that part of the land which they did not receive in 1948, and by hardening the hearts of the different Arab leaders ... He impelled Israel to react. The result of what became known as the Six Day War was

that Judea and Samaria—heartland of biblical Israel—and the ancient city of Jerusalem—King David's capital—were returned to their original owner ... Thus, the Lord, by hardening the hearts of the Arab leaders, caused His people Israel to inherit the rest of the land, especially their ancient city, in a war of self defense! ... God has His own sovereign way to fulfil His Word and promise (van der Hoeven 1993: 151).

Moreover, the Third International Christian Zionist Congress (February 1996) reaffirmed that Israel had an absolute right to possess all the land of what it terms Judea, Samaria, Gaza and Golan. (ICEJ 1996). This leads ICEJ to support the settlements.

The Jewish settlements in the Occupied Territories

The ICEJ's support for the occupation and settlement of the West Bank is in part politically motivated as well as theologically. It remains implacably opposed to the peace process. Essentially the ICEJ uses the same arguments as those of secular Zionists. Thus, e.g.:

Jan Willem van der Hoeven
Today, most of the relatively uninformed journalists and politicians in the West are of the misguided opinion that as long as Israel withdraws from the 'Occupied Territories,' namely Gaza, Judea and Samaria (the 'West Bank') and the Golan Heights, there will be a chance for peace in the Middle East. The reason they think this is their false perception of the conflict as basically over land—rather than the reality that what is being sought is the elimination of Israel from the map of the Middle East (van der Hoeven 1993: 133).

Benyamin Netanyahu
Today too we are told that it is we who provoke terrorism. We provoke it by building apartments in Jerusalem, we provoke it by providing for the natural growth of our communities ... The real provocation ... is not a housing project, it is not the settlements. The real provocation is pure and simple. It is our existence here. That is what is causing the provocation. It is not a provocation. This is our country, this is the Land of Israel; it is the country that belongs to the people of Israel, and we have an inalienable right to this land (Netanyahu 1997).

115

In its support for the confiscation, occupation and settlement of the West Bank, the ICEJ has, according to critics, turned God into '... a cosmic real estate agent who will allow one people to suffer and be removed from their cities and farms ...', thereby reducing '... eternal truths to material terms. This truncated gospel of reductionism is inconsistent with the message of Jesus' (Wagner 1995: 111).

Jerusalem the eternal undivided capital of Israel

The ICEJ, like other Christian Zionists, regards Jerusalem as the undivided eternal capital of Israel, and central to God's future purposes for the Jews on earth. The following forms part of the address, given in the presence of the mayor of Jerusalem, at the opening ceremony of the ICEJ on 30 September 1980:

> Dear Mr Teddy Kollek,
> We are here from many different nations of the earth, representing, as we believe, millions of Christians who would have loved to be here with us ...
>
> These last weeks must not have been easy for you, as you have seen all the embassies, one after the other, leave Jerusalem where you have worked so hard to create a place where all people could be respected and live in freedom under the same roof of this eternal City ... Today, we open in this, your City, the International Christian Embassy and, because we believe in God, the God of Israel, and in the promises of His Book, the Bible, we will remain in Jerusalem to pray for its peace and work for its good, knowing that in the end, all shall be well. May this International Christian Embassy then, be a sign of hope; hope for your people, and hope for your City so that it may become what it was always destined to be under Israel—a new dawn for all mankind (van der Hoeven 1993:159-160).

Furthermore, Jan Willem van der Hoeven, the founder of ICEJ, whose book *Babylon or Jerusalem*, carries a foreword by Teddy Kollek, sees the prediction of Jesus made in Luke 21.24 to have now been fulfilled in the Israeli occupation of East Jerusalem.

In 1997 the ICEJ gave support to a full page advert placed in the *New York Times* (18 April) entitled, 'Christians Call for a United Jerusalem' signed by ten evangelical and fundamentalist leaders, including Pat Robertson, chairman of *Christian Broadcasting Network* and president of the *Christian Coalition*; Oral Roberts, founder and chancellor of Oral Roberts University; Jerry Falwell pastor of Liberty Road Baptist Church, Lynchburg and founder of *Moral Majority*; Ed McAteer, President of the *Religious Roundtable*; and David Allen Lewis, President of *Christians United for Israel*:

> We, the undersigned Christian spiritual leaders, communicating weekly to more than 100 million Christian Americans, are proud to join together in supporting the continued sovereignty of the State of Israel over the holy city of Jerusalem. We support Israel's efforts to reach reconciliation with its Arab neighbors, but we believe that Jerusalem or any portion of it shall not be negotiable in the peace process. Jerusalem must remain undivided as the eternal capital of the Jewish people (ICEJ 1997b).

Readers were invited to:

> Join us in our holy mission to ensure that Jerusalem will remain the undivided, eternal capital of Israel. The battle for Jerusalem has begun, and it is time for believers in Christ to support our Jewish brethren and the State of Israel. The time for unity with the Jewish people is now (ICEJ 1997b).

Moreover, in 1999 the ICEJ launched another world-wide petition to demonstrate 'Christian' support for Israel's sovereign rule over Jerusalem to be presented to the Israeli government in March 2000 during the next Christian Zionist Congress, when '... tremendous pressure will be exerted to re-divide the city.' The petition invited supporters to add their signature to the following resolution:

> We the undersigned, support Israel's exclusive claim to sovereignty over united Jerusalem as the capital of Israel. We commend Israel for its exemplary record in guaranteeing

access to the biblical sites in Jerusalem and throughout Israel, and support the continuation of Israel in this role (ICEJ 1999).

Tom Getman, then director of World Vision in Palestine, responded with an open letter to the ICEJ calling them 'either hopelessly naive or liars':

> Two things you may want to consider in your blatant partisan support:
>
> 1. For 5000 years any time this city has been under the exclusive control of one power it has been the cause of untold bloodshed; and 2. Israel's so called 'exemplary record in guaranteeing access to biblical sites' has been significantly sullied in recent years, and even over this past Easter weekend, when in and around the Old City, streets were blocked off to all traffic except Jewish Pessah worshippers. For those of us who could not get to Good Friday and Easter services, and for your Palestinian brothers and sisters in Christ who could not even get out of Bethlehem, you are setting yourselves up to be perceived as either hopelessly naive or liars. Jerusalem is the spiritual home for 2 billion people ... Only 15 million are Jewish. The better part of wisdom would be for 'God's chosen' to share it or they will absolutely guarantee being proven the world's rejected once again (Getman 1999).

ICEJ, along with other Christian Zionist agencies such as Bridges for Peace, of course, continues to oppose the peace process.

The rebuilding of the Jewish Temple

The ICEJ has been careful to avoid controversy, at least publicly, concerning the religious Zionist conviction that the Jewish temple must be rebuilt. In an open letter to Benjamin Netanyahu, then Israel's ambassador to the United Nations, the ICEJ affirmed its commitment

that like Muslims, Jews be able to worship again on the Temple Mount, implicitly within a rebuilt Jewish Temple.

> The International Christian Embassy Jerusalem fervently hopes and prays that the day will soon come that the Temple Mount—or as the Bible calls it, the Mountain of the Lord— will no longer be a reason for religious divisiveness, but a place where all mankind will unite in worship to God according to His declared purposes. The Bible foresees the day when all nations will flow to the Mountain of the Lord irrespective of race or colour, and says that: 'His house shall be called a house of prayer for all nations (van der Hoeven 1993: 169).

Van der Hoeven insists that a new Temple will one day be built on the Temple Mount. He quotes from the speech made by Teddy Kollek, then mayor of Jerusalem, at the 1985 Feast of Tabernacles celebration, held at the Binyanei Ha'Uma auditorium. Behind him was a futuristic painting of Jerusalem showing a rebuilt Jewish Temple:

> Thank you for being here, for coming here faithfully, every year. Your faith gives us strength ... I am glad I am speaking here against the background of this beautiful painting of Jerusalem. It is not yet the Jerusalem of today. If you look properly, you will see that the Temple, the Holy of Holies, has been restored! ... Our return is the first sign that the city will be existing again as it is in this painting! (van der Hoeven 1993: 163).

Moreover, the ICEJ has been implicated in funding the Jerusalem Temple Foundation, founded by Stanley Goldfoot, which is committed to the destruction of the Dome of the Rock (Rapoport 1984). As a member of the Stern Gang, Goldfoot was responsible for planting the bomb at the King David Hotel in Jerusalem on 22 July 1946 which killed, among others, over 100 British soldiers and officials. In 1948 he was also convicted and jailed by an Israeli court for the murder of UN envoy Count Bernadotte. Goldfoot has subsequently been influential in raising large sums of money, allegedly up to $100 million a year for the

Jerusalem Temple Foundation through American Christian TV and Radio stations and evangelical churches (Halsell 1986: 106).

Antipathy toward Arabs and Palestinians

Although the ICEJ claims to have sponsored humanitarian projects among Arab Palestinians, it is consistently critical of Islam and Arabs generally, and has been a divisive influence between Jewish Israelis and Palestinian Christians. Comparisons between Hitler and Arabs are also made frequently within ICEJ material. It is ironically the indigenous churches of the Middle East who receive the strongest criticisms from the ICEJ. Van der Hoeven's cynicism toward the established Church is clear.

> Their concern nearly always falls on the side of Israel's enemies, hardly ever on Israel's side. Through their frequently misguided and unilateral statements, they present an evil and negative influence. Maybe we should not be too surprised about this present allegiance of the traditional Church to sometimes violent or murderous people or organizations. Isn't this as it has often been during the long history of the Church? (van der Hoeven 1993: 49-50).

In 1997, he was even more outspoken claiming, 'Palestinians are under Israeli occupation because they asked for it ... It was not because Israel was so aggressive, but because they wanted to throw the Israelis into the sea. The Jews are kind enough to let them live here without killing them' (Corley 1997: 7). The result of the ICEJ's uncritical endorsement of Zionism essentially demonises the Palestinians and 'negates Palestinian claims to their land, livelihood, beliefs and very presence in the land' (Wagner 1995: 106).

The emigration of Soviet Jews to Israel

The ICEJ has been proactive in encouraging, coercing and facilitating the immigration of Soviet Jews to Israel/Palestine. This is based on the theological conviction that it is God's intention to '*bring back His people*'

to Palestine. Claiming that an estimated three million Jews still live in the 'land of the north' ICEJ believes that 'God has promised an exodus that would exceed in greatness the Exodus from Egypt' (ICEJ 1993: 11)

Since 1991, the ICEJ has paid for the transportation of 40,000 immigrants, 15,000 of whom were taken to Israel on 51 ICEJ-sponsored flights. ICEJ Russian team members are especially active in the more remote regions of the FSU. Basing itself on Jeremiah 16.16 (see below) the ICEJ describes its ministry in terms of 'fishing' for Jews,. It locates Jews, persuades them to emigrate, helps them obtain documents to prove their Jewish origins, distributes humanitarian packages and pays for exit permits, passports, debt repayment, transport and accommodation while their applications are processed by the Jewish Agency in the larger Russian cities. Once in Israel, the ICEJ assists émigrés with their resettlement costs, providing food, clothing, blankets, kitchen and school supplies as well as medical equipment, if needed.

In 1992, the ICEJ conceded that the number of Soviet immigrants was declining and therefore a new, more intimidating strategy was devised, to persuade Jews to leave Russia for Israel. Jeremiah had promised repentant Jews of his own day they would eventually return to Israel from their Babylonian captivity. Under the banner 'The 'Fishers' Task,' the ICEJ applied Jeremiah 16.16 to its own work.

> 'But now I will send for many fishermen,' declares the LORD, 'and they will catch them. After that I will send for many hunters, and they will hunt them down on every mountain and hill and from the crevices of the rocks' (Jeremiah 16.16).

Believing that '*Many Jews in the former USSR are sitting on the fence concerning Israel,*' the ICEJ initiated the production of 'educational' material and videos distributed among Jewish communities in the Soviet Union to persuade Jews to leave before it was too late. Using a concert tour and a double-decker bus equipped with a theatre and audio-visual exhibition about Israel, an ICEJ team also toured the Soviet Union between 1990-1992. Reinterpreting Jeremiah 16, the ICEJ claimed,

> The task of the fisher is to encourage them with a 'good report' of the land like Joshua and Caleb, before God sends

the hunters. The biblical fact is that in Israel, they have a 'future and a hope' (ICEJ 1993: 10).

The implication is clear, as in pre-war Germany, the Jews should leave before 'God sends the hunters', and 'it is too late.'Van der Hoeven is convinced that even Jews living in the United States will emigrate to Palestine and that God may use antisemitism to achieve it. 'Even if it takes anti-Semitism in America, God may use it to get his millions back to Israel. So we must have enough room there. So if we have six million American Jews coming we cannot give up the West Bank, can we?' (Wikstrom 1994: 76). In 1996, at the Third International Christian Zionist Congress, the following affirmation was endorsed.

> Regarding Aliyah, we remain concerned for the fate of imperilled Jewish People in diverse places, and seek to encourage and assist in the continuing process of Return of the Exiles to Eretz Israel. To this end we commit to work with Israel and to encourage the Diaspora to fulfil the vision and goal of gathering to Israel the greater majority of all Jewish People from throughout the world (ICEJ 1996).

Controversially, the ICEJ has been active in encouraging Soviet Jews to move into new settlements in East Jerusalem and the Occupied Territories, largely oblivious of the fact that they were being used to displace the indigenous Palestinians, in violation of international law. It has also raised funds for the settlements. For example, at the Feast of Tabernacles celebration in 1991, ICEJ representatives from twelve countries presented the Israeli Prime Minister, Yitzhak Shamir with cheques to help finance the settlements (Wagner 1995: 109).

In sum, the political activities of the ICEJ which range from defending Israel politically, lobbying Western governments on the status of Jerusalem, aiding the settlements and funding the emigration of Russian Jews, are both significant and comprehensive.

A critical summary of the distinctive Christian Zionism of ICEJ

The ICEJ's distinctive form of Christian Zionism is best summarised in its own words in the following way.'To stimulate Christian leaders, churches and organisations to become effective influences in their countries on behalf of the Jewish people' (ICEJ 1995: 5). Despite its endorsement by the Israeli government, the ICEJ is a self-appointed and self-regulated organisation unaccountable to the wider Christian community and working against the interests of the indigenous Christian community of the Middle East.

Theologically, the ICEJ has, without precedent, transformed the Christian mandate to proclaim the Gospel of Jesus Christ 'to the Jew first' into a highly politicised gospel serving the expansionist agenda of the contemporary State of Israel. The ICEJ's justification of Israel's racist and apartheid policies on biblical grounds is contributing to the ethnic cleansing of Palestinians from their historic homelands. Many Christians regard this as nothing less than apostasy and, 'an anachronistic return to the Judaizing tendency the early church rejected at the first ecumenical council, recorded in Acts 15' (Wagner 1995: 104).

Politically, the ICEJ has repeatedly identified itself uncritically and unconditionally with the Israeli political Right, defending, against international criticism, Israel's military occupation and settlement programme within Syria's Golan Heights and the Palestinian Occupied Territories. The ICEJ has from its inception remained implacably opposed to the aspirations of the Palestinians for political autonomy in the pre-1967 borders of the West Bank, a shared Jerusalem, or the right of return for refugees.

Wagner offers seven reasons why the ICEJ should be rejected as a 'Christian' organisation. The following is a summary of his arguments.

1. The ICEJ allows the gospel and lordship of Jesus Christ to become subservient to the modern political ideology of Zionism.
2. The International Christian Embassy is guilty of the sin of idolatry by worshipping state power in Israel and benefiting from its praises.
3. The ICEJ obscures the call to reconciliation in the Christian gospel, especially as it applies to Palestinians and

Israelis.

4. The ICEJ reduces the gospel to material and partisan political dimensions while it ignores the ultimate principles of the Christian message and its immediate kingdom implications.

5. The ICEJ has become a heretical cult by reducing the Christian church to a mere 'parenthesis', and by rejecting the local Christian community.

6. The ICEJ represents anti-mission activity in the Middle East, in relation to both Islam and Judaism.

7. The ICEJ does not take Jesus Christ as its alpha and omega but focuses on Zionism in theory and practice (Wagner 1995: 109-13).

The ICEJ, it appears, is a sectarian, pseudo-Christian organisation of dispensational origins which has unconditionally endorsed contemporary political Israel as the exclusive fulfilment of God's promises and purposes made under the Old Covenant. In doing so it has ignored or disregarded the means by which these promises and purposes find their ultimate fulfilment in Jesus Christ and in his Church.

References

Corley, Felix. 1997. 'Is Radical Zionism an Option for Christians?', *Church of England Newspaper,* 7 February

Darby, J.N. 1962. 'Our Separating Brethren', *Collected Writings of J.N. Darby*, Eccl. III, Vol. XIV, edited by William Kelly, 34 volumes (Kingston on Thames, Stow Hill Bible and Trust Depot.

Getman, Tom. 1999. 'A Response to Christian Zionist Exclusivism', *Cornerstone*, Issue 15 (Spring): 19

Halsell, Grace. 1986. *Prophecy and Politics, Militant Evangelists on the Road to Nuclear War.* Westport, Connecticut: Lawrence Hill

ICEJ. 1985. *Declaration of the First International Christian Zionist Leadership Conference.* Jerusalem: ICEJ

ICEJ. 1988. *The Second Christian Zionist Congress.* Jerusalem: ICEJ

ICEJ. 1993. *International Christian Embassy Jerusalem.* Jerusalem: ICEJ

ICEJ. 1996. *International Christian Zionist Congress Proclamation.* Jerusalem: ICEJ

ICEJ. 1997a. *Feast of the Tabernacles Conference.* Jerusalem: ICEJ

ICEJ. 1997b. 'Christians Call for a United Jerusalem', *New York Times,* 18 April, www.cdn-friends-icej.ca/united.html

ICEJ. 1998. 'About the International Christian Embassy Jerusalem', http://www.icej.org.il/about.html

ICEJ. 1999. *'The Jerusalem Petition, Statement of Support'*. Jerusalem: ICEJ, 9 April.

ICEJ. n.d. *Prepare ye The Way of the Lord*. Jerusalem: ICEJ

Lukoff, Johann. 1985. *A Christian Response to Israel*. Jerusalem: ICEJ

Maoz, Baruch. 1990. 'The Christian Embassy in Jerusalem', *Mishkan*, 1(12. 3).

Netanyahu, Benyamin. 1997. Speech delivered to the ICEJ Feast of Tabernacles celebration, 21 October 1997. www.pmo.gov.il/english/library/sp-211097.html

Rapoport, Louis. 1984. 'Slouching towards Armageddon: Links with Evangelicals', *Jerusalem Post International Edition*, June 17-24

Ross, John S. 1990. 'Beyond Zionism: Evangelical Responsibility Towards Israel', *Mishkan*, 1, 12. 17

van der Hoeven, Jan Willem. 1993. *Babylon or Jerusalem?* Shippensburg, Pasadena: Destiny Image Publishers

Wagner, Donald. 1995. *Anxious for Armageddon*. Scottdale, Pennsylvania: Herald Press

Wikstrom, Lester. 1994. 'The Return of the Jews and the Return of Jesus: Christian Zionism in the 1970's and 1980's', *Al-Liqa' Journal* 3

MAINSTREAM CHRISTIAN ZIONISM
Peter J Miano

Christian Zionism is attracting more and more popular and scholarly attention, an attention which generates lots of heat, but, so far, not very much light. Until recently, attention has been focused almost exclusively on a select band of the Christian Zionist spectrum, leaving a wide and conspicuous band of that spectrum almost totally ignored. This essay argues that Zionism is far more pervasive among Christians than it is usually regarded to be. While Christian Zionism is reasonably well known to occur among 'fundamentalists' it is not usually associated with mainstream Christians.

Christian attention to the phenomenon of Zionism is appropriate, because, paradoxically, Zionism originated as a Christian phenomenon and continues to be an overwhelmingly Christian ideology. The significance of this point should not be ignored, because Zionist apologists often advance the erroneous and specious complaint that criticism of Zionism is a new and evolved form of antisemitism (Merkley 2001: 4). Zionism, however, cannot be equated with Judaism, if only because the ranks of Zionists are overwhelmingly populated by Christians, especially once Christian Zionism is properly understood. Indeed, for every Jewish Zionist, there are at least ten Christian Zionists.[1] Historically considered, before there were Jewish Zionists, there were Christian Zionists. Since the application of Zionism has had enormous and far-reaching consequences on a national and global level, the examination of Christian Zionism by Christians of all persuasions is an important historical enterprise. What is more, since Zionism has produced catastrophic consequences for many people, Jews as well as non-Jews, an examination of Christian Zionism is a moral obligation as well.

Christian Zionism is very much in the news. In the US, on Sunday, 8 June 2003, the TV programme *Sixty Minutes* devoted a segment to it. The programme focused exclusively on fundamentalist, evangelical

---

[1] I will argue below that the proportion is even greater still.

Christian support for the State of Israel. Furthermore, the 2 February 2003 issue of *The Washington Post* also devoted an entire page of its Sunday edition to fundamentalist Christian Zionism. It never hinted that Christian Zionism could be anything other than a fundamentalist ideology. Similarly, Paul Beran, a member of the Board of Directors of *Evangelicals for Middle East Understanding,* equates Christian Zionism exclusively with *fundamentalist* Christian biblical interpretation and with figures such as Jerry Falwell.[2] Corinne Whitlatch, the Executive director of Churches for Middle East Peace, asserts that the definitive characteristic of Christian Zionism is '... the belief in the abiding relevance of the promise God made to Abraham in Genesis 12.3 ...' (*Christian Commitment to Peacemaking is Distorted by Christian Zionists,* June 2003). She likewise identifies Christian Zionism with Pat Robertson, Jerry Falwell, Tom Delay (US House of Representatives Majority Leader) and the Christian Coalition of America, among many others.

In England also, Giles Fraser, writing for *The Observer,* identified Christian Zionism exclusively with the 'lunatic ravings' of the Christian right and fundamentalist Christians, such as Hal Lindsey.[3] Moreover, Stephen Sizer's doctoral dissertation on Christian Zionism, which contains the most comprehensive analyses of the subject to date, is devoted entirely to evangelical, fundamentalist Christian Zionism. Meanwhile, even in the Holy Land itself, Bishara Awad, founder and President of the Bethlehem Bible College, defines Christian Zionism solely in terms of dispensationalist theology.[4]

Fundamentalist Christian Zionism: an easy target for liberals

It is not surprising that most contemporary attention focuses exclusively on *fundamentalist* Christian Zionism. This, to a large extent, is because fundamentalist Christian Zionists are vocal, visible and, therefore, easily identified. Due to their distinctive and sometimes bizarre biblical interpretations, they are also easily critiqued. Notwithstanding the recent

---

[2] '*Christian Zionism*', 6 May 2003.

[3] 'Apocalypse Soon. Evangelicals in the US Believe There is a Biblical Basis for Opposing the Middle East Road Map', 10 June 2003.

[4] Address to the Third International Conference of the Holy Land Christian Ecumenical Foundation, 19-20 October 2001.

popular attention focused on Christian Zionism, the dimensions of the phenomenon are widely misunderstood and over simplified. Accomplished scholars have invested considerable attention in identifying the dimensions of fundamentalist Christian Zionism and exposing its moral, biblical and theological inadequacies (see, e.g., Wagner 1995 and Sizer 2003). Such efforts, however, either ignore or insufficiently illuminate Christian Zionism. Almost without exception, contemporary mainstream scholarship ignores a dimension of Christian Zionism that attracts much more sympathy than does fundamentalist Christian Zionism, wields far more political influence and translates to overwhelmingly greater financial support for the State of Israel than its fundamentalist cousin. I refer to this phenomenon as *mainstream Christian Zionism*. This is a distinct variant of Zionism that is almost wholly ignored by Christian scholarship. Examination of the much more pernicious and numerically superior strain of mainstream Christian Zionism is a rather stunning lacuna in scholarship on Zionism.

Recent popular and scholarly assessments of fundamentalist Christian Zionism are not wrong. Indeed, as far as they go, they render an important service. Fundamentalist Christian Zionism is a particularly virulent strain of Zionism based on a distorted reading of the Bible. It is politically potent. Its popularity is alarming. But in defining that particular tree, too many have neglected the forest.

Evangelical Christians have demonstrated exemplary vigour in distinguishing between fundamentalist Christian Zionism and evangelical Christianity. Mainstream Christians, however, have not addressed in a corresponding fashion the phenomenon of mainstream Christian Zionism—a much broader and more potent variant of Christian Zionism. The phenomenon of *mainstream* Christian Zionism is so poorly understood that the term is not even in the scholarly lexicon. Even when Jewish Zionist scholarship and contemporary Christian critique of Zionism recognize the Christian origin of Zionism and stress the originally secular nature of Jewish Zionism, Christian scholars have restricted their attention exclusively to fundamentalist Christian Zionism, not its secular, mainstream partner. *Mainstream* Christian Zionism, then, deserves closer inspection.

Fundamentalist Christian Zionism is correctly regarded as a religious ideology that sees the establishment of the State of Israel as the fulfilment of biblical prophecy occurring in the end time. Accordingly,

God has a special role for the Jewish people in their covenanted land, and Christian devotion to God requires support for God's plan of salvation, including the establishment of the State of Israel. In this view, a covenanted promise, in a covenanted book, to a covenanted people is being actualised in modern-day Israel. The violence associated with the creation of the State of Israel and its continued struggles with episodic violence is understood, not as the result of political struggle between coloniser and colonised, but as the predicted and necessary birth pangs of a new eschatological age. Thus, the earthly struggle between Israel and the Palestinians is interpreted in apocalyptic terms as part of a broader cosmic struggle between the forces of good and evil, the defining battle of which will take place on the plain of Armageddon, as the Book of Revelation foretells. This ideology was originally, and still is to this day, a predominantly Christian one, although Jewish Zionism now includes a fundamentalist variant as well.

Fundamentalist Christian Zionism was conceived by 19th-century Christian dispensationalist and millenarian theologians before there were any Jewish Zionists. Christians who adhere to this ideology today vastly outnumber Jewish Zionists, simply because Jews are relatively few in number compared with fundamentalist Christians. Moreover, not all Jews are Zionists. A high profile example of fundamentalist Christian Zionism can be found in the *Left Behind* series of novels by Tim Lahaye and Jerry B Jenkins. These reached *The New York Times* bestsellers' list, and stayed there for twenty months. There are currently eleven volumes, and a 'kids' collection as well. In Jerusalem itself, fundamentalist Christian Zionism is centred at the so-called International Christian Embassy. It is predicated on the tenets that 'the restoration of the nation of Israel in its ancient soil is evidence of the redemption promised for the whole world,' and, 'to support Israel … is to work in harmony with God.'[5]

When European Jews began to develop Zionism as a political ideology later in the 19th century, it was devoid of the theological underpinnings that defined its elder Christian cousin, even though the first Jewish Zionists recognised the utility of exploiting evangelical Christian support for their nationalist agenda. Even after religious Jews adopted the Zionist enterprise, it remained an overwhelmingly Christian phenomenon. Early in the 20th century, liberal Christian politicians in

---

[5] International Christian Embassy, Jerusalem, 'Biblical Zionism, Cutting Edge Theology for "the Last Days" ', in *Word from Jerusalem*, 2001, 9.

Britain began to recognize that the Zionist enterprise could help advance Britain's foreign policy objectives in the Near East. In the 1930s, Jewish Zionists began actively to exploit mainstream, liberal Christian support and the two have been wedded ever since. Why, one wonders, is this marriage between mainstream liberal Christian and Jewish Zionists so widely ignored?

Fundamentalist Christian Zionism deserves all the critical attention it gets and more, but no one should be deluded into thinking that by delineating its defects we have isolated the extent of the problem. Fundamentalist Christian Zionism should be carefully distinguished from Jewish Zionism in all its varieties. For one, fundamentalist Christian Zionism is, in fact, virulently anti-Jewish, notwithstanding its pretences to be a form of love for Jews. For the fundamentalist Christian Zionist, support for Jews is not for the sake of the Jews themselves, but as a means to another end. In that scenario Jews are not valuable in and of themselves, but merely as useful devices for God's plan of salvation, a plan—in their eyes—that will ultimately require Jews to convert to Christianity, or, if refusing to do so, perish with unbelieving Christians. Fundamentalist Christian Zionism, then, should be distinguished from *mainstream* Christian Zionism which is far more pervasive, far more mercurial and far more pernicious. It is also much more difficult to expose and critique.

Mainstream Christian scholarship has overlooked mainstream Christian Zionism. This is partly the case perhaps, because many scholars—to say nothing of a growing number of lay observers—incorrectly associate Christian Zionism with exclusively *fundamentalist* biblical interpretation. It is important to note that no variant of either Jewish or Christian Zionism requires any particular form of biblical literalism. If biblical literalism were a necessary component in the definition of Zionism even most modern Zionist Jews themselves would not qualify. Moreover, many contemporary, conscientious Zionist Jews are 'secular', and do not subscribe to the idea that the establishment of the State of Israel is a fulfilment of biblical prophecy. They certainly do not harbour the idea that the 'ingathering' of the Jews in the land of Israel is a necessary precondition for the return of the Christian Messiah. Moreover, many of the founding fathers and mothers of Jewish Zionism were agnostics and atheists. Theodor Herzl himself did not subscribe to the idea that establishing the State of Israel was in any way related to fulfilling biblical prophecy. He had little use for Jewish spirituality even when he realised—

rather later than other Zionists—that Palestine would make a convenient place for the Jewish state due to its perceived historical connection with Jewish history. The same can be said for Chaim Weizmann, David Ben-Gurion, Golda Meir and a host of contemporary Jewish Zionists, including Yitzhak Rabin, Shimon Peres and Ariel Sharon.

If Jewish Zionists can be defined as such without reference to a fundamentalist biblical interpretation, why cannot the same be true of mainstream Christian Zionists as well? The fact is that biblical literalism is not a precondition for Zionism. Christians no less than Jews can be Zionist without being fundamentalists and even without being particularly 'religious', however that term is defined.

If Zionism is defined strictly in terms of a specific biblical interpretation or theological orientation, fewer than 20 percent of Jews in Israel would qualify as Zionists. Those excluded would include the vast majority of the Knesset, not to mention millions of grassroots, street level Jewish Zionists. Yet no one there makes the mistake of identifying Zionism exclusively with this fundamentalist Jewish minority. In Israel, fundamentalist Jewish Zionists are particularly active and exert enormous influence on the political processes of the nation. The influence of this fundamentalist Jewish minority in mainstream Israeli politics is widely recognised in Israel (see, e.g., Mezvinsky and Shahak 1999). It is disproportionate to their actual numbers. Most secular Israelis regard it as a nuisance, if not a danger to Israeli society. Fundamentalist Jewish Zionism is well studied and well understood within Israel. But without the co-operation of non-fundamentalist Israeli Zionists, the activism of the concentrated minority of fundamentalist Jewish Zionists in Israel would amount to very little.

Just as in Israel where fundamentalist Jewish Zionists cannot advance their agenda without the co-operation of secular Jewish Zionists, so in the United States, the Zionist Christian right needs—and gets—the active support of mainstream Christians to advance their agenda of supporting the State of Israel at almost any cost. In the United States, fundamentalist Christians represent no more than 30 percent of the Christian population. While the activism of this fundamentalist minority is highly effective, the success of promoting the Zionist agenda in America cannot be attributed solely to this dedicated minority. On the contrary, in American political systems, support for Israel and the Zionist agenda comes overwhelmingly from mainstream, progressive, liberal Christians,

whether they identify as Zionists or not. Christian Zionism extends throughout the Churches, and the biblical academy too. If I am correct in redefining Christian Zionism to include mainstream Christian Zionists, then Christian Zionists as a group easily outnumber Jewish Zionists by some one hundred to one. Such a proportion makes the success of the Zionist agenda much easier to understand.

Why, then, do concerned mainstream Christians equate Christian Zionism exclusively with a minority of fundamentalist Christians who are heavily influenced by dispensationalist theology? Why do mainstream Christians restrict the definition of Christian Zionism solely to those whom they consider to be representative of a fringe group? The answer to these questions, I suggest, is twofold.

First, it is easy to identify fundamentalist Christian Zionists, due to their distinctive biblical orientation. Second, it is difficult to identify and critique mainstream Christian Zionism, since mainstream Christian Zionists are usually progressive and liberal. They often do not declare their Zionist orientation. Their affinity for Zionism is often masked by a sincere and notable concern to correct past wrongs by Christians against Jews. They usually do not endorse the extreme policies of the State of Israel against the Palestinians in the West Bank and Gaza, although their sensitivity toward Palestinians does not usually include the Palestinian experience in 1948. The ranks of mainstream Christian Zionists include highly regarded academics, Church leaders and politicians who otherwise champion cherished causes of liberal, progressive Christianity and democratic society.

Is biblical literalism an essential ingredient of Zionism?

What then defines a Zionist and Zionism? To answer this question, one must discern the characteristics of the ideology to which Zionists subscribe. What do those who call themselves Zionists believe about Zionism?

In Israel, among both Jews and Christians, Zionism occurs in a rich variety of forms. There are Zionists, non-Zionists, post-Zionists, anti-Zionists and arch-Zionists. There are also '1948' Zionists and '1967' Zionists. There are 'hard' Zionists and 'soft' Zionists. I have even heard one person describe herself as a 'zionist with a small *z* '. There are

fundamentalist Jewish and Christian Zionists. More importantly, there are mainstream, progressive, liberal Jewish and Christian Zionists. The distinctions between these various forms of Zionism are significant to those who use the terms for themselves. This rich diversity is reflected in the political life of Israel where there are 41 registered political parties and 12 different parties holding seats in the Knesset.

Among all these varieties of Zionists the claim that Jews constitute a distinct ethnic group is one of the most frequently enunciated components of Zionism. The identity of this ethnic group is inextricably bound to the territory of the biblical Land of Israel, itself a by no means unambiguous designation. Like other ethnic groups which are organised into nation states, it is said that Jews, too, should have a state with all the apparatus the modern world associates with statehood, including a specific land. In this view, the modern State of Israel is a political necessity. Indeed, for modern Jewish Zionists, fundamentalist and secular alike, the identification between the people and their land is paramount in their self-understanding. It is almost axiomatic among Jews inside and outside Israel that they can trace their cultural, spiritual and biological ancestry in the land of Israel to the time of Jesus and even earlier. Indeed, some even advance the argument that Moses and Abraham were *Jews*, as if such a phenomenon as Judaism could exist even before there ever was a Judah.

Moreover, the land in question is overwhelmingly identified with the biblical land of Israel, even when the one who articulates the claim is neither fundamentalist nor even particularly religious. Jewish people, in this view, have a distinct association with the land of Israel, not necessarily because the Bible says it, or foretells it or covenants it, but because, historically, the Jews as a distinct people are believed to have emerged and flourished in the land of Israel. According to one articulation of this ideology, 'Zionism is the national liberation movement of the Jewish people, which holds that Jews are entitled to a homeland in the land where they lived thousands of years ago following their exodus from Egypt.'[6] In mainstream Jewish Zionist ideology, the establishment of the State of Israel and its preservation are political necessities, because Jews often experienced mistreatment when living

---

[6] AIPAC press release, 28 August 2001.

among non-Jewish majorities. The need for a state, then, is not predicated on a fundamentalist reading of the Bible.

A second component of Jewish Zionism is the notion that the State of Israel represents restitution and moral compensation to Jews in the diaspora for generations of persecution and suffering at the hands of Christians, especially in the 20th century. This entitlement is earned, it is claimed, because Jews have suffered uniquely throughout their long history, going back to the time when they lived as a people in the land of Israel. Many Israeli and non-Israeli Jews share this sentiment and consider themselves Zionists for holding it. Thus, Rabbi Michael Lerner, editor of *Tikkun* magazine, explains his Zionism in such terms. Rabbi Lerner identifies himself as a Zionist, notwithstanding his strong and open rejection of Israel's policies with respect to the Palestinians. When I asked him on what basis he considers himself to be a Zionist, he said, 'Because I believe that the Jewish people deserve a state of their own where they can be secure.'[7] Jewish Zionists believe that there should be *a place* where Jews can be safe and that Jews as a people should be protected in their land. The establishment, protection and continued preservation of the State of Israel is considered in this view to be a moral imperative. Such an appeal to moral legitimacy, however, does not require any concomitant appeal to biblical prophecy, or to theology. Zionism, then, requires neither a fundamentalist biblical interpretation, nor the extreme positions of highly exclusive, maximalist Zionists. Those progressive, mainstream Christians who express sentiments similar to self-defined Jewish Zionists should be identified as Zionists also.

When one considers the two foregoing characteristic features— each of which involves elaborate corollaries—of the thought and self-identification of contemporary, mainstream Israeli and non-Israeli Jewish Zionists, one begins to get a feel for *mainstream* Zionism in contradistinction to *fundamentalist* Zionism. These two characteristics— that the establishment of the State of Israel is both a moral imperative and a political necessity—are common to those who identify themselves as Zionists. These two primary characteristics define religious and secular, fundamentalist and mainstream, elite and grassroots, Jewish and Christian Zionists.

Why, then, are Christians who harbour similar convictions not identified as Zionists unless they are biblical literalists? It is clear that

---

[7] See also Zion's Herald Interviews, *Zion's Herald* May/June, 2002.

many have incorrectly equated Christian Zionism exclusively with biblical literalism and the millenarian, dispensationalist theology that frequently accompanies it. Fundamentalist Zionism does not represent the dominant form of Jewish Zionism. By the same token, fundamentalist, dispensationalist Christian Zionism is not the dominant form of Christian Zionism in America or anywhere else. If it were, it would be easy to critique and confront it, because biblical fundamentalism is neither historically sophisticated, hermeneutically sound, nor theologically satisfying to mainstream Christians.

Christian Zionism, the mainstream

Mainstream Christian support for Zionism in the US occurs in the halls of Congress, in churches and in the biblical academy, all of which are overwhelmingly sympathetic to the Zionist enterprise. Mainstream Christian Zionism is defined by the notion that supporting a distinctively Jewish state is both a political necessity and a moral imperative. It is a political necessity, because Jews are a distinct ethnic group and the nation-state is the natural and normal political organization for ethnic groups. It is a moral imperative, because the State of Israel represents a form of restitution to Jews for past sufferings. These notions are often paired with the perception that support for the State of Israel is harmonious with national interests (US interests in the case of American Christian Zionists). Mainstream Christian Zionism is invigorated by sincere Christian sensitivity to the horrific suffering of Jewish people, especially, but not exclusively in light of the Holocaust. It is often accompanied by *philosemitism* expressed in various ways, including the ascription of a unique moral quality to Jews as a group, the belief that Western civilisation is rooted specifically in ancient Jewish culture and the idea that Jews are owed a particular measure of gratitude for the Western values that are rooted in ancient Jewish culture and modern Jewish contributions to humanity.

Mainstream Christian Zionists tend to reject the maximalist features of much contemporary Jewish Zionism. They often oppose the policies of the State of Israel in the occupied Palestinian Territories, even though they usually do not object to the violence against Palestinians that took place during the 1948 war. They often recognize the legitimate

demands of the Palestinian people for justice even while rationalising Jewish nationalism by appeal to justice and morality. On the other hand, some prominent mainstream Christian Zionists display no regard for the plight of the Palestinians even when they staunchly and sincerely advocate solidarity with the suffering endured by Jews. Sometimes, mainstream Christian Zionists who themselves are accomplished academics in various fields even express the most naïve historical understanding of the birth of Israel. They are nonetheless difficult to critique precisely because they are prominent, respected figures and sincerely concerned with justice. These qualities, however, do not remove them from the ranks of Zionists. Many Jewish Zionists display similar qualities.

While fundamentalist Christian Zionists in the US Congress are easily identified by their willingness to associate themselves explicitly with Zionism, the mainstream Christian variety evades identification, not only because the phenomenon is largely unrecognized, but because mainstream Christians generally do not claim affinity with Zionism. This, however, should not insulate them from scrutiny.

Illustrations of mainstream Christian Zionists in Congress who usually evade detection include US House of Representatives Minority Leader Richard Gephart (Democrat-Missouri), Sen. Hillary Clinton (D-New York) and Sen. John Kerry (Democrat-Massachusetts), currently the favourite candidate for the Democratic nomination for the presidency, none of whom is either a fundamentalist or millenarian Christian. All three, however, are staunch supporters of the State of Israel for the same reasons that Theodor Herzl was. Sen. Kerry's rationale for supporting the State of Israel includes his beliefs that such support is in US national interests, that the Jews as a people deserve a nation-state of their own, like other ethnic groups, and that Jews are particularly deserving of restitution for past sufferings.[8]

Moreover, each year, the American Israel Public Affairs Committee (AIPAC) hosts a conference during which liberal, progressive members of Congress clamour for the opportunity to express their devotion to the ideals and results of the Zionist enterprise. Tom Wuliger, the President of AIPAC stated, 'The Congress continues to show unwavering bipartisan support for the State of Israel.'[9] Congressional

---

[8]   Personal interview with Chris Wyman, an aide to Senator John Kerry, 5 November 2001.

[9]   AIPAC press release, 14 November 2001.

resolutions expressing support for Israel are abundant. They invariably pass with near unanimity in the Senate and with 95 percent majorities in the House of Representatives. The Congress annually approves a budget that includes billions of dollars in support for the State of Israel, thereby raising far more financial support for the Zionist agenda than the most effective right wing Christian Zionist activists. The Congress, however, does not hold a monopoly on Zionist support among mainstream Christians in the US political apparatus. No one has ever accused Dick Cheney, Donald Rumsfeld or Colin Powell of being soft in their support of Israel. One wonders what more they would have to do to earn the Zionist label.

Zionism and the mainstream academy

In the scholarly arena, where does one find Christian Zionism in the biblical academy? In recent years, prominent biblical scholars, including Keith Whitelam, Thomas Thompson, and Michael Prior have produced groundbreaking works demonstrating that both biblical archaeology and the broader field of biblical studies are dominated by scholars whose ideas are sympathetic to, and indeed attempt to, validate the Zionist enterprise.[10] They illustrate that, notwithstanding the scholarly pretence to objectivity and historical impartiality, the biblical academy colludes with Zionism purposely or inadvertently. Thus, in the course of his comprehensive demonstration that Western biblical scholarship is overwhelmingly sympathetic to Zionism, Whitelam points out,

> Biblical scholarship ... has attempted to ignore or deny its intricate involvement in the political realm ... Biblical scholarship has been and continues to be, despite the many protestations of innocence, involved in the contemporary struggle for Palestine (Whitelam 1996: 89).

Moreover, many scholars and lay people alike have got a whiff of the odour produced by historiography put to the service of nationalist

---

[10] See, e.g., Keith Whitelam (1996a; 1996b; 1998), Michael Prior (1997a; 1997b; 1998; 1999a; 1999b; 2000; 2002a; 2002b; 2003a and 2003b), and Thomas L Thompson (1974; 1987; 1992; 1995; 1998).

ideology. Neil Asher Silberman explores this theme vigorously as it pertains to Zionist historiography (Silberman 1982; 1989). One outstanding example, among many, is the archaeological excavation of Masada. Yigal Yadin, an avowed Zionist who directed the dig and first published its findings, is the author of the popular myth of Masada. Yadin's findings and the story were subsequently debunked, but, nevertheless, live on because they fit so well with the worldview of contemporary Israelis and their sympathisers. That Zionist archaeology finds significant evidence of the roots of the State of Israel in the soil it claims is hardly an objective coincidence. Whitelam's citation of B Trigger clarifies the point: 'In modern Israel, archaeology plays an important role in affirming the link between an intrusive population and its own ancient past and by doing so asserts the right of that population to the land' (Trigger 1984: 358, in Whitelam 1996: 16). It should be observed that the archaeologists and historians whose histories are so harmonious with the Zionist enterprise, more often than not, are Christians who are neither fundamentalist nor dispensationalist. For example, William Foxwell Albright, whose shadow looms over the field of 20th century biblical archaeology, was a mainstream Christian who produced profoundly influential theses that would be labelled Zionist if he were Jewish. Albright, incidentally, had no qualms about the plunder attendant upon Joshua's enterprise of the genocide of the indigenous population of Canaan, which he understood in a largely historically reliable way—and this only a decade after the full horrors of the Nazi 'ethnic cleansing' had been revealed (Albright 1957: 280-81). Albright also judged that, through Zionism, Jews would bring to the Near East all the benefits of European civilisation (Albright 1942: 12-13). In addition to reflecting conventional Western colonialist attitudes, then, this mainstream Christian was a Zionist.[11]

In some cases, Zionist sympathies form the point of departure for scholarly work. Michael Prior points out that W D Davies, a leading New Testament scholar, states unequivocally that he was impressed by modern Israel's victory in the Six Day War and began his work on the territorial dimensions of ancient Israel at the encouragement of certain 'friends' in Israel (Prior 1997a: 253-59). Davies never questions the

---

[11] For further discussion of the role of the Bible in the alleged justification of Zionism see Prior 1997b; 1999a: 169-70; 2000; 2002a; 2002b, and 2003a.

notion that the Jews as a distinct people can trace their ethnic lineage, along with the claim to the territory now claimed by modern Israel, to ancient Israel. When scholars uncritically accept and promulgate the ideas that there is a continuous ethnic lineage between an ancient people called Jews and modern people by the same name who claim the ancient territory, why do they escape being labelled Zionist? Why also do they evade critique for anachronistic historiography?

Throughout the 19th and 20th centuries, biblical archaeologists were motivated to excavate in Palestine by their desire to uncover the roots of the Christian West in 'Ancient Israel'. Until recently, the presumption that the civilisation identified as ancient Israel formed the taproot of modern Western civilisation was completely uncontested. During these years, biblical scholars uncritically presumed that modern Jews were descended from the ancient Israel of Jesus in an uninterrupted line, thereby helping to validate the notion that Jews, as a distinct people, have a unique, historic claim to the territory of their presumed ancestors. Most biblical scholars continue to conceptualise ancient Israel in terms that are remarkably reminiscent of modern Western monarchies and even nation-states. Such assessments are not only unduly sentimental and nostalgic, but are hopelessly anachronistic. That they are remarkably congenial to Zionist ideology suggests that closer examination is warranted.

Upon closer inspection, it seems an unusual coincidence that Zionist ideology depends so heavily on the idea that a distinct modern ethnic group, claiming to originate in the territory of ancient Israel and with an uninterrupted lineage to ancient Israel, possesses a modern claim to the distinct piece of historic property associated with ancient Israel. Zionism appeals to biblical archaeology to validate its contemporary claims to ethnic identity and territorial integrity. But the scholarship is not merely congenial to Zionist ideology. The scholars themselves assume uncritically the ethnic identity, territorial legitimacy and nationalist aspirations at the root of Zionism. If the assumptions of the scholars are identical with those of Zionists, why do we not consider the scholars Zionists? If we see a creature that looks like a duck, walks like a duck and sounds like a duck, we call it a duck. When a scholar talks like a Zionist and writes like a Zionist, we seem to say instead, 'I wonder what it is?'

Mainstream Christian Zionism, however, is not restricted to the ranks of biblical scholars, archaeologists and historians. The history of

collusion between mainstream, liberal Christians and the Zionist enterprise is neither obscure nor relegated to a narrow band of the mainstream spectrum. While mainstream, liberal Christians have little interest in fundamentalist biblical hermeneutics, or in restorationist theology, from early in the 20th century, they were predisposed to support Jews in what were largely perceived to be noble ambitions, and were intrigued by the utility of the Zionist enterprise in advancing Western national interests in the Middle East. Thus, many saw Zionism as a mechanism to project Western civilisation into a largely retrograde cultural backwater, devoid of worthwhile people, but rich in resources and strategic value.

While European political support for Zionism was spawned in the pools of fundamentalist Christian Zionism, it took diplomatic form only when mainstream European Christians saw support for Zionism as an imperative to advancing their imperial objectives. The notorious Balfour Declaration of 1917, for example, was not formulated by fundamentalist Christian Zionists, but by liberal Christians. Chaim Weizman's access to the British government was not restricted to fundamentalists, but included access to others, such as Winston Churchill, who was religious, but supported the Zionist enterprise for its utility in advancing Britain's imperial interests. In the United States also, liberal Christian support for the Zionist enterprise took root among Christians who were predisposed to Zionism by their religious foundations, but were not themselves fundamentalists.

Mainstream Christian Zionism depends on several critical elements. Among these, there is sympathy for the Jewish people in their struggle against injustice, and appreciation of the cultural accomplishments of the Jews throughout history. For example, in 1931, Charles Edward Russell, a journalist and a social activist who was one of the founders of the National Association for the Advancement of Colored People, took the chair of the mainstream Christian Organization called The Pro-Palestine Federation of America. Its agenda was explicitly Zionist (see Merkley 1998: 106-14). It promoted support for Jews against bigotry, sympathy for the distinct problems of Jews living as a minority people among gentiles and advancement of the goals of the Balfour Declaration. Emmanuel Neumann, a prominent American Jewish Zionist, recognised that there was a distinct 'Christian consciousness' that could be exploited to support the Zionist political agenda. Russell is an illustration of this Christian consciousness. Predisposed to sympathise with the Zionist

agenda by his infatuation with the Jewish people, he was converted to Zionism by Rabbi Stephen Wise. He wrote:

> It was long ago, in either 1897 or 1898, when I was a managing editor on the *New York Morning Journal*, you came in one day ... and talked with me about Zion, talked so interestingly and so convincingly that from that day I was a Zionist ... I owe to Jews such a debt of gratitude that I can't easily forego the opportunity to work with them in a cause like this (the Pro-Palestine Federation) ... There are many things in this world that I am ignorant of, but at least I know the Jewish spirit and the Jewish heart (in Merkley 1998: 108).

Reinhold Niebuhr is another example of a mainstream Christian Zionist. By no means a fundamentalist, Niebuhr's support for Jewish causes was unwavering. He was motivated not by restorationist theology, but by moral outrage over the experience of Jews in Nazi Germany. His conscience was attuned by his theological disposition to issues of justice and the moral obligation on Christians to respond to social challenges. He cultivated close friendships with Jewish clerics who themselves were Zionists and encouraged him to support Zionist causes. He spoke frequently in support of Zionism to Jewish audiences. Leaders of Zionist organizations identified him as one who could be counted on to advance their agenda among Christians and he agreed to write a two-part pro-Zionist article that appeared in *The Nation* (in Merkley 1998: 133-43). He wrote:

> The problem of what is to become of the Jews in the postwar world ought to engage all of us, not only because a suffering people has a claim upon our compassion but because the very quality of our civilisation is involved in the solution ... The Jews require a homeland, if for no other reason, because even the most generous immigration laws of Western democracies will not permit all the dispossessed Jews of Europe to find a haven in which they may look forward to a tolerable future ... The Anglo-Saxon hegemony that is bound to exist in the event of an Axis defeat will be in a

position to see to it that Palestine is set aside for Jews (in Merkley 1998: 137).

No doubt informed by Christian philosophical moral underpinnings, Niebuhr was also predisposed by his theological orientation and experience toward empathy for and affinity with Jews. Just as clearly, he had no interest in fundamentalist biblical hermeneutics. Does that fact alone, however, disqualify him from the ranks of Zionists? On the contrary, his orientation toward Zionism perfectly illustrates that fundamentalism is not a precondition for Christian Zionism. He wrote,

> Many Christians are pro-Zionist in the sense that they believe that a homeless people require a homeland; but we feel as embarrassed as anti-Zionist religious Jews when messianic claims are used to substantiate the right of the Jews to the particular homeland in Palestine … History is full of strange configurations. Among them is the thrilling emergence of the State of Israel (in Merkley 1998: 141).

Mainstream Christian Zionism also pervades one of the most hallowed precincts of liberal, mainstream Christianity, namely the Jewish–Christian dialogue. It is in this realm that it is at once most virulent and unchallenged. It is no surprise that Jews involved in the dialogue display obvious Zionist sympathies, but their Christian counterparts are often equally and unapologetically Zionist. It is also in this realm that the challenges associated with identifying and critiquing mainstream Christian Zionism are most apparent. Unlike the ranks of fundamentalist Christian Zionists, whose opinions are often shrugged of as 'lunatic ravings', mainstream Christian Zionists are not easy targets. Not only is the group of expositors and prime examples of mainstream Christian Zionism populated by icons of liberal, progressive Christianity, their motivation for assuming obviously Zionist positions is theologically competent and grounded in sincere moral concern. Introducing one of the issues that prompts considerable hesitation on the part of Christians to criticise Israel, Michael Prior writes:

> The role of the *Shoah* in Western Christian thought has been critical. Jewish–Christian dialogue has been dominated

by Holocaust theology, with its emphasis on suffering and empowerment, frequently making Christians silent partners to Israeli policy (Prior 1999a: 134).

Nowhere is the reality of Jewish suffering more prominent in Christian thought than in the formal circles of Jewish-Christian dialogue where it propels Christian participants in the dialogue to adopt clearly Zionist positions.[12] Almost without exception, their concern grows out of sincere regard for Jewish suffering and the demands of justice and restitution. Rarely, however, does their concern extend to other peoples, especially the Palestinians who experience Zionism as an instrument of catastrophe. Among many Christian participants in Jewish-Christian dialogue groups, the suffering and experiences of the Palestinians do not merit the same regard as that accorded to Jews. One notable example among many is Father Robert Drinan, formerly Dean of the School of Law at Boston College, and now professor of law at Georgetown University. Drinan is a well-known activist in liberal social causes throughout his long and illustrious career. However, in describing Zionism, Drinan uses language that would have surprised even Herzl, whom, he says, pursued his 'messianic pilgrimage' with a zeal 'infused with a compelling humanitarianism combined with traces of Jewish mysticism'. The 'mystery' and 'majesty' of Zionism appears in its glory from Herzl's tomb. Now that the state is established, Christians should support it 'in reparation or restitution for the genocide of Jews carried out in a nation whose population was overwhelmingly Christian' (Drinan 1977: 32, 39 and 1). Moreover, Drinan not only uncritically subscribes to standard Zionist canards about the formation of the State of Israel and the virtues of the founders of Zionism, the moral indignation he displays toward to the suffering of the Jews is nowhere in evidence in relation to the suffering of the Palestinians (see Prior 1999a: 126-27).

The reader should not ignore Father Drinan's distinguished, ten-year career as a member of the US House of Representatives (Democrat-Massachusetts) during which he had numerous opportunities to express his enthusiasm for Zionism by voting in favour of legislation and resolutions that were staunchly pro-Israel. He is, thus, also an example

---

[12] See the recent discussion in Prior 2003b.

of the way in which mainstream Christian Zionism pervades US political institutions. Neither can Father Drinan be dismissed as a member of the lunatic fringe, which illustrates one of the unique challenges endemic to isolating and critiquing mainstream Christian Zionism. Mainstream Christian Zionism is by no means as easy to isolate as its fundamentalist cousin, and its proponents are not as easily shrugged off.

Very few topics generate fervent debate, arouse passions and evoke confusion like the Israeli-Palestinian conflict. This is because it veers into the volatile areas of religion and politics. Personal faith, interpretation of scripture, personal loyalties, moral convictions and deeply-held political opinions overlap and collide in a confused sea of facts, perceptions, images and realities. Notwithstanding these treacherous emotional waters, conscientious American Christians have no choice but to attempt to navigate them, because their Churches and their government are both deeply complicit in the sadness and suffering of the people of Israel and Palestine. What is more, their Churches and their government can make positive contributions to resolution of the conflict for the benefit of all parties involved—provided, that is, that the dimensions of the conflict and US complicity in it are properly understood. This last condition is not satisfied even by passionate activists. Activists and novices alike badly misunderstand Christian Zionism as a phenomenon restricted to fundamentalist Christians.

Conclusion

It is clear that a more pervasive, pernicious and sophisticated form of Zionism has been overlooked, which I call *mainstream Christian Zionism*. Were it not for this form of Christian Zionism, the more easily identifiable, easily critiqued, unsophisticated form of Christian Zionism would not have the effect that it has. Mainstream Christian Zionism does not depend on biblical authority for its legitimacy. It is rooted in the genuine moral sensitivities of mainstream Christians. Its appeal is to moral imperatives and political necessity rather than personal piety. As we have seen, it is cultivated throughout mainstream churches and in the biblical academy, and it is entrenched in the political institutions of the West, especially in America. It is far better organised, far better funded and far more politically potent that its fundamentalist cousin.

Reconsidering Christian Zionism in its mainstream form leads inevitably to vexing moral conflicts. It requires re-examination of widely held assumptions about ethnic identity and nationhood and the moral implications of these. If Zionism as a nationalist ideology is susceptible to critique—and it certainly is—so also are other nationalist ideologies. Indeed, reconsidering Christian Zionism demands a re-evaluation of the moral principles upon which liberal, progressive Christians base their unwavering support for Zionism. Many are not willing to examine these. Reconsidering Christian Zionism requires us to understand Zionism in much more sophisticated terms than Christians typically do. It raises issues that are considered taboo in the Church and takes us into perilous academic 'no-fly zones'. But intellectual honesty requires no less.

It is, of course, conspicuously convenient for mainstream Christians to identify Christian Zionism exclusively with evangelical, fundamentalist Christians. It is always easier to identify other people's defects than one's own. Zionism, to be sure, is too diverse a phenomenon to be denounced in a simplistic fashion. Nevertheless, mainstream, liberal Christians cannot absolve themselves of complicity in the Zionist enterprise, simply because they are not fundamentalists. If they espouse views that are identical to the nationalist assumptions of self-confessed secular and religious Jewish Zionists, then they should be identified as Zionists themselves. After all, Ariel Sharon is neither a fundamentalist, nor a dispensationalist theologian. Indeed, if Zionism were defined solely in fundamentalist or dispensationalist terms, not even Sharon himself could not be considered a Zionist! Moreover, although Reinhold Niebuhr and Robert Drinan are neither colonisers, abject racists nor biblical literalists, if they are not counted among the ranks of Zionists, then many self-defined Zionists would not qualify either.

As long as Christian Zionism is considered to be the exclusive domain of Christian fundamentalists, mainstream, liberal Christians do not have to do much more than point the incriminating finger at them. It needs to be acknowledged that Zionism is not only primarily a Christian phenomenon—as opposed to the misconception that it is primarily a Jewish phenomenon—it is fundamentally and primarily a *mainstream, liberal* Christian phenomenon.

Equating Christian Zionism so thoroughly with evangelical, fundamentalist Christians, or with the Christian Right is highly misleading, and ignores the reality that Christian Zionist support for the

State of Israel comes overwhelmingly from mainstream Christians. To reduce the phenomenon of Christian Zionism to a particular style of biblical interpretation (fundamentalist), or to a particular type of theological orientation (dispensationalist or millenarian) grossly oversimplifies the range of Christian Zionism. Christian Zionism is not restricted to fundamentalist Christians. Until we understand Christian Zionism in its *mainstream* aspects, however, we have not begun to appreciate how pervasive Zionism really is.

References

Albright, William F. 1942. 'Why the Near East needs the Jews', *New Palestine* 32: 12-13

Albright, William F. 1957. *From the Stone Age to Christianity: Monotheism and the Historical Process*, New York: Doubleday

Drinan, Robert F. 1977. *Honor the Promise: America's Commitment to Israel*. Cape Town, NY: Doubleday

Merkley, Paul C. 1998. *The Politics of Christian Zionism 1891-1948*. Portland: Frank Cass Publishers

Mezvinsky, Norton and Israel Shahak. 1999. *Jewish Fundamentalism in Israel*. London: Pluto Press

Prior, Michael. 1997a. *The Bible and Colonialism. A Moral Critique*. Sheffield: Sheffield Academic Press

Prior, Michael. 1997b. *A Land flowing with Milk, Honey, and People* (The Lattey Lecture 1997) Von Hügel Institute, St Edmund's College, Cambridge University

Prior, Michael. 1999a. *Zionism and the State of Israel: A Moral Inquiry:* London and New York. Routledge

Prior, Michael. 1999b. 'The Bible and the Redeeming Idea of Colonialism', in Marcella Althaus-Reid and Jack Thompson (eds), in *Studies in World Christianity*, Vol. 5 (2, *Postcolonialism and Religion*). Edinburgh: Edinburgh University Press and Maryknoll, NY: Orbis: 129-55

Prior, Michael. 2000. 'Zionist Ethnic Cleansing: the Fulfilment of Biblical Prophecy?' *Epworth Review* 27(2): 49-60

Prior, Michael. 2002a. 'Ethnic Cleansing and the Bible: A Moral Critique', *Holy Land Studies. A Multidisciplinary Journal* 1: 37-59

Prior, Michael. 2002b. 'The Israel-Palestine Dispute and the Bible', *Scripture Bulletin* 32: 64-79

Prior, Michael. 2003a. 'The State of the Art: Biblical Scholarship and the Holy Land', *Holy Land Studies. A Multidisciplinary Journal* 1 (no. 2): 65-92

Prior, Michael. 2003b. 'Speaking Truth in the Jewish-Christian Dialogue', in *A Faithful Presence. Essays for Kenneth Cragg*, ed. David Thomas and Clare Amos. London: Melisende: 329-49

Prior, Michael. 1998 (ed.). *Western Scholarship and the History of Palestine.* London: Melisende

Silberman. Neil Asher. 1982. *Digging for God and Country: Exploration in the Holy Land, 1799-1917.* New York: Doubleday

Silberman. Neil Asher. 1989. *Between Past and Present: Archaeology, Ideology, and Nationalism in the Modern Middle East.* New York: Doubleday

Sizer, Stephen R. 2003. *Christian Zionism: Historical Roots, Theological Basis and Political Consequences.* CD rom. Virginia Water: Stephen Sizer

Thompson, Thomas L. 1974. *The Historicity of the Pentateuchal Narratives. The Quest for the Historical Abraham.* Berlin/New York: de Gruyter

Thompson, Thomas L. 1987. *The Origin Tradition of Ancient Israel. 1. The Literary Formation of Genesis and Exodus 1-23.* JSOTSS 55, Sheffield: JSOT Press

Thompson, Thomas L. 1992. *Early History of the Israelite People from the Written and Archaeological Sources,* Studies in the History of the Ancient Near East, 4, Leiden: Brill

Thompson, Thomas L. 1995. 'A Neo-Albrightean School in History and Biblical Scholarship', in *Journal of Biblical Literature* 114: 685-98

Thompson, Thomas L. 1998. 'Hidden Histories and the Problem of Ethnicity in Palestine', in Prior (ed.) 1998: 23-39

Thompson, Thomas L. 1999. *The Bible in History. How Writers Create a Past.* London: Jonathan Cape (US title: *The Mythic Past. Biblical Archaeology and the Myth of Israel.* Basic Books)

Trigger, B. 1984. 'Alternative archaeolgies: nationalist, colonialist, imperialist', Man 19: 355-70.

Wagner , Donald E (foreword by Elias Chacour). 1995. Anxious for Armageddon: A Call to Partnership for Middle Eastern and Western Christians. Scottdale & Waterloo, Penn: Herald Press

Whitelam, Keith W. 1996a. The Invention of Ancient Israel. The Silencing of Palestinian History, London and New York: Routledge

Whitelam, Keith W. 1996b. 'Prophetic Conflict in Israelite History: Taking Sides with William G Dever', in Journal for the Study of the Old Testament 72: 25-44

Whitelam, Keith W. 1998. 'Western Scholarship and the Silencing of Palestinian History', in Prior (ed.) 1998: 9-21

POLITICS AND MULTI-FAITH
IN THE HOLY LAND:
A CHALLENGE FOR CHRISTIANS
Duncan Macpherson

This essay explores the importance of Israel–Palestine in Christian theology and in particular in relation to an appropriate interfaith perspective to such a theology. Political issues, and Zionism in particular, raise questions that make a genuinely ecumenical and open approach especially difficult.

For a Christian, the world of the Holy Land is the world of the Gospels. Whenever and wherever the Gospel is read and preached, understanding of that world is an essential part of the background to the text.[1] The geography and archaeology of the Holy Land can illuminate the world of the Gospel texts. This world includes historical, religious, political, and cultural elements that are often complex and unfamiliar to the modern reader. Sometimes these elements can provide avenues towards understanding analogous realities in the Holy Land today. Significantly, however, they can also illuminate Christian theological understanding of the world beyond the Holy Land, what is represented in the Acts of the Apostles as the 'the uttermost parts of the earth' (Acts 1: 8).

A Christian theology firmly situated within the perspective of the Holy Land takes place within the religious context of ecumenical and interfaith realities. It also takes place in an area of contested secular historical and political issues, any or all of which constantly confront the pilgrim or anyone else interpreting the Gospel message against the background of an informed interest in contemporary Israel–Palestine.

It is not always easy for European Christians to acquire the necessary sensitivity for Christian spirituality against such a varied, confusing, and frequently challenging background. As Kenneth Cragg has wisely remarked:

---

[1] This perspective is explored in its wider aspects with special reference to the concerns of the Christian preacher in Duncan Macpherson, *Pilgrim Preacher: Palestine Pilgrimage and Preaching*, published in March 2004, London: Melisende.

> The sacrament of geography is too much for our qualities
> of soul. Feeling becomes either sour or over-indulgent and,
> in either case, is religiously unreal. A score of temptations
> await the Christian in the precincts of his redemption and
> are multiplied again when he takes up his ministries in its
> meaning to the other religions which in their diversely
> passionate ways possess the same territories (Cragg 1969:
> 571).

In the wider context of Christian understanding there is a range of other realities and issues. Some of the realities and issues are specific to the local situation. Others are of global significance and must contribute to a fuller interpretation of the Gospel texts. Likewise, there are some realities and issues that are specific to the Holy Land itself, but there are others that have importance for everyone. These provide opportunities to explore the relevance of Christianity to wider issues than those that concern the Holy Land. Nevertheless, Israel-Palestine can never be far from the mind of people who hear or read the Gospel story, wherever they may be. This is partly because human beings live increasingly in a 'global village' in which regional issues have world-wide significance. For historical and geopolitical reasons the Israeli-Palestinian conflict is just such an issue. The Holy Land has a special significance for Christians, Jews, and Muslims everywhere. In the Christian tradition the biblical text itself constantly refers back to the land that is proclaimed as being in some special way the arena of God's revelation and saving actions in history. The fact that those who take sides in the modern Israeli-Palestinian conflict frequently invoke the Bible makes it even more difficult to ignore what is taking place in the land where it all began.[2]

Three faiths

One of the primary religious realities of the Holy Land is that it is holy to the three Abrahamic and Semitic faiths: Christianity, Islam, and

---

[2] Michael Prior offers an account of the use of Scripture to justify oppression in the Holy Land and explores parallels with religious justification of other rapacious colonial enterprises (Prior 1997).

Judaism. In Israel today there are approximately six million people of whom 81.45 percent are Jews, a further 16.3 percent are Palestinian Muslims and 2.3 percent Palestinian Christian (Bissio 2001-2: 302). In the West Bank (including East Jerusalem) and Gaza, there are approximately three million people, a figure that includes 400,000 Jewish settlers and a mere 51,000 Palestinian Christians. Nearly all of the remainder is Muslim Palestinian (Prior 1999: 424).

Those with a narrowly exclusivist Christian perspective may be able to ignore this reality and concentrate on the significance of the land in terms of biblical sites associated with the Christian story alone. However, one or other, or both, of the other two faiths also revere many of the sites referred to in the Bible and revered by Christians. Those Christians who are influenced by more inclusivist currents of thinking—for example those of the Second Vatican Council's *Nostra Aetate* (Austin Flannery 1975: 783-47)—are obliged to provide a perspective that addresses the significance of some of these sites to Judaism and Islam.

For Jews, the Holy Land is the land promised to Abraham and Moses, the land of David and Solomon. Long before modern Zionism succeeded in giving it political significance, the Holy Land, and Jerusalem in particular, served as a spiritual symbol of religious identity and of eschatological hope for Jews throughout the world.

For Muslims, Jerusalem, al-Quds ash-Sharif, is associated with the offering of Ishmael as a sacrifice by Abraham and also with the furthest *qibla,* the destination from the Ka'ba of the Prophet Muhammad on his miraculous night journey. Other associations with the prophets of Islam include Adam, as well as Jacob, David, and Solomon, who are credited with having contributed to the building and extension of al-Aqsa (Gibb and Kramers 1974: 267-69). There are many other associations with the prophets of Islam in Israel-Palestine, as well as a number of pious associations often shared either with Christianity and/or Judaism.

For each of the three faiths these common associations can and should provide a special impetus towards dialogue and mutual understanding. Christian scholars and communicators can build on inter-faith understanding with appropriate references to these shared associations. To do this with any degree of honesty, however, requires reference to the problematic, often bloody, history of relations between

these faiths in past centuries—no one faith is above reproach[3]—as well as to the Israeli-Palestinian conflict of the last fifty years.

The Christian experiences a constant tension between faith in the Prince of Peace and the ever-present reality of violence and the threat of violence between Israelis and Palestinians. This is a tension between belief that the '*light has come*' and the evidence, so near to hand, that '*night still covers the earth and darkness the people*' (Isaiah 60.1).[4] Christians have the option of ignoring the issue and concentrating on the purely 'spiritual' character of the Holy Land. For those who take this option, understanding of the historical and the political issues underlying the conflict between Israelis and Palestinians is of secondary importance, and seeking to understand the issues is always conditional upon maintaining a position of strict neutrality between the contending parties. Such an approach seems to this writer both to be morally shallow and to betray a weak understanding of the doctrine of the Incarnation. The alternative approach requires facing the challenge of doing justice to the issues of the Israeli-Palestinian conflict. This involves the examination of controversial questions requiring historical judgements.

The Israeli–Palestinian dispute and relationships between the three religions

The Israeli-Palestinian conflict, like the conflicts of earlier centuries includes religious and political factors that are not always directly related. Unfortunately it does not take long for them to become so. Thus, for most Jews today the Jewish state has become 'part of their self-understanding' (Prior 2003: 327-47), Zionism was initially a project of secular Jewish nationalists. Indeed the leader of the founders of the Zionist

---

[3]   Consider Jerusalem, for example. According to the Byzantine chronicler Antiochus Strategos, the Jewish allies of the Persians massacred Christians in 614. In 1009 Muslims under Caliph Hakim, 'the mad', massacred Christians, and in 1244 Muslim mercenaries fighting on behalf of the Ayyubids engaged in similar bloodletting. More terrible than any of these was the massacre of Muslims and Jews by Christian Crusaders in 1099. In the modern period the emergence of Zionism and the establishment of the State of Israel has been at the cost of the indigenous Muslim and Christian population.

[4]   This text is taken from the section of the Book of Isaiah from chapters 40 to 66, which reflects the period in Palestine around 520 BC during uncertain conditions that prevailed after the return from exile in Babylon in 538 BC.

community of Petah Tikvah (Jacobs 1998: 101) 'though an observant Jew, was excommunicated (put into *herem*) by the orthodox rabbis of Jerusalem, because it was heresy for Jews to redeem the soil and so to anticipate the Messiah' (Arberry 1969: 62). Despite this earlier opposition of religious Jews to the Zionist project, 'In recent times no group of Jews is more enthusiastic for the state' (Prior 1999: 67-102).[5] Unsurprisingly then, the issue of Israel and Zionism invariably overshadows Jewish-Christian dialogue. Where the Jews are Israelis and the Christians are Palestinian Arabs, the issue can be said to preclude the possibility of genuine dialogue altogether. As Bishop Kenneth Cragg has wisely observed, theological dialogue separated from justice can be a snare and a delusion (Cragg 1997: 217).

Today the religious right includes uncompromising Zionists who interpret the setting up of the Jewish state in 1948 and the capture of Jerusalem in 1967 as precursors of the rebuilding of the temple and the coming of the Messiah. Meanwhile a minority of very observant Jews follows the earlier religious opinion that the coming of the Messiah must come before the return to Zion. These traditionalists are opposed on principle to the existence of the State of Israel. It should be borne in mind, however, that Jews across the political spectrum, from ultra-Zionist to anti-Zionist, might belong to either religious or secular groupings.[6]

Christian perspectives on the Israeli–Palestinian conflict

Christians have adopted quite different perspectives on the Israeli-Palestinian conflict, ranging from identification with one or other of the two contending parties through to relative indifference. Those western Christians identifying more or less uncritically with the Israeli side of the conflict divide into two main categories. The first and the most extreme of these consists of Christian Zionists who regard the State of Israel as fulfilling biblical prophecy, and consider that Christians owe a debt of

---

[5] Prior here traces the evolution of Jewish religious evaluation of Israel and of Zionism from anathema to sacred significance.

[6] Zionism was originally an ideology espoused by non-religious Jews. However, after the occupation of the West Bank (including East Jerusalem), Sinai, Gaza, and Golan Heights in 1967, the majority of religious Jews became supporters of Zionism (Prior 1999: 134-56).

loyalty and support for the most uncompromising and expansionist policies of the Israeli government.

Beliefs of Christian Zionists can be summarised as follows. Biblical prophecies are literal and predictive. The true Church will enjoy rapture into heaven, and Israel will become God's primary instrument. There are seven epochs or dispensations in human history. There is a dispensation of grace before the millennium. The coming 'tribulation', the battle of Armageddon, and the Second Coming of Christ are all events for which Christians must try to discern the signs (Wagner 1995: 199-214). This revival gained its strength from the influence of the televangelists, the emergence of the 'Moral Majority' right-wing Christian fundamentalist movement, and the Christian Broadcasting Network. Influenced by their literalistic interpretation of biblical prophecies, they maintain that the return of the Jews to Sion is a necessary prelude to the Second Coming of Christ. This movement which has its origins in millenarian Christian Zionism going back to 16th century England, gained wider support, particularly in the United States, after the founding of the Jewish State in 1948. However, it was the capture of Jerusalem in 1967 that fired the apocalyptic imagination and led to the Christian Zionist revival of the 1970s.

The second category of Western Christians considers that the terrible sufferings which the Nazis inflicted on the Jews during the Second World War gives them a moral right to a state of their own. They also consider that the crimes committed against the Jews by Christians of past generations need to be compensated for by giving strong support for a secure Jewish homeland.

Then there are those Christians who are critical of Israel and who identify with the Palestinian case, who see the Palestinians as the innocent victims of the setting up of the State of Israel and emphasise that a small but important section of the Palestinian people is Christian. The Holy See and the Anglican Communion, in particular, are concerned about the continuation of an indigenous Christian presence in the Holy Land. They are also anxious that Jerusalem should not be in the hands of followers of just one of the three faiths for which it is holy.

Palestinian Christians themselves have generally supported the moderate nationalist camp and have rejected the infusion of religious zeal into political fanaticism, many of them advocating non-violent resistance to the occupation. They are conscious that they have shared in

the sufferings inflicted on the Palestinian people as a whole and that many of their number have left the country to escape from situations of conflict and discrimination. Their leaders try to draw attention to the implications for the Christian world of the gradual disappearance of communities that have maintained a continuous presence in the Holy Land since the outpouring of the Holy Spirit at Pentecost.

Other Christians have more nuanced approaches supporting the existence of the State of Israel, while being critical of oppressive Israeli government policies. Thus, for example, the statement of the Holy See of 1976 recognised 'the rights and legitimate aspirations of the Jews to a sovereign and independent state.' This is balanced by a demand that there should be a reciprocal recognition of 'the rights and legitimate aspirations of another people, which have also suffered for a long time, the Palestinian people' (*Acta Apostolicae Sedis*, January–March 1976: 134).

The main criteria governing the attitudes to the conflict by Christianity at the official level have been concern for the safety of the holy places and the preservation of free access to them, the protection and survival of the indigenous Christians, and more general considerations of peace and justice. Thus in his audience with American Jewish Committee leaders in February 1985, Pope John Paul II expressed the hope that 'The Lord give to the land, and to all the peoples and nations in that part of the world, the blessings contained in the word *shalom* and 'that the sons and daughters of Abraham—Jews, Christians and Muslims—may live and prosper in peace' (Fisher, Rudin and Tannenbaum.1986: 58-59). Since 1948, there has been also a concern by some to support the existence and safety of Israel as a way of atoning for past Christian crimes against the Jews. From this perspective, 'Disregard for Israel's safety and welfare is incompatible with the Church's necessary concern for the Jewish people' (Council of Churches for Britain and Ireland 1994: 14).

Inter-faith relations between Christians and Jews clearly have considerable influence upon attitudes to the conflict, but there is an increasing realisation that this needs to be balanced by a parallel concern to promote good relations between Christians and Muslims.

From a Christian point of view it is also important to retain a sense of theological perspective. Contemporary preachers are rightly warned against interpreting the New Testament in ways that are detrimental to Jewish-Christian relations or supportive of antisemitic ideologies. From this unexceptionable perspective, however, some writers

wish to go further and talk as though there were no sense in which Christ fulfils the earlier covenant.[7]

From this distorted theological perspective in which Judaism and Christianity are seen as parallel covenants with equivalent value, the political perspective of Christian Zionism follows easily. If Christ does not fulfil the Law and the Prophets, the modern State of Israel emerges as an alternative candidate. There is a danger in giving a nation-state the status of being divinely promised. Politics is a grubby business, and any state is liable to be involved in oppression towards the defenceless, aggressive policies towards its neighbours, espionage, wars and deceit. In the case of Israel, many would regard the negative case as overwhelming. Unless or until some measure of justice is achieved for those who have endured the evils of displacement, exile, and military occupation, Israel should be one of the last states to have its nationalism validated by Christian preachers. For Christian critics of Zionism, the acceptance of Zionism involves collusion with the injustice done to the Palestinians. (Prior 1999: 147-52). Meanwhile, for some religious Jews the granting of messianic status to the State of Israel is not only dangerous but also blasphemous (Prior 1999: 227-29).

Christian Liberation Theology perspective

The impact of the Liberation Theology perspective that emerged primarily out of Latin America in the 1960s and 70s has obvious relevance to the Israeli-Palestinian conflict. The fundamental tenets of Liberation Theology are those of the 'preferential option for the poor'[8] and 'praxis'[9]— breaking down the distinction between abstract theory and its practical application. Both these tenets have as their premise the recovery of the

---

[7] For example, John Pawlikowski (1990: 155-70), or Paul van Buren (1980). In a debate with Messianic Christian theologian David Stern, Friedrich-Wilhelm Marquardt argues that traditional christological doctrines must be rejected. Stern counters this by asserting that Jesus must continue to be regarded as the Messiah both of the Jews and of the gentiles (see Hegstad 1997: 112).

[8] 'Jesus, like the prophets, concentrates on those areas where the life of individuals is most precarious, most threatened, or even non-existent. For this reason the program of his mission is one of partiality and announces a God of partisan life to those who lack it at the most elementary levels' (Sobrino 1987: 107-108).

[9] 'Existing liberation theology is a theology directed upon praxis—precisely a praxis of social transformation ... at once critical and utopian' (Boff 1993: 65).

communal dimension of Christianity, rejecting preoccupation with 'soul saving' individualism that does not also embrace the imperatives of affirming bodily and material needs, and the liberation of communities experiencing exploitation and oppression. The application of these principles clearly invites an active concern for the plight of the Palestinians—Muslim and Christian alike. It also provides a commitment that transcends the limitations of nationalist ideology. Rather, it looks beyond the redressing of an historic injustice towards a liberation that includes all the parties to the present conflict. In the words of Naim Ateek, the pioneer of a Palestinian Liberation Theology,

> The challenge of jubilee implies the possibility of a new era, a new beginning between Palestinians and Israelis. In other words, when the oppressed are set free, their dignity and humanity is restored to them, and they become free human beings. When the land is returned to its legal owners, it means that people can cultivate it and live from the gift of the land and its produce which God has given them. When the debt of the poor is cancelled they can have a fresh start with hope for a better future for themselves and their families. The jubilee allows for new attitudes to develop and new perceptions to be created. The Palestinians and Israelis will not perceive each other anymore as enemies, but as neighbours and potential friends and partners (Ateek in Ateek and Prior 1999: xiv-xv).

Christian Zionism and Jewish-Christian dialogue

It is evident that some Western Christians ignore the honourable anti-Zionist currents of Orthodox Jewry and give more or less uncritical support to Israel and its policies towards the Palestinians. A large group of Western Christians, mainly American and other Evangelical believers, are motivated by apocalyptic speculation. For them, the 1967 Israeli conquest of Jerusalem is the fulfilment of biblical prophecy and a presage of the Second Coming of Jesus.[10] Others are motivated by a desire to

---

[10] Indeed, in response to the refusal of the international community to recognise the Israeli annexation of Jerusalem or to establish embassies there, a particular group of the Evangelical constituency has set up a 'Christian Embassy' in Jerusalem. (Sizer 1998: 18).

improve relations with Judaism, even if that excludes consideration of Muslim-Christian relations. At the theological level this can be understood in terms of the special status given to Judaism. Whether Judaism is seen as the Old Covenant fulfilled and superseded by the New, or whether it is seen as the Older Covenant retaining an enduring value in parallel with Christianity,[11] for Christians, Judaism remains a special case among the religions of the world. Western Christians are also more vividly aware of past Christian wrongs against Jews than of those committed against Muslims. This lack of even-handedness in approaches to the two religions is often mirrored in Western Christian attitudes to the Israeli-Palestinian conflict and to the status of Jerusalem. By contrast, the leaderships of the major Christian Churches have insisted on the special status of Jerusalem, and in common with the Islamic world they have protested against Israeli attempts to claim a special monopoly over it for one religion at the expense of the others (PASSIA 1996: 32-33).

Neither of these approaches takes serious account of the injustice suffered by the Palestinians, whether Muslim or Christian. Michael Prior highlights the historical misunderstandings or falsifications that have been used by some of the Christian participants in the dialogue. Among North American Catholic writers, he cites Father Edward Flannery as a spokesman for the view that Israel is an essential part of Judaism and that 'support for it is a *sine qua non* of the dialogue' (Flannery 1986: 73-86).

Flannery further characterises criticism of Israel and anti-Zionism as 'not necessarily, but ... almost always a symptom of the antisemitic virus' (Flannery 1986: 82).[12] In contrast he himself sees Israel as having quasi-messianic significance and, as in some degree at least, fulfilling prophecies of the First Covenant that remained unfulfilled by Christianity. Father Robert Drinan, too, argues that Christians should support the State of Israel 'in reparation or restitution for the genocide of Jews carried out in a nation whose population was overwhelmingly Christian' (Drinan 1977: xi).

Prior catalogues how Flannery and Drinan accept a whole range of distortions and falsifications and omissions of the historical record

---

[11] Sensitivity to 'supercessionalism' influences one influential North American Theologian, Douglas John Hall, to avoid the terms Old and New Testaments in favour of 'Older' and 'Newer Testaments' (Hall 1996: 303, 407).

[12] For a recent discussion of the relationship between antizionism and antisemitism see Prior 2002.

regarding the exodus of the Palestinians and subsequent events in 1948. In the case of these and other contributors to the Jewish-Christian dialogue, Prior draws attention to the asymmetries in the relationship. On the one hand, according to Professor Walter Harrelson and Rabbi Randall M Falk, Christians are required to say, 'I am sorry for what my Christian forebears and contemporaries have done to Jews. And I am sorry for my own part in it.' Collectively, the Church should observe the Days of Remembrance of the *Shoah*, and the worldwide Christian community should erect a memorial to the victims of the *Shoah* (Harrelson and Falk 1990: 195-97). On the other hand, as Prior points out,

> There is no question of a collective of Jews acknowledging Zionist responsibility for the catastrophe perpetrated on the Palestinian Arabs in furtherance of the Zionist enterprise to establish a state for Jews, all in Rabbi Falk's own lifetime (Prior 2003: 339).

The example of the Second Vatican Council

This same contradiction was evident during the debates of the Second Vatican Council. The impact of Middle Eastern politics on Christian-Jewish and Christian-Muslim relations provided clear evidence of the way in which cultural and political issues can impede the growth of better relations between world faiths. Nowhere more is this the case than in the Holy Land.

It was the political issue of the Israeli-Palestinian conflict that compelled the council to broaden its discussion on the Catholic Church's relations with the Jews to include consideration of relations with Islam and then with other religions. The inspiration for the discussion of relations with the Jews stemmed from the conviction that, over the centuries, Christian teaching and preaching had contributed to the antisemitism that had led in turn to the Nazi extermination of the Jews. The decision to include Islam in the discussion derived directly from the political realities of the Middle East.

The proposal to condemn the long-held prejudice that the Jews shared a common guilt for the death of Jesus Christ may have seemed overdue at a distance in time of only sixteen years from the discovery of

the extermination camps in Europe. However, it also came only thirteen years after the *Nakba*—the flight and expulsion of some three-quarters of a million Palestinians from their homes. Arabs and Muslims responded with indignation that although such a statement might help Jews and Christians to live together in peace in the West, it would nevertheless advance the cause of Israel.

Representatives of Arab Catholic communities in the Middle East spoke of the dangers of a backlash against Christians in the Middle East. Reassurance was offered from Cardinal Bea that the statement on the Jews was 'a merely religious question, there is no question that the Council will get entangled in those difficult questions regarding the relations the Arab states and the State of Israel, or regarding so-called Zionism' (in Rynne 1966: 22) Further reassurance came with Pope Paul VI's pilgrimage to the Holy Land in January 1964 giving practical expression to just such a pastoral and politically even-handed approach by the Church.

In response to further opposition it was finally agreed to enlarge the declaration on the Jews to embrace all the major world religions. Pope Paul VI's first encyclical *Ecclesiam Suam* (August 1964) centred on the theme of dialogue between the Catholic Church and other traditions and belief systems.[13]

The new approach failed to silence all criticism. When the revised document, *Nostra Aetate*, was carried by the council fathers on 20 November 1964, Arab reaction followed speedily. A Syrian radio broadcast referred to 'a facelift which would fool nobody' (*Herder Correspondence*, March 1965, 80).

For most Arabs, it seemed that the wrongs done to the Jews were being acknowledged but that the injustices suffered by the Palestinians were being ignored. The theologian René Laurentin considered that the Israelis themselves gave credibility to hostile Arab interpretations by themselves claiming that the denial of Jewish responsibility for the death of Christ had a hidden Zionist agenda. One noted Catholic supporter of Israel, revealed just such an agenda when he expressed the hope that the

---

[13] 'We refer first briefly to the children of the Hebrew people, worthy of our affection and respect, faithful to the religion of what we call that of the Old Covenant. Then to the adorers of God according to the conception of monotheism, the Moslem religion is especially deserving of our admiration for all that is true and good in their worship of God. And also to the followers of the great Afro-Asiatic religions' (Pope Paul VI, *Ecclesiam Suam*, August 1964, paragraph 107).

new dialogue would eventually lead to the recognition of the State of Israel by the Church. John Oesterreicher suggested that the immoderate attack on the document by the Arab states had 'deprived them of the sympathies which they had enjoyed before, and thus the hearts of Christians turn to the forward-looking (*sic*) State of Israel' (in Laurentin and Neusner 1966: 303).

Sympathetic statements on Islam did little to alter this. Nevertheless some Muslim commentators appreciated the new, positive attitude towards Islam by the council. One article in the Beirut newspaper *L'Orient* argued that Arabs should have welcomed the awakening of the Christian conscience to the truth in other religions. 'It is a pity that the fear of Zionist exploitation prevents them from examining its contents. Islam is presented as a sister religion. The Christian is exhorted to end all disrespect not only to Jews but also to all non-Christians' (in *New York Times*, 26 November 1964). In this respect the author considers that Christianity is moving closer to the greater inclusiveness of the Qur'an.

Christian-Muslim relations

In retrospect, it can be argued that the Second Vatican Council did unwittingly give some encouragement to commentators sympathetic to Zionism. Nevertheless, since the Council there have been many examples of Christian-Muslim solidarity at both the international and the local level that have strengthened relations between the two faiths. Thus, in respect to the Holy Land, Roman Catholic and other Christian bodies have expressed common concern over Jerusalem. In 1980, contrary to United Nations resolutions and in total disregard of responsible world opinion, the Israeli Knesset passed the Geula Cohen law annexing Jerusalem as 'the eternal capital of Israel' and the *de jure* capital of Israel. In the same year, the Central Committee of the World Council of Churches responded (PASSIA 1996: 24), affirming Jerusalem as a city of Christians, Jews and Muslims whose future could not be considered in isolation from the destiny of the Palestinian people. The Holy See protested in similar vein:

> It must be understood that the declaration in 1980 that Jerusalem is the 'central and indivisible capital of Israel' is

contrary to international law, based as it is on military occupation without the consent of the interested parties or the United Nations and condemned as it immediately was by the Security Council; the fact that almost no countries have moved their embassies to Jerusalem is further proof that the international community rejects the legitimacy of the unilateral declaration (Address by the Permanent Observer of the Holy See to the United Nations, Archbishop Renato R. Martino, concerning Jerusalem, 10 April 1989, in PASSIA 1996: 24).

These and other Muslim and Christian statements about Jerusalem have turned on the idea that Jerusalem is not just a place where human and religious rights must be protected. It is also a place where the three religions should find common ground.

Evidently there has been common ground between Muslims and Christians at the popular level too, particularly in the Holy Land. Some of this can be attributed to the sense of common cause arising from shared suffering. This solidarity had its roots as early as the beginning of the British Mandate in Palestine when Palestinian Christians were actively involved in anti-Zionist Palestinian politics. In 1918, the Muslim-Christian Society (*A1-Jam'iyyah al-Islamiyyah al-Masihiyyah*) had been formed to develop a common front against the encroachment of Zionism on Palestinian rights. Christians generally made up some 20 percent of the membership despite constituting less than 8 percent of the population of Palestine as a whole.

This sense of common cause has not only expressed itself in solidarity but also in inter-faith dialogue. In the 1980s, a small but significant and influential group of Palestinian Muslims and Christians formed *Al-Liqa'* (literally 'The Meeting'), with the aim of discovering more about each other and building upon solidarity to make new openings in inter-faith dialogue between Christianity and Islam. *Al-Liqa'* was launched after a conference on 'Christian-Muslim Arab Heritage in the Holy Land' at Bethlehem University in 1983. In a personal interview, spokesmen for the organisation emphasise that the foundation was not just a Christian initiative, but a joint Muslim-Christian Palestinian one.

Members of *Al-Liqa'* saw the occupation as an attempt to drive a wedge between the Christian and Muslim communities. However,

Muslims had demonstrated that they shared Christian concern over the decline in the numbers of Christians in the historic Holy Land of Palestine. Nevertheless, this sense of common purpose had not been matched with real insight into what members of the other community really believed. In the understanding of *Al-Liqa'*, the time had come for a mutual discovery that went beyond mere tolerance and friendship to the beginnings of real Muslim-Christian dialogue. The hope remained that this discussion might ultimately include Judaism.

Conclusion

The issues raised in this essay illustrate some of the difficulties attendant upon such a desired three-way inter-faith discussion. As long as the conflict between Israelis and Palestinians remains unresolved, Christians will find an even-handed approach difficult to achieve. The Holy Land may help in providing historical-critical understanding of the Gospel narrative. The Holy Land may also provide insights into contemporary issues in the same geographical area. It may even cast light on issues in the wider world beyond Israel-Palestine. Religious pluralism is one such issue. Appreciation of the fact that the land is sacred to the three great monotheistic faiths is significant for inter-faith relations world-wide.

However, in the context of Israel-Palestine, as elsewhere, inter-faith issues continue to be complicated by politics. Thus Zionism can be seen to distort not only Jewish-Christian and Jewish-Muslim relations but Christian-Muslim relations as well. Nor is it only the politics of the Holy Land that provide such unwelcome complications. There have been conflicts and bloodshed between Christians and Muslims in Indonesia and Nigeria, between Hindus and Muslims in Kashmir, Buddhists and Hindus in Sri Lanka—and, indeed, between Catholics and Protestant Christians nearer to home in Northern Ireland. None of these unhappy conflicts should prevent honest and politically informed attempts at an inclusive Christian theology. However, the example of the interplay of politics and religion in the Holy Land provides the important lesson that the task of religious dialogue can never be divorced from the work of justice and peace.

References

Arberry, J. 1969. *Religion in the Middle East*, vol. 1. Cambridge: Cambridge University Press

Ateek, Naim S and Michael Prior. 1999. *Holy Land—Hollow Jubilee: God, Justice and the Palestinians*. London, Melisende

Bissio, Robert. 2001. *The World Guide. An Alternative Guide to the Countries of our Planet 2001/2002*. Oxford: New Internationalist Publications

Boff, Leonardo. 1993. 'Epistemology and Methodology of the Theology of Liberation,' in Ellacuría. and Sobrino 1993: 57-85

Council of Churches for Britain and Ireland. Commission for Inter-Faith Relations: Christians and Jews. 1994. *A New Way of Thinking. Guidelines for the Churches*. London: Council of Churches for Britain and Ireland

Cragg, Kenneth. 1969. 'The Anglican Church', in Arberry 1969: 570-95

Cragg, Kenneth. 1997. *Palestine. The Prize and Price of Zion*. London and Washington: Cassell

Drinan, Robert F. 1977. *Honor the Promise: America's Commitment to Israel*. Cape Town, NY: Doubleday

Ellacuría, I and J Sobrino (eds). 1993. *Mysterium Liberationis. Fundamental Concepts of Liberation Theology*. Maryknoll NY: Orbis

Fisher, Eugene J, A James Rudin and Marc H Tanenbaum (eds). 1986. *Twenty Years of Jewish-Catholic Relations*. New York: Paulist

Flannery, Austin. 1975. *Vatican Council Documents*. Dublin: Dominican Publications.

Flannery, Edward H. 1986. 'Israel, Jerusalem, and the Middle East', in Fisher, Rudin and Tanenbaum 1986: 73-86

Gibb, H A R and J H Kramers. 1974. 'Kubbat al-Sakhra', *Concise Encyclopaedia of Islam*. Leiden: E J Brill

Harrelson W and R M Falk. 1990. *Jews and Christians: A Troubled Family*. Nashville: Abingdon

Haddad. H and D Wagner. 1986. *All in the Name of the Bible*. Vermont: Armana Books

Hall, Douglas J. 1996. *Professing the Faith: Christian Theology in a North American Context*. Minneapolis: Fortress Press

Hegstad, H. 1997. 'Der Erlöser der Heiden oder Israels Messias? Zur Frage der theologischen und christologischen Bedeutung des Judeseins Jesu', *Kerygma und Dogma* 40(1994): 33-44, from the summary in English, 'Saviour of the Gentiles or Israel's Messiah?' *Theology Digest* (Summer 1997): 111-16

Jacobs, D. 1998. *Israel and the Palestinian Territories: Rough Guide*. London: Rough Guides

Laurentin, R and J Neusner. 1966. *Commentary on the Documents of Vatican II*. New York: Herder

Le Strange, Guy. 1890. *Palestine under the Moslems*. London: 89-114

Macpherson, Duncan. 2004. *Pilgrim Preacher: Palestine Pilgrimage and Preaching*. London: Melisende

PASSIA. 1996. *Documents on Jerusalem*. Jerusalem: Palestinian Society for the Study of Academic Affairs

Pawlikowski, John T. 1990. 'Ethical Issues in the Israeli-Palestinian Conflict', in Ruether and Ellis (eds) 1990: 155-70

Prior, Michael. 1997. *The Bible and Colonialism. A Moral Critique*. Sheffield: Sheffield Academic Press

Prior, Michael. 1999. *Zionism and the State of Israel: A Moral Inquiry*. London and New York: Routledge

Prior, Michael. 2002. 'Antizionism = Antisemitism?' *Doctrine and Life* 52. 339-47

Prior, Michael. 2003. 'Speaking Truth in the Jewish-Christian Dialogue', in Thomas and Amos 2003: 327-47

Ruether, Rosemary and Marc Ellis (eds). 1990. *Beyond Occupation: American Jews, Christians and Palestinians Search for Peace*. Boston: Beacon Press

Rynne, Xavier. 1966. *The Fourth Session*. London: Faber and Faber.

Sizer, Stephen. 1998. 'Christian Zionism: True Friends of Israel?' *Living Stones*, Autumn, 18-24

Sobrino, J. 1987. *Jesus in Latin America*. Maryknoll, NY: Orbis

Tanenbaum, Marc H. 1986. 'A Jewish Viewpoint on Nostra Aetate', in Fisher, Rudin and Tanenbaum 1986: 39-60

Thomas, David. and Clare Amos (eds). 2003. *A Faithful Presence. Essays for Kenneth Cragg*. London: Melisende

Van Buren, Paul. 1980. *Discerning the Way: A Theology of Jewish Christian Reality*. New York: Seabury

Wagner, Don. 1992. 'Beyond Armageddon', in *The Link* (Americans for Middle East Understanding) 25 (no. 4): 1-13

Wagner, Don. 1995. *Anxious for Armageddon: A Call to Partnership for Middle Eastern and Western Christians*. Scottdale & Waterloo: Herald Press

Wagner, Don. 1999. 'Reagan and Begin, Bibi and Jerry: The Theopolitical Alliance of the Likud Party with the American Christian 'Right', in Ateek and Prior 1999: 119-215

THEOLOGISING, TRUTH AND PEACEMAKING IN THE PALESTINIAN EXPERIENCE

Jean Zaru

I have struggled most of my adult life with issues of theology and liberation. One of the great insights of the liberation theology which was reborn in Latin America in the 1970s was the importance of the place in which one does theology. Is a library or a university lecture hall the most appropriate setting for it? Or is theology best done within the terms set by a Church which enjoys the friendship of the powerful? 'No!', the liberation theologians insisted. Theology must be done among the oppressed. Its questions must address their real conditions. Authentic theology must be rooted in the realities of peoples' lives, rather than proceed in some kind of metahistorical, ethereal manner that has no real contact with such realities.

While embracing that insight, however, I consider the Latin America liberation theologians' use of the Bible's Exodus narrative as a paradigm for liberation to be not only naive, but also one that embraces violence against an indigenous people. As Michael Prior observes, conformity with the biblical narrative requires that the liberational Exodus from Egypt cannot be separated from the Eisodus (entrance) into the land of the Canaanites, which, in the narrative, demanded the genocide of the indigenous peoples. On that account, the authentic biblical narrative of Exodus-Eisodus could well be used to justify the behaviour of the *conquistadores* rather than support the indigenous peoples, and, of course, has been used to justify a range of colonialist adventures.[1] The Exodus, then, is not a paradigm for liberation, but one that simply transfers power from one group to another, without leading to the transformation of society. Violence is at the heart of the Exodus.

It has also been my life experience also, rather than a library, that has served as my source of inspiration. My experience has taken me to all five continents where, over the years, I have been enormously

---

[1] See Michael Prior's *The Bible and Colonialism passim,* and in particular his critique of the Exodus narrative (Prior 1997: 278-84).

enriched by contact with activists and theologians engaged in various struggles for liberation. But, neither is it sufficient, the liberation theologians insisted, for theological reflection merely to describe reality. It must also adjudicate on it, evaluate it, and, finally, outline programmes that will bring about transformation of peoples' lives for the better.

My purpose here is to attempt to theologise from the context in which I find myself in Palestine, in a town under military occupation. In addition to reflecting my human values I draw on the great Christian tradition in which I have lived all my life. My life experience is rooted in my identity as a Palestinian Quaker woman struggling to find a way of transformation in our broken world.

1. Palestine, my theological place

I am one of eight million Palestinians world-wide. I come from the heart of Palestine, a land besieged and violated by Israeli military occupation, from the midst of an indigenous people, a nation held in captivity. Fifty-four years ago, we were cast outside the course of history, our very identity was denied, and our human, cultural and historical reality was suppressed. We became victims of the cruel myth of 'a land without a people for a people without a land'. And we continue to be victims of an exclusivist agenda, an agenda that usurped our rights, our lands and confiscated, as well, our historical narrative. We became victims of a colonialist programme.

More than 500 Palestinian villages were depopulated and destroyed in what became the State of Israel. Over 750,000 indigenous Palestinians became refugees outside their homeland, while another approximately 150,000 became internally displaced refugees. Those Palestinians who remained in what became the State of Israel still experience discrimination and repression on a daily basis.

Those of us who came under Israeli occupation in 1967 in the West Bank, the Gaza Strip and East Jerusalem have since been subjected to a unique combination of military occupation, settler colonisation and systematic oppression. Today, together with their descendants, the Palestinian refugees number over 5.5 million, making our refugee crisis the largest and the longest standing in the world. Those who remain continue to experience exclusion and discrimination in their historical

homeland. The State of Israel continues to entrench an occupation which consistently violates United Nations resolutions, international humanitarian law, and the Fourth Geneva Convention.

At various stages over the last few years, the Israeli Defense Forces invaded our cities and villages, imposing a permanent closure and siege that has impoverished more than two-thirds of the West Bank and Gaza, whose inhabitants were forced to survive on less than $1.90 per day. The closures produced chronic malnutrition rates and anaemia among children which has reached emergency levels. Tens of thousands of Palestinians were imprisoned without charge or trial, and great numbers of activists and innocent bystanders were assassinated or murdered. There was also widespread destruction of the carefully built public infrastructure, private homes and businesses. The Israeli assault on our towns and villages severely damaged schools, hospitals, and the offices of civil society.

As someone who has lived all her life in Ramallah, and more than half of it under Israeli military occupation, I can assure you that life has never been as difficult as it is today, at the beginning of the fourth year of the new millennium. While Israeli troops are amassing in the Occupied Territories and with the siege tightening, we are increasingly subjected to a policy of persistent shelling, political assassinations, abductions, house demolitions, and the systematic destruction of crops and trees. Our lands are being further confiscated, our water resources are still being taken away, and subsequently rationed back to us, at exorbitant prices. Fledgling government offices have been dynamited and bombed by US-supplied F-16 fighter jets. Occupation soldiers were allowed to loot personal property and force Palestinian civilians to become human shields. Altogether, an entire people was put behind barbed wire, checkpoints and walls, and its movement has been severely restricted. Humiliation has become our daily routine. There has been no security, since even civilians have been targeted and killed inside their own homes and properties. Restrictions on movement, checkpoints, closures, confiscation of land and water resources, are making life almost unliveable for all.

Our country is becoming a gigantic prison and a vast cemetery. The people, land, houses and trees have been brutally treated. Fear and insecurity have replaced compassion and trust. Relations have become hard and tense. When almost every aspect of life is framed in oppression

and humiliation, moral space in diminished. Our very humanity is threatened and role models for our children become hard to find. People are tired and depressed. They are traumatised by the violence that is perpetrated against them which affects both their physical and mental health. My people need time to mourn, to heal their wounds, to pacify their children and to find their daily bread.

2. The challenge of truth-telling

A Japanese poet wrote: 'The world grows stronger as each story is told'. And yet there is a tendency to ignore personal stories, preferring sterile history books, or the authoritative voice of the CNN newscaster. People prefer truth to be simple. However, every time we insist on such simplicity we diminish truth and deprive ourselves of its richness. Storytelling makes our world stronger because stories reveal the complexity of our truth. By telling our stories, we resist watering down our truths into vague and generalised abstractions; we maintain the urgency and intensity of the concrete. My story reflects a narrative of exclusion: the denial of basic human and community rights. But, I also have a message of hope, one embodied in the spirit and will of all those throughout the world who refuse to submit to forces of oppression, who refuse to submit to violence, injustice and structures of domination.

It is vitally important too to insist on a prophetic ministry in today's threatened world, to expose the lies and myths that have been created mainly by the powerful to cover up the pain and grief of our world. This ministry should resist the monopoly of knowledge and the power exercised by the dominant. It should struggle to forge a new discourse, one that includes critique from the margins. Therefore, it is essential that all engaged in a prophetic ministry should make contact in each and every place with the dispossessed, the prisoners, the immigrants, and the downtrodden. Spaces must be created for such people, so that they may be able to share their stories, to grieve, and to express their anger and hope.

Those engaged in prophetic renewal are called to be 'truth-tellers', rather than people who cover up. Contemporary culture is marked by the great cover-up. Half-truths and lies fill government halls, institutions and the media, reminding one of the lament of the prophet Jeremiah,

They all deceived their neighbours and nobody speaks the truth; they have taught their tongues to speak lies (Jer 9.5).

It is the duty of all who know it to tell the truth, to uncover the scars and wounds of the oppressed. This requires courage, sometimes even great courage. Yet, it is the only way to disarm 'the principalities and the powers' whose lies and deceit are fed by silent co-operation. How many realise, for example, the truth that within Israel the option of 'transfer', that is, ethnic cleansing of Palestinians from the Occupied Territories, or of Palestinian citizens from inside Israel, is discussed openly today in Israeli society? Truth, however, can never make friends with violence.

Some Palestinians, in their anger and despair, have resorted to violence. I do not think that violence can lead us anywhere, either morally or strategically. Indeed, all recourse to violence as an instrument of change has to be rejected. However, that should by no means lead one to have a merely passive attitude to the circumstances that confront one. Fortunately, many Palestinians, as well as faith-based organisations and NGOs, have adopted an active, and indeed pro-active posture. For Palestinians in general, the very act of living on a daily basis has itself become an act of non-violent resistance to a brutal occupation. Thus, tending one's garden, going to school, walking through checkpoints, and even harvesting one's own crops are all ways in which Palestinians demonstrate their determination to survive and carry on with life. Over recent times, large numbers of Europeans have joined us in our peaceful protests. These, however, remain largely unknown to the world. Instead what is being instilled in a naive Western public is that we Palestinians are the terrorists, even while we are occupied, shelled by US-manufactured helicopter gunships and F-16 fighter jets. In the absence of truth-telling, the war crimes of Israel against our people are masked by the myth of the 'purity of arms' of the forces of the Israeli government.

The false symmetry between occupier and occupied

The most fundamental deception in this crisis is the false symmetry that is predicated to exist between occupier and occupied, oppressor and victim. Thus, the violence of the powerful Israeli occupation army which uses live ammunition, tanks and helicopter gun ships is put on a par with

the violence of Palestinian civilians protesting their victimisation and their continued loss of rights, of their land and even of their lives. An offshoot of this perception it that, if we Palestinians do not show ourselves to be grateful for the occupation, with its colonisation and the isolated bantustans under Israel's apartheid system, we deserve to be pounded into submission.

The Israeli occupation cannot in any sense be understood as a reaction to 'terrorism', or as a means of self-defence. It is, rather, an expression of the policy of *de facto* annexation that began immediately after 1967. Nevertheless, Israel customarily presents its military actions and policies of repression to the world as if they were no more than reactions to Palestinian violence. In doing so, it tries to ensure that the term 'occupation' disappears altogether from the dominant discourse.

It should surprise no one that the current Palestinian generation refuses to inherit more pain and powerlessness. Resistance is our right and our natural response to Israel's illegal occupation. This is especially true, as our young generation looks back at the Oslo 'peace process', only to realise that the occupation has only become more entrenched. The illegal settler population has doubled to 400,000 persons since Oslo began in 1993. Moreover, thousands of homes have been demolished, leaving tens of thousands of Palestinians homeless and destitute.

Nevertheless, the talk one hears consistently on the US media and from US politicians of 'stopping the violence' refers exclusively, of course, to the violence of the Palestinians, invariably designated 'terror'. Thus, the fundamental imbalance of the situation is ignored. Israel, in systematic violation of human rights in order to make its occupation permanent—killing thousands, and maiming tens of thousands, with massive US aid to fund its efforts—is one of the most powerful military forces in the world (including some 200-300 nuclear warheads), and has an economy some twenty times larger than that of the Palestinians. The aggressor has become the victim. The refusal of the international community to intervene makes it complicit in Israel's war crimes and violations of human rights.

The situation calls upon all our Palestinian resources, physical, mental and spiritual. And, in this darkest night of our communal soul, we Palestinians seek the active intervention of the international community, especially its masses, since its governments and power systems have consistently failed to provide the protection which is our right. They

have thus far failed to exercise their responsibility and obligations, presumably for some combination of power politics, absence of will, and short-sighted self-interest.

It is clear to me that, minimally, the Israeli military occupation of the West Bank, Gaza and East Jerusalem must end. It remains a most pervasive form of violence (both direct and structural), human rights violations, and immoral enslavement of a whole nation. It is the ultimate provocation at both the individual and collective levels. Conflicts can only be resolved politically and legally, on the basis of parity of rights and the global rule of law. There should be an insistence that all parties concerned adhere to the relevant United Nations Security Council resolutions and the terms of international law. Israel should not be above the law.

Despite the current Israeli government's determination, no amount of its violence could subjugate the will of a people, or destroy their spirit as they struggle for their freedom, dignity and their right to sovereignty on their own land. All Israeli attempts at intensifying the brutality of the occupation against the Palestinians have only led to the escalation of the conflict and increased our determination to gain our liberty. I do hope that the Israeli public and the international community will realise the extreme danger of the Israeli policies before it is too late, and before even more blood is shed. And I do hope that the United States government will realise that its unswerving support for, and military aid to Israel is not in the best interests either of the Jews and Israel, or of the US government.

3. Testifying to suffering and hope

I have been challenged in numerous ways by the suffering and hope arising within my own context—the experience of the breakdown of life in Palestine—and within the experience of all people on the margins of life. The suffering arises when I listen to pleas from young people for solidarity and support. Or, when I see the blank stare of pain in the eyes of Palestinian refugees who have remained displaced for more than fifty years. Or, when I recall that thousands of people who have been injured over the three recent years of crisis, consider how they are not remembered and, as a consequence, feel abandoned by the world community. But, even in the midst of daily humiliations hope is generated, and the human

spirit rises, even to greatness. The quotidian reflects something of the grandeur of the eternal.

Crossing the Bridge

Recently I needed to go to Amman to be with my mother who is critically ill. I had to cross the King Hussein Bridge on the River Jordan, just as I have to do whenever I leave the country for my lecture tours. Crossing this bridge, however, is not like crossing a bridge in a car and in your country, or paying the toll. For us Palestinians, it entails moving from our occupied country in stages, firstly by securing permits, then having our papers, identity cards and passports checked, all achieved without any respect for our human dignity.

Travelling from Ramallah to the bridge takes usually less than an hour. This time, however, it took five hours, and I had to take three different cars and three different buses. The tolls we pay at this bridge are difficult to describe. They drain our lives, impair our health, and increase our separation anxiety as neither leaving nor returning is ever guaranteed. Throughout the last thirty-six years Israel has claimed that these measures were for security. As they check our bodies, our shoes, our belongings, piece by piece, I often wonder whether they can, with all their sophisticated devices, check our hearts and minds as well. Can they see how we feel? Do they notice our pain? Or is this not part of the security check? Or not part of building bridges with one's neighbour?

So often I feel like screaming at the Israelis: 'Why do you treat us this way? We are sacred, God's creation.' Other times, I felt like crying out the words of the psalm:

> My God, my God why have you forsaken me?
> Why are you so far from helping me,
> from the words of my groaning?
> O my God, I cry by day,
> but you do not answer;
> and by night, but find no rest (Psalm 22.1-2).

As I look at the people around me during the long waiting hours at the checkpoints or in the bus, and listen to their conversations I hear

individual stories of pain, of families being torn apart, of despair and suffering, of longing and hope. Hope is strengthened when I see the sharing of food and water, the compassionate offers of help to the elderly and to young mothers with children. Hope is strengthened when I see resilience to resist humiliation and the longing to cross frontiers in spite of difference. And again, hope is strengthened, when we see the divine quality in those with whom we differ or even in those who impose the persecution!

Without a doubt, the way of transformation calls us to stand against the forces of death and evil, both within and around us. It challenges us to resist the temptation simply 'to re-arrange the furniture', whether that re-arrangement be in the structures of our own psyche, or those of our planet. Crossing the bridge, invariably, brings up profound thoughts about the deep things of life, and even about the passage from death to life.

Holiness in the ordinary

My mother herself provides another example of hope in the midst of distress. She lost her mother at a very early age, then three of her brothers, as well as her husband and her two sons. My older brother, Hanna, was only forty years old when he was among the disappeared in the civil war in Lebanon, and my younger brother was only five years old when he passed away. My mother suffered further, in that she was not able to see my oldest sister who left for the US to study for several years because of the 1967 war. Moreover, my youngest sister and I were widowed very young, and this gave my mother extra worry. She refers to herself sometimes as being like Job, and is forever speaking of patience.

My mother loved to recall the wisdom of Henry Nouwen:

> No one can help anyone without being involved, without entering with [one's] whole person into the painful situation, without taking the risk of becoming hurt, wounded or destroyed in the process ... [without a willingness] to make one's own painful and joyful experiences available as sources of clarification and understanding ... the great illusion of leadership is to think that [humankind] can be led out of the desert by someone who has never been there (*The Wounded Healer*).

I often visit three Palestinian refugee camps, in connection with several YWCA projects. When I ask women whose homes were demolished, who had no work or security, and whose husbands, fathers, or brothers were in jail, 'How do you manage?', they say such things as, 'God who created us will not forget us. Sometimes we wake up in the morning to find food supplies on our doorstep.' One Easter, some young people tried to share eggs with their neighbours. Every house they knocked at to offer a gift of eggs referred them to a more needy person, for, they said, 'Thanks be to God, we are not starving.' Their faith challenged me, gave me hope, and reminded me of the passage in the Apostle Paul's Letter to the Corinthians concerning faith, hope and love (1 Corinthians 13). It reminded me also of what Jesus said: 'Your God will feed you; see how God feeds the birds and clothes the flowers; therefore be not anxious.' Jesus told us not to worry, but to seek first and find God's kingdom, and align ourselves with its righteousness (Matthew 6.25-33).

I was visiting Jalazone refugee camp during the first *Intifada*, after three weeks of curfew and closure. The camp residents had been collectively punished by having their electricity cut off and their gas supply curtailed. Women told me how determined they were to find a way to bake their own bread. Collecting wood and rubbish they made a communal fire, kept alight by burning old shoes and rags. When the Israeli soldiers came to put the fire out and throw away the dough, the women resisted, shouting, 'Go tell your leaders that no matter what you do, no matter what kind of restrictions you impose on us, we will not allow our children to starve. We will find a way to bake bread, and all your efforts to destroy our spirits are not going to succeed. What God has created, no one can destroy!'

If the divine glory is to be found anywhere on earth, it is to be seen in the humanity and wisdom of talented men and women who live in the midst of oppression. Such people are an inspiration. Mahatma Gandhi, Martin Luther King Jr, and Nelson Mandela immediately come to mind. But it is not just among the famous that the spark of the Divine is to be seen: one finds it also in the countless ordinary people who, despite the grave constraints and oppression in which they live, witness to the power of truth in their everyday lives.

The divine virtues of hope and justice, then, manifest themselves at the very heart of human experience, certainly in Israel and Palestine, but elsewhere also, in those who courageously challenge and resist

oppressive powers without dehumanising the human being hidden behind 'the enemy'. While these 'communities of hope' often change directions and patterns of thought, they can also affect political decisions and economic transactions. The growing networks of non-governmental organisations that co-operate across the globe also are an encouraging sign. However, without the support of great majorities of people—large numbers of women and men—who see themselves as responsible human beings in a world created for mutual justice, care and compassion, millions, I am afraid, will continue to suffer oppression and injustice. Our mobilisation efforts, then, must be broad-based and as diverse and inclusive as imaginable.

4. Crying out in distress

The real turning point in the liberation experience is the public voicing of pain that is an intentional, and often communal act of expressing grievance. While it is sometimes unheard and always includes risk it is nonetheless crucial, for with the cry of pain begins the formation of a counter community around an alternative perception of reality. Thus, the act of crying out and groaning is at one and the same time an act of subversion and an act of hope. For Jeremiah, indeed, grief was a radical form of criticism and of de-legitimising. As he publicly mourned over Judah, Jeremiah exclaimed

> My anguish, my anguish! I writhe in pain!
> Oh, the walls of my heart!
> My heart is beating wildly;
> I cannot keep silent,
> for I hear the sound of the trumpet, the alarm of war.
> Disaster follows hard on disaster,
> The whole land is laid waste (Jer 4.19-20).

In Palestine today you will hear the cry of every Palestinian, man, woman and child. A cry. A cry from the depths. A cry of grief and lamentation. A cry with the hope that this grief might possibly penetrate the numbness of history and open a way towards newness.

Jesus and Jeremiah wept over Jerusalem. And so do we. The

words of the prophets can be our words, describing exactly our situation and our lives. And in the wilderness of occupation, oppression and exile, we need more than ever to look to the ancient prophets who used grief as a critique to energise people, who used grief as a means to find alternatives for newness of life, and to make a commitment to work for justice and peace.

Not alone

I find it difficult to retreat into a hope that centres primarily on the individual and on heaven beyond. Rather, I find hope in communities of people and their movement towards liberation. The experience of the everyday world is an essential part of the knowledge of God. In the theology of liberation the primary text is 'reality': the reality of oppression, poverty and circumstances. Knowledge of that primary text makes theologians out of all God's people. I find often that I am not satisfied with, or consider myself bound by, the letter of scripture alone; that must certainly be subordinated to the inner understanding that comes through the Spirit.

For the last couple of years, International Solidarity Movement volunteers and Israelis from a number of peace groups joined hands with Palestinian farmers to collect the year's abundant olive crop. This was done against the background of threats of violence by militant settlers, who in fact did kill Palestinian farmers and threatened and brutally beat several other Palestinians, internationals and Israeli activists, while the Israeli army watched on. These Solidarity people have crossed boundaries to recognise the humanity of the other. Many have literally risked their lives, and a number have given them, for peace. The meaning and impact of their actions should not be underestimated. Such acts of solidarity will surely change the tide.

In my own journey of struggle I walk alongside many others, who help me to carry on in the hope that society can change from using oppressive and destructive power to deploying a power that is liberating and life-enhancing. The task ahead for me as a Palestinian woman goes beyond merely seeking the transfer of power from men to women, or from Israelis to Palestinians. Rather, what we should struggle for is the transformation of our communities from:

◻ militarist, coercive power to the power of mutual trust;

◻ ethnic and religious exclusiveness to the celebration of diversity;

◻ racist and sexist discrimination to the protection of human rights for all;

◻ neutrality and objectivity to compassion and ethically based priorities;

◻ exploitation of nature to gentle co-operation with it; and, finally,

◻ God above to God within, from death to resurrection.

To hope is a duty

That the Spirit of God inspires is a central theme of the New Testament. Jesus promises to send the Spirit who would be an advocate to remind the disciples of his words and to guide them into truth. The Spirit was open to all, women and men. Access to the Spirit not only gave an important position to women but also disrupted those who sought a monopoly on truth. The way of Jesus takes radical Christianity back to the Gospel story of non-violent protest and the implementation of the reign of God on earth. Jesus rejected the strategy of recourse to violence as an instrument of change. However, that should not lead us to suppose that he had a passive attitude to the circumstances that confronted him.

Clearly, violence should be excluded as an option for those who seek to offer hope and transformation. My vision for peace, however, must contend with the charge that Christians have failed to promote a just peace in the world, and more seriously that they have collaborated with injustice by encouraging the poor and the oppressed to accept patiently their misery, promising abundant rewards in the afterlife. This understanding of faith merely alienates people from their proper task in life and induces irresponsibility.

Sometimes we try to look for hope in what seems to be a hopeless situation. But if there is hope after such a brutal death of the resurrected Jesus Christ, then there surely is no situation devoid of hope and promise. Let us encourage ourselves with the words of Cardinal Suenens.

Who would dare to say that the love and imagination of

God were exhausted?
To hope is a duty not a luxury.
To hope is not to dream, but to turn dreams into reality.
Happy are those who dream dreams and
are ready to pay the price to make them come true.

5. The demands of peace and reconciliation

Before considering the demands of peace and reconciliation, as I see them, I need to remind you of my context. As a Palestinian, I am one of the approximately eight million around the world. Some half of us were uprooted and forcibly driven out of our land and out of our homes, in many cases more than once. The other half has been subjugated and made strangers in our own land. We continue to be denied our basic right to self-determination, which is the basis of the other forms of human rights violations and abuses perpetrated against us. One of the key elements for self-determination is 'land'. For us as a people to exercise our political, economic, social, and cultural rights, we must be able to exercise them in our own land. However, the continuing expropriation and confiscation of our land is one of the key manifestations of the denial of our right to self-determination. Many of my people have little or no security or guarantee for their own lives or those of their children. Daily they are being denied the right to develop their full human potential due to the continuing oppressive policies of the Israeli government. So as people and as a nation, we are seeking freedom, justice, and equality.

As a woman in a male-dominated culture I have no equality with my brothers. In my culture, girls do not have equal opportunities in health care, education, and even sometimes in nutrition. Girls are supposed to serve and to conform, and they are often condemned if they choose a style of life that is different from what society expects. There is always a double standard used when it comes to judgements about boys and girls, as is the case with all comparisons between the powerless and the powerful in the world. Women do a lot in my society and their work is recognised, but they are not part of the decision-making processes in society.

As a Christian, however, I am also held responsible by my brothers and sisters to speak out when the Bible is abused in a way that

leads to the worship of false gods such as wealth or racism, or other present day idols. Also I am expected to speak out when individual interests are justified by quoting biblical passages out of context, and when the dispossession of my people, the Palestinians, and the situation of my sisters is justified by quoting the Bible.

As a Christian living in the Holy Land, I have witnessed how some Western churches, to promote their 'presence' in the Holy Land divided us, and made many feel inferior and alienated from our own culture and language by demanding loyalty to a foreign leadership, whether in Rome, England, Germany, or the United States. While the Church in Jerusalem is the mother church, Western Christians often forget, or do not even realise that there are Palestinian and Arab Christians—the forgotten faithful witnesses, the descendants of the disciples of Christ.

As an active member of the ecumenical movement and interfaith commissions for the last two decades, I have witnessed new pressures and obstacles in our work. In the view of fundamentalist Christians I, as a Palestinian, am not among the chosen. I am, rather, one of the cursed. As they see it I stand in the way of the fulfilment of the prophecy of God. Even for some liberal Western Christians who are influenced by Holocaust theology, European history, and guilt, I am not part of their agenda. My very existence and insistence on justice, as in the case of the widow in the Bible, disturbs them. For these Christians, to have dialogue with the Jewish people has meant that they have had to accept the 'self-understanding' of the Jewish people and their historic right and connections to the 'Land of Israel', which allows no room for us as Palestinians, even Palestinian Christians. I fail to understand until this day why all the Church commissions involved in dialogue with the Jewish people do not criticise fundamentalist Christians, such as the International Christian Embassy in Jerusalem, for their theology, which has no respect for Judaism, while they express alarm when some Christians speak out for the rights of the Palestinians, and against their oppression. When Westerners think of fanatical fundamentalists, the first thing that comes to mind are Muslims, forgetting that there are foreign Christian fundamentalists and Jewish fundamentalists, all of whom are against the peace process, and, typically also are against the emancipation of women.

As a Quaker woman, I have to struggle on yet another front, for I am labelled a 'pacifist'. This is often misinterpreted as being passive or submissive or even accepting of the injustice we receive at the hands of

our oppressors. We are all the victims of violence. However, a double standard is applied when speaking about violence. When the oppressed use violent means to bring about change, they are considered 'terrorists'. When the oppressors use violent means to meet their goals they are 'taking care of their security needs and enforcing law and order'. Thus, the root causes of violence are not considered.

In my lifetime I have been confronted by many structures of injustice, political, social, economic, and religious. These structures have been at work in a destructive way throughout our community. What has made me take an active part in the struggles against such injustices? Two ideals spur me on:

1. The message of the Gospel has sensitised me to the suffering in the world and has opened me to God's redeeming love and activity.
2. The concept of the divine nature existing in harmonious relationship with human nature and with the natural order in Judaism, Christianity, and Islam has inspired me.

The teachings of the faiths in my part of the world have helped to undergird the belief that human beings have rights, that we are created in the image of God, and that our value comes from this likeness. God's nature is loving, free, and just. God's purpose is to liberate human life from inhuman conditions. These inhuman conditions exist because humans with free will have chosen behaviour that disrupts the intended harmony that provides justice, peace, and freedom for all.

Directed by my faith, I became involved in the struggle for justice on all fronts. I could not be selective. I could not reconcile myself to structures of domination and oppression, covered over with words of peace and reconciliation. Such hypocrisy became problematic for me because the words of peace were preached without regard to any genuine change in the oppressive situation created by the powerful. Too often in our talk about peace and reconciliation the victimised are called upon to forgive and reconcile in a way that perpetuates, rather than rectifies, the root causes of injustice, alienation, and division. While reconciliation suggests a genuine change in relations, reconciliation can also mean a collapse into acceptance of the *status quo* because of the belief that nothing can be done.

In the Israeli-Palestinian case, there were hopes for the kind of change that would lead to justice, and that would bring about reconciliation and peace. These aspirations, however, are being betrayed as the peace process shows its real face, by which the Israeli government consolidates its occupation over us in terms of both demography and land. Nevertheless, stirring events in recent years in South Africa, Europe, and the Middle East have pushed the topic of reconciliation to centre stage. What does the message of Jesus contribute to the building of a new order in situations dominated by so much violence? Indeed, what do we mean by reconciliation?

Reconciliation involves a fundamental repairing of human lives, especially of those who suffered. It requires restoring their dignity to the victims of violence. It has four dimensions: political, economic, psycho-social, and spiritual. Christ did not merely announce the good news that the sick can be healed. He healed them, and in his very action He proclaimed the Kingdom. Word and deed, then, are one. They are inseparable. Reconciliation is central to the Gospel, and Christians must be active in reconciling—in repairing lives and proclaiming the good news.

> 'If you take away the yoke, the pointing of the finger ... if you pour yourself out for the hungry and satisfy the desire of the afflicted ... your ancient ruins shall be rebuilt ... you shall be called the repairer of the breach, the restorer of paths to dwell' (Isaiah 58.9-12).

All the while, however, both as Palestinians and as women, we were being told to be peaceful, in the sense of being passive, and 'nice', and also to allow ourselves to be walked over. Many talked to us about that peace that could be achieved by pounding the opposition into submission, peace that was maintained by crushing protest against injustice, in a word, a peace for the rulers and the oppressors, and all at the expense of the oppressed. Sometimes the call for 'reconciliation' comes to us from even our oppressors, the perpetrators of violence against us, in the hope, presumably, that they will be spared any punishment, and will be acquitted of their responsibility to transform their structures of violence. We are directed towards 'reconciliation' also, of course, by people who are outside the situation, and who invariably have accepted the

narrative of the lie—the lies about our true situation, and the reasons for it. People who aspire to being people of truth, however, must never give in to the lies and myths that were created either to demonise the Palestinians, or to conceal the appalling human cost we suffered as a result of the very creation of Israel, and continue to suffer from its continuing domination and oppression. We can never move towards authentic reconciliation if the truth about our human hurt and human hope is not known. We have to find, then, a redeeming narrative to restore truth.

But the fact remains that many Israelis do not feel any guilt for what they did to us. They do not feel that they have done anything wrong in virtue of their Zionist ideology. For them, therefore, reconciliation is not an issue. Many, nevertheless, do talk to us about 'reconciliation' to be achieved through a hasty peace, or a reconciliation in place of liberation, or, of reconciliation merely as a managed process. These calls to reconciliation want us, the victims of violence, to 'let bygones be bygones', and to exercise Christian forgiveness. In trivialising and ignoring a history of suffering the victims are forgotten, and the causes of the suffering are never uncovered and confronted. True reconciliation, however, is not a hasty peace that tries to escape from an examination of the causes of suffering. But, if the causes are not addressed, suffering is likely to continue, and, thus, the wheel of violence will keep turning, and more and more people will get crushed.

Sulha: Palestinian reconciliation

Let me share with you our Palestinian and Arab way of making peace and granting forgiveness. If my neighbour, or any member of the community, has violated my dignity in any way, or has taken my land, or has injured any of my family members, the first step in making peace is for the person who wronged me to choose a mediator, always a person who is well-respected in the society for his or her values of justice and reconciliation. Then we proceed in the following way:

1. A date is set to visit me in my home in the presence of my extended family members—the community participation in reconciliation.

2. he person who wronged me will come with the mediator and his/her extended family members—the expression of humility in reconciliation.

3. The person who has wronged me recognises the hurt that was done. Then a commitment is made to repair the damage, and forgiveness is asked for—the expression of truth in reconciliation

4. The mediator takes the responsibility of ensuring that the damage is repaired—the demands of justice in reconciliation.

5. Then forgiveness is pronounced (*ahli samah imnah*) by saying: 'You are in our home. You are one of us, and we take it upon ourselves to help and protect the person who has done us wrong.' It is then proclaimed: 'Forgiveness is a gift from God' (*samah min Allah*)—forgiveness in reconciliation.

6. All, then, share in eating, breaking bread together, which commits everyone to friendship and sharing, rather than enmity and exploitation—communion in reconciliation.

This way of making peace and reconciliation—the Arabic term for it is *Sulha*—respects and restores the dignity of both parties. How different is the reconciliation on offer in our political life.

In the last few years, first in Madrid and then in Oslo and Washington, we all watched anxiously the Mideast peace process unfold. We should not forget that the real issue in these talks was Palestine. The Palestinian people had already accepted an extraordinary set of compromises, with nothing corresponding required of any other participant. Israel, for example, was not committing itself to withdrawal, or to end settlements, or to negotiate on Jerusalem, nor was there any question of compromise on Palestinian self-determination.

Our land is fragmented. The movement of the people is not allowed between Gaza and the West Bank, and no one is allowed to enter Jerusalem, even for worship. The economic situation continues to worsen and the violations of all basic human rights are continuing. Collective punishment is still used against the entire population, which is leading to economic and social strangulation. The only peace that Israel is ready to

offer the Palestinians is for us the surrender of our national identity, of our political rights, and of most of the land on which we live. But such a vision is a formula for unending conflict.

No one can suppose that, having resisted Israeli rule for decades, we are about to give up. The realities on the ground are too tragic, too violent. Cosmetic peace for us is not enough. We have no allies, but we have hope, and we cannot be reconciled with hopelessness. We do have a more just picture of the future than Israel, one built on reconciliation and peace, rather than on empty promises that are contradicted by the worsening reality. Peace does not derive from exclusive and unending hostility. It comes about, rather, by sharing and community. There is no military option for the Palestinians and Israelis. We must live together and discover how to share the land together—we have to learn how to become true neighbours.

We Palestinians have agreed to work for peace. We have co-operated with the convenors of the peace process and with the Israelis. What worries us is the silence and indifference to our plight, particularly in the United States. The issues are clear, and the dangers are obvious. Moreover, peace is meant to be for everybody, not just for the powerful. We need to build with different materials, ones that are not combustible and that will not produce other wars! With the signing of Oslo I and II the world thinks that we have peace and reconciliation, but without liberation both are difficult to attain. On the surface one might see less direct violence, but the structural violence is present more than ever before, and suffering goes on and on. Two comments from Hebrew prophets come to mind:

> 'Justice is turned back and righteousness stands at a distance
> for truth stumbles in the public square and uprightness cannot
> enter. Truth is lacking and whoever turns from evil is
> despoiled. The Lord saw it and it displeased him that there
> was no justice' (Isaiah 59.14-15).
> 'Because they misled my people saying peace when there is
> no peace' (Ezekiel 13.10).

To have peace we have to tell the truth—without truth telling, there can be no peace and no reconciliation.

Without justice there is no peace, even in the absence of open

strife. Justice has two connotations. One is fairness, which is not sufficient for lasting peace. The other is the observance of the divine law, righteousness, the state of being just before God: when the bonding force of love unifies the temporal and the spiritual, the task of the peacemaker is fulfilled. At that point, peace has been established, true justice reigns, and the outcome is reconciliation. Reconciliation is not a strategy or a skill to be mastered, but rather something discovered—no less than the power of God's grace welling up in one's life. It is a gift of God and a source of new life.

At the beginning of his ministry, in the synagogue of Nazareth, Jesus, quoting the prophet Isaiah, proclaimed, 'the acceptable year of the Lord' (Luke 4.19). Many scholars suggest that the expression refers to the Jubilee year (Leviticus 25) which was to be celebrated by the Israelites in intervals of fifty years, in order to redress injustice and oppression, and to recognise the limits placed on the human claim on God's creation.

One remembers that in 1998 the modern State of Israel celebrated its fiftieth anniversary, while the Palestinians recalled their fiftieth year of dispossession. Sadly, there was little by way of a Jubilee, a year of restoration, a year of proclamation of the good news of liberation and transformation for all God's people who were struggling for life in its fullness.

And yet, the Christian Church should be encouraged by Jesus' proclamation of a permanent jubilee, and be driven by the constant task of witnessing to the demand of justice, peace, liberation, reconciliation, and the dignity and rights of nature. The task ahead is to break through to become a community of friends that crosses boundaries, deconstructs the dominant ideology that normalises sin, darkness and injustice, and that shapes an alternative praxis of mutuality.

> We form a circle of hope
> We pass the flame to one another
> If my candle goes out, yours will light it.
> Together we enable a brighter light ...
> And each candle promises something of its own
> That darkness is not the last word (David McCauley).

6. Overcoming direct and structural violence

These are very hard times in Palestine. We have been working for a long time to end occupation, oppression and destruction, without any political gains. Fear and loss surround us, and many forces are at work to make us feel isolated, marginalised and disempowered. At best the work ahead seems overwhelming. Death and loss rearrange our priorities, and teach us how much we need each other.

Many activists mistrust religion and spirituality, sometimes for good reasons. But those of us who work for peace and justice do so because something is sacred to us, so sacred that is means more than convenience or comfort. It might be God, or the Spirit, or the sacredness of life and mother earth, or belief in freedom. Whatever it is, it can nurture us.

For more than thirty-six years, I have been walking that edge where the spiritual meets the political. For me, the two have always been integrated. My spirituality is rooted in the human dignity and human rights of all people, and the sacredness of mother earth. I do feel compelled to take action to work for a world in which human freedom and dignity can flourish. Spirituality can bring life and vibrancy and imagination into my struggle, but the mixture of religion and politics can also fuel the most extreme and violent acts, and lead to systems of great repression.

We should be rightly suspicious when religion is exclusive, nationalistic, chauvinistic and against the emancipation of women. I do not want to believe in a religion which has a set of standards or dogma determining who are the worthy people, and who are the others. Religion for me is to re-link, to bind ourselves with others.

Political work is hard. Without a spiritual base to renew my energies and my sense of hope, and without a community to share them with, I suffer from frustration and despair. My work involves my taking many risks. But involvement in any action has a price. The question, of course, arises, am I ready to pay that price?

Lecturing outside of Palestine is, for me, an act of faith. My children and family often ask me, 'Why, mother, why?' Some think it is courageous to do so. Perhaps. Courage involves rising to the occasion wherever you happen to find yourself. It is not easy to carry the burden of 'being courageous' all the time, particularly in a fragile and mortal body. Nevertheless, I feel obliged to bear witness to what is happening

in my land, to expose the principalities and powers, to bring them out into the Light. Courage is not only doing what I do, but in my daily struggle to remain open to love, to the beauty of the world, to be open to tell our story.

There is nowhere left to go but forward. If we hold on to hope and vision, if we dare to walk with courage, and to act in the service of our values and beliefs, the barriers holding us back will give way. The road, of course, is unmapped and dangerous, but the powers of life, hope and creativity empower us to work toward a viable future.

There are many different modes of a 'politics of despair'. We usually associate that phrase with secretive, militant, political bombings which, in desperation, offer a type of ultimate hope that the extreme nature of such actions might spark a revolution. But it can also apply to those who opt to be virtuous, balanced, or neutral in the face of doom, and who have lost sight of any possibility of victory. Such people reduce significantly their chances of being in any way effective, and simply reinforce the focus on individuals that systems prefer to address. Rather than being isolated actors they ought to encourage all to ask: 'how do we collectively take power and bring about change?' In the case of Palestine people prefer to focus on Arafat, Sharon, Abu Queri and suicide bombings, without addressing the main issue, which is the structures of domination, the violence, and the military occupation which is enslaving a whole nation.

We Palestinians are constantly told that non-violence and dialogue are the key to solving our problems. I do agree, and have committed my life to it. As women, we have embraced suffering all along, and we have been taught to suffer and sacrifice for others. We have been conditioned to swallow our anger, and not to strike back. Yet women's empowerment involves acknowledging our anger, owning our rage, allowing ourselves to be powerful and dangerous, as well as being accommodating and understanding. We women have to understand how violence functions, and how systems of domination function.

Structural violence is silent. It does not show. Television captures only the direct violence, more often than not, the violence of the powerless and the hopeless. Invariably, this violence is equated with terror. Certainly, terrorist violence is vile. It violates the sanctity of God's creation, and defaces creation itself. A striking weakness of the concept of violence in the Israeli-Palestinian conflict, however, is the assumption of symmetry, which views the contending parties as being

equal. In reality, of course, there is a conflict precisely because of the inequality between the two parties.

The consequences of those who use violence, whether it be freelance or state-supported, is the filling of our mental and emotional space with rage, fear, powerlessness and despair, and our being cut off from the sources of life and hope. How might we work to overcome structural and direct violence? I suggest the following pattern for overcoming the different forms of violence:

▫ overcome direct violence (killing, imprisonment, etc.) by building multiple non-violent strategies for resistance;

▫ overcome economic structural violence (exploitation of water, land, etc.), by advocating economic rights, water rights, land rights and ecological sustainability, etc.;

▫ overcome political structural violence (military occupation, settlement, etc.), by advocating for political rights according to international law and UN resolutions, etc.;

▫ overcome cultural structural violence (stereotyping of Palestinians, Arabs, women in the media, education, language, Anti-Arabism, discrimination against women, etc.), by media and education strategies, etc.;

▫ overcome religious structural violence (chosenness, disunity among the churches, demonisation of Islam, Christian Zionism, etc.), by working for ecumenism and unity, challenging fundamentalisms, educating Christians on Islam, constructing a contextual liberation theology based on non-violence etc.;

▫ overcome environmental structural violence (confiscation and destruction of agricultural land, uprooting of trees, theft of water resources, etc.), by insistence on adherence to international environmental conventions and protocols, and on international human rights, etc.).

Conclusion

I have learned that the struggle for justice is one struggle, and that an action taken to subvert violence and strengthen human rights in one

area is an action on behalf of people everywhere. In his 'Letter from a Birmingham Jail' (16 April 1963), Martin Luther King reminded us that, 'Injustice anywhere is a threat to justice everywhere.'[2] That is the international context. I now understand even more that our global responsibilities and relationships have a local face, and, no matter where we live, we can work for human rights and a culture of non-violence. The kinships we form as we do so serve as a prototype of a new community, one that knows no boundaries, national, racial or gender/sexual.

Those of us committed to theologising, truth-telling and peacemaking, whether with respect to the Palestinian experience or to any other issue, must not give up, for to give up is to give in to the forces of darkness. We must continue, rather, to fan the embers into flames of light, no matter how small they are, because these embers of light give hope to those in the forefront of the struggle. They will keep the work for justice and peace in the Middle East alive. Martin Luther King defined peace, not as the absence of war, but as the presence of justice. In that same 'Letter from a Birmingham Jail', he defended his movement against the charge of 'extremism' his fellow religious leaders had levelled at him: his activities were 'unwise and untimely'.

> So the question is not whether we will be extremists, but what kind of extremists we will be. Will we be extremists for hate or for love? Will we be extremist for the preservation of injustice or for the extension of justice?

and added,

> More and more I feel that the people of ill-will have used time much more effectively than have the people of good will. We will have to repent in this generation not merely for the hateful words and actions of the bad people but for the appalling silence of the good people.

---

[2] The full, unedited text of King's 'Letter from a Birmingham Jail' is available at http://almaz.com/nobel/peace/MLK-jail.html, accessed on 21 December 2003.

SPEAKING THE TRUTH TO JEWS
Paul Eisen

What Israel and Zionism have done, and are doing, to the Palestinians is indefensible, yet so many Jews defend it. How and why do they do this? And why does the rest of the world seem complicit and unable to speak out?

The Original Sin

Many arguments can be advanced in favour of a Jewish state in Palestine, from the simple right of the Jewish people to national self-determination, the right of Jews to return to their ancestral homeland, and the need of a suffering and persecuted people for a haven where they can be safe and secure.

Jews can define themselves as they wish. If they feel themselves to be a nation, then they are a nation. But, in accordance with the dictum, that 'your freedom to swing your arm ends where your finger touches my nose', it is when this self-definition impinges on others that the problems begin. It is then that others may ask whether this Jewish sense of nationhood—often an emotional and religious matter based on a perceived sharing of history and even of destiny—can ever be realised politically. What it boils down to is this: Jews, like any other people, may have the right to establish and maintain a state of their own, but, do Jews have the right to establish and maintain a state of their own in Palestine, already the home of the Palestinians? All this may, and will be argued, but what is beyond dispute is that, for Jewish national self-determination and statehood, it is the Palestinians who have paid a terrible price.

By 1947-48, Palestinians had been reduced to a state of anxiety and insecurity, and in 1948, when the State of Israel was established, a traditional Palestinian society was no match for its democratic, egalitarian and fiercely ideological foe. As a consequence, an entire way of life was obliterated. At least 750,000 Palestinians were driven from their homes

and into exile, more than 450 of their towns and villages were destroyed or pillaged and people who had lived a settled life for generations ended up either in tents in Lebanon, Syria or Jordan, or as a bereft and traumatised diaspora in every corner of the earth.

Nor was all this an unintended by-product of war. Although the idea that the Palestinians just 'ran away' has, in the main, been dispelled, we are still left with many stories, obfuscations and downright lies about where responsibility lies for this ethnic cleansing. The critical issue now centres on the question of intentionality.

The ethnic cleansing of Palestinians, like most instances of ethnic cleansing, was intentional, premeditated and planned. But we need not bother looking for direct documentation. Although there is mounting evidence for the desires and intentions of the Zionist leadership to cleanse the land of Palestinians, the architects of the *Nakba* left no 'smoking gun'. There was no written order, because there was no need for a written order. Like other instances of ethnic cleansing, the expulsion of the Palestinians was done on 'understandings'. As Ilan Pappé has noted, every local Haganah commander, and all the men under their command at every village and town, knew exactly what was required. Sometimes a few shots in the air would be sufficient, and sometimes a full-blown massacre was needed. However, the result was always the same.[1]

This was the original sin. Since then, the sin has been compounded many times over, as Israel has continued its assault on Palestinians and Palestinian life. From border raids and massacres to the occupation and the settlements, to the slaughter of 20,000 in Lebanon, through provocations, closures, expulsions, demolitions, arrests, torture and assassinations, right up to the chicaneries of Oslo and the Roadmap where Palestinians were to be bamboozled into going into their cage quietly, Israel and Zionism have sought to destroy the Palestinians, if not always physically, then certainly as a people in their own land.

'... While we babble and rave ...'

... Only then will the old and young in our land realise how great was our responsibility to those miserable Arab refugees

---

[1] Ilan Pappé, in a lecture given at the School of Oriental and African Studies (University of London), 10 September 2002.

191

in whose towns we have settled Jews who were brought
from afar; whose homes we have inherited, whose fields we
now sow and harvest; the fruits of whose gardens, orchards
and vineyards we gather; and in whose cities that we robbed,
we put up houses of education, charity and prayer while we
babble and rave about being the 'people of the Book' and
the 'light of the nations!' (Buber/Chofshi).[2]

For a relatively small number of Jews, support for what is being
done to the Palestinians is a relatively easy matter. God gave the land to
the Jews, the Palestinians are Amalek, and if they will not submit to
Jewish rule they must, and will, be destroyed. Just like those Germans
who relinquished Nazism only when the Russians were on the streets of
Berlin, such Jews will abandon their militant, eliminationist Zionism
only when the options finally close down.

But for most Jews things are not so simple. Defending the
indefensible is never easy, and many Jews, intellectually sophisticated, secular
and liberal in their instincts, require more than just careful selections from
the Bible to justify what is being done to the Palestinians. These Jews have
had, over the years, to tell themselves a lot of stories. For some this has been
easier than for others. For some, perhaps the majority, it has been simple
enough to swallow the Israeli and Zionist line whole: Jews came to a land
inhabited only by rootless peasants, and battled against overwhelming odds
to establish their state. Since then, Israel, an island of Western decency in a
sea of Arab decadence and decay has had to battle for its very survival.

But for some, after 1967, and the occupation of the West Bank
and Gaza, the illegal settling of the land, and, later, the war in Lebanon,
the *Intifadas*, and the work of the new Israeli historians in uncovering the
truth of Israel's birth, the story has had to be revised.

'End the occupation!'

Many Jews, now aware of the injustice associated with the establishment
of Israel, but still unable to relinquish their belief in Israel's essential

---

[2] It is unclear which of the men actually wrote this, but it appeared in the Jan/Feb 1961
issue of *Ner* (Light), the journal of the binationalist movement *Ichud* (Unity), with which
they were both associated.

innocence, have congregated around the slogans: 'End the occupation!' and 'Two states for two peoples!' That there is no 'occupation', and that there will never be a true Palestinian state on the West Bank and Gaza, are simply denied.

The long-term Zionist strategy for the conquest of Palestine was always to wait for what Ben-Gurion called 'revolutionary situations', meaning situations which would provide cover under which the take-over of Palestine could be completed. The first of these 'revolutionary situations' presented itself in 1947 and 1948, when, under the cover of the conflict, 78 percent of historic Palestine was transformed into Israel. Another such situation presented itself in 1967.

Israel in 1967 was not the innocent party threatened with annihilation by the Arab states (though its population probably thought it was). Israel had been preparing for such a war for years. Neither was Israel's victory anything other then totally expected by anyone who was even a little bit in the know. Like the 1947-48 conflict, the war of 1967 was an opportunity gladly taken for the take-over of the remaining 22 percent of Palestine. This was the fulfilment of Zionism's historic mission.

There is, then, no occupation. There never was an occupation. If there had been an occupation, and the Israelis had the slightest intention of ending it they would have done so years ago. The fact is, that no Israeli government, either of the left or the right, has ever shown any intention of fully withdrawing back to the 1967 border. No Israeli government, left or right, has shown the slightest inclination to permit anything even remotely resembling a real Palestinian state to be established on the West Bank and Gaza. Any state that could emerge would be tiny, fragmented and weak, being simply a legitimisation of Palestinian surrender. The occupation, in fact, has been a fig-leaf to conceal the reality of the final conquest of Palestine.

Nevertheless, for many Jews the occupation is the bedrock of Israel's essential innocence. Occupations are temporary and can be reversed, and this one, they believe, was the result of a war which Israel did not seek. So, Israel and Zionism are still, at heart, innocent. The Jewish state, established at the expense of another people's national life, is still blameless. It is the occupation that has 'forced' Israel into the role of oppressor, and if only Israel would withdraw to the borders of 1967 all would be as it had been, only better: the gains of 1948 would then be secured, Jews would have their Israel with its 'moral foundations', and

the Palestinians would be contained within a bantustan with a semblance, but not the reality, of justice. For many Jews, this would mean that they could have both their empowerment and their consciences.

The sin of moral equivalence

> To talk about 'a cycle of violence' in the Middle East between Israelis and Palestinians is to commit the sin of 'moral equivalence.'[3]

Conceived in the Israeli and Jewish peace camps, taken up by the mainstream and pretty much the entire solidarity movement, and now underpinning all acceptable discourse on Israel and Palestine, is the notion that the conflict in Israel/Palestine is not the brutal dispossession and oppression of one people by another, but a tragic conflict between two equal, but conflicting rights. This notion emerged after 1967 when doveish, more moderate Zionists, realising that the story of a blameless innocent Zionism could no longer be sustained, but still unable to acknowledge Israel's guilt, after years of denying the very existence of the Palestinian people, began to concede that the Palestinians also had a story which ought to be heard.

In this new narrative Israel is not guilty, because no one is guilty, and Israel is not the oppressor, because there is no oppressor. Everyone is an innocent victim. Variations on the theme include the *I've suffered, you've suffered, let's talk* approach, and what has been called the psychotherapy approach to conflict resolution, *You feel my pain and I'll feel yours.* Proponents of this theory say that the two sides are not listening to each other. If only each side would hear the other's story a solution would surely be found.

But it is not true that neither has heard the other's story. Palestinians have heard the Zionist story *ad nauseam*, and they have certainly heard enough about Jewish suffering. It is not, then, both sides that need to listen: it is Israelis, and Jews who need to listen.

But, as is heard so often from inside the Jewish and Israeli peace camps, both sides have a point of view, and both sides must be heard;

---

[3] Walid Khalidi, in a lecture, 'The Prospects of Peace in the Middle East ', delivered at Brunei Gallery (SOAS), 8 October 2002.

both sides have suffered, and right or wrong is *never* on one side only. This, of course, is true, but did these same Jews, then struggling against apartheid and now campaigning for the 'justice' of a disempowered statelet for Palestinians on a mere remnant of what was once their homeland— and many were the same Jews—say then that we had to see both sides of the picture? They did not. They acknowledged that white South Africans were as deserving of peace and prosperity as black South Africans, but they never lost sight of who was the victim and who was the perpetrator.

Nor are the two sides in Israel-Palestine equal in power, or in moral weight. Israel, a modern Western-style state, with the fourth most powerful army in the world, faces a civilian population with a few poorly armed militias, and enforces a claim which is highly questionable. Jewish claims to Palestine are not only more complex than Palestinian claims, but are also more contentious. Even whilst acknowledging a Jewish connection with Palestine, and even if one might wish to see a Jewish presence there, the historical evidence can hardly justify exclusive Jewish ownership

This recasting of the struggle as a conflict between equals means that Jews do not have to see Israel for what it is: a powerful state, founded and maintained on injustice, oppressing a weak and defenceless civilian population. Instead, they see it for what they would like it to be: a tiny, embattled state, well-intentioned, but caught up in a tragic conflict of equal but opposing rights. So, an assault by the fourth most powerful army in the world on a largely undefended refugee camp becomes just part of a continuing 'cycle of violence', and the imposition of surrender on an exhausted and defeated people can be recast as 'negotiations', or 'peace talks'.

Good cop/bad cop

Zionism's eternal good cop/bad cop routine has for years deflected criticism, and provided for Jews and others a means of reconciling what they see with what they want to see. The good cop is the secular 'left', meaning the Labour Party and its offshoots, descended from the old Labour Zionism of David Ben-Gurion, while the bad cop is Likud, descended from the old revisionists founded by Ze'ev Jabotinsky, and now joined by the religious fanatics and the settlers. And the argument

runs, that Israel and Zionism are not themselves responsible for their crimes, but only extremist elements therein. If only the good guys were in power, things would be alright for the Palestinians.

History, however, does not bear this out. The fact is that certainly as much, if not more suffering has been inflicted on the Palestinians by Labour governments and the left, than by Likud and the right. It was Labour Zionism which created the pre-state society that excluded Palestinians, particularly in the organisation of labour. It was Labour Zionists, good, humanistic, left-wing kibbutzniks who directed the ethnic cleansing of 750,000 Palestinians, and the destruction of their towns and villages. It was Labour Zionism which established the present state with all its discriminatory practices, and it was a Labour government that held the Palestinian citizens of Israel under military government in their own land for eighteen years. Finally, it was a Labour government which conquered the West Bank and Gaza, and first built the settlements, and it was a Labour government that embarked on the Oslo peace process, coolly designed to deceive the Palestinians into surrendering their rights.

The difference between the good cop and the bad cop is not their final destination but only how they get there. Both Labour and Likud, indeed the whole of mainstream Zionism, has as its aim the complete conquest of the whole of Palestine, from the Mediterranean Sea to the Jordan River, with as few Palestinians therein as possible. The only difference is that, whilst Likud and the 'right' understand, as they have always understood, that the only way to achieve this was through force, Labour would prefer, along with the use of force when necessary, to deceive their victims into going into the cage quietly. And, when the good cop has failed, and the victims have proved themselves unwilling to walk into the cage unaided, as they did at Camp David at the end of the Oslo process, what do they do? Why, they call in the bad cop, in this case, the butcher, Ariel Sharon.

The Palestinians have had 100 years of good cop, bad cop, good cop, bad cop. The good cop led them down the Oslo path and made them the generous offer of a tiny, fragmented and trashed statelet on just part of 22 percent of what is their own land, under the political and economic control of Israel, and under the guns of the Israeli military. And, shock, horror, they turned it down. So the Israelis called in the bad cop, Sharon, who has done his worst. Now after more than two years of relentless assault the victim is nicely softened up. So, in comes the good

cop. In his hand is a piece of paper. On the piece of paper is a new peace plan. The peace plan offers just that, peace for the victor, but very little justice for the victim. All the Palestinians have to do is to sign, and the pain will go away. There is little doubt that the overwhelming majority of Jews, including many in the peace camp, will be clamouring for them to sign.

A light unto the nations

'*Le tzionut, le sozialism ve le achvat amim* ('For Zionism, socialism, and internationalism')
Motto of *Hashomer Hatzair* ('The Young Guard')

Within many Jews there is the deep and abiding wish for the return of the 'Beautiful Israel' of their childhoods. This was the Israel that was conceived in universal ideals of socialism and justice to be 'a light unto the nations'. That such an Israel never existed, and could never have existed, is ignored.

The notion of 'Beautiful Israel' lies at the very foundations of Political Zionism with roots deep in Jewish history. Zionism, which connects a modern Jewish state in Palestine with its supposed biblical antecedent, never saw itself as just another colonial enterprise, though it certainly was that. But it was much more as well. Zionist thinkers, though generally secular, used Jewish religious sentiment to further their cause, but this was not just cold-blooded political manoeuvring. Like so many ideologues, the early, and also later and present-day Zionists, believed their own stories.

Even for the least observant Jew, Jewish identity is a complex and resonant issue, and Jewishness may be experienced a long way from the synagogue, the *yeshiva*, or any other formal aspect of Jewish life. Jewish history, inextricably linked with Judaism, is also the bedrock of many secular Jews' sense of Jewish identity. The founders of modern political Zionism, as secular a bunch as one could meet, still had a powerful sense of their history, and even destiny, with all the inevitable emotional and religious overtones. For many of them, and certainly for many of the Jewish masses who offered their allegiance, the founding of a Jewish state in Palestine was, if not overtly religious, still profoundly emotional and spiritual.

Many of the founding fathers of the modern state defined themselves as socialists. Unable to choose between their socialism and their Zionism, they tried to combine the two, believing that Zionism and Socialism could go hand in hand in building a Jewish state, founded on principles of equality and social justice, an absurdity really, since the one stood for universal principles and the other for Jewish ethnic interests. The motto of *Hashomer Hatzair* (The Young Guard), which formed the core of the 'left-Zionist' Mapam party, *Le tzionut, le sozialism ve le achvat amim* (For Zionism, socialism, and internationalism) is significant in that Zionism always came first.

Loftier than most run-of-the-mill colonial enterprises, pre-state Zionism did not so much rob the natives—though they certainly did plenty of that—as ignore them. Central to the pre-state society and the state itself were socialist structures such as the Histadrut trades union, which presided over both the organization of Jewish labour and the exclusion of non-Jewish labour. That their lofty socialist principles rarely extended in practice to non-Jews need not be attributed only to cynicism, but also to a moral schizophrenia that has always made Zionism so hard to analyse and therefore so hard to oppose.

But there was another Zionism: Cultural or Spiritual Zionism that envisioned a Jewish community, a spiritual, religious and cultural centre in Palestine, living in peace and equality with the Palestinians. These voices of bi-nationalism, led by such as Ahad Ha'am, Martin Buber and Judah Magnes, were small in number and increasingly marginalised. In retrospect it is hard to see that they had any effect on Zionist policy, or made much difference to present-day Zionist ideology. But these traditions were, and are, very important to Jews theologically and had an enormous cultural effect—the revival and development of the Hebrew language and literature, and the establishment of centres of learning, such as the Hebrew University and the Haifa Technion, were to have a huge and positive effect on the scientific and cultural progress of the pre-state Yishuv and of Israel.

But the theological and cultural effects of this Spiritual Zionism were nothing compared to the effects they had on the marketing of Political Zionism. One need not doubt the sincerity of these voices, nor of those Jews who hold them dear, to note how, with that particular blend of conviction, hypocrisy and self-delusion on the part of Political Zionists, they have been used to mystify and obfuscate, and so better promote, a

far less scrupulous vision. Many leftist Zionists, such as those in *Hashomer Hatzair*, took great pains—whilst working for a Jewish majority through immigration, directing and participating in the ethnic cleansing of 1948, and subsequently building their socialist and utopian (but only for Jews) kibbutzim on stolen Palestinian land—to cloak themselves in the rhetoric of bi-nationalism. The sincerely held beliefs of Buber, Magnes, Ahad aham and others were used to give Zionism that messianic, moral tinge which has done so much over the years to bamboozle us all. Today, these traditions are often cited as evidence of Zionism's essential goodness, and many Jews today now look back on them with nostalgia, and cling to them for comfort, and also to conceal from themselves and others Political Zionism's manifest character.

These moral ambiguities are evident, not only in the divisions within Israel, the Zionist establishment and the Jewish community world-wide, but also often within many individuals. Zionism, the drive for the return of an ancient and suffering people to their God-given homeland, is for Jews a compelling ideology. This surge of power to the powerless, this messianic story of return, the utopianism, the intensity, the near religious fervour of Zionism, blended with enormous dollops of self-delusion, constitute a heady mix which has gone straight to the head of many an otherwise sober and rational Jew, and has led to some strange and contradictory behaviour: left-wing Jews at solidarity demonstrations calling over loudhailers for justice for Palestinians, whilst at the same time vigorously defending Israel's right, as a Jewish state, to discriminate officially against non-Jews; the 'progressive' Rabbi Michael Lerner claiming that Israel cannot be discriminatory, since it accepts Jews of all ethnic backgrounds, and that the establishment of Israel with the attendant obliteration of Palestinian society amounts to 'affirmative action' for Jews;[4] and the appearance at Palestine solidarity rallies of organised Jewish youth in full Zionist regalia, blue shirts with stars of David on their badges and flags, carrying placards calling for an end to the occupation.

It is within these ambiguities and contradictions that so many Jews have found places of refuge from the moral condemnation of the crimes committed in their names. When confronted with the crimes of Israel and Zionism or the charge that Israel and Zionism are, by definition,

---

[4] Michael Lerner, 'Say "No" to the Zionism is racism lynch mob', in an email from Rabbi Lerner (13 August 2001),

discriminatory, many Jews will answer 'Ah, but that's not the Israel I love', or 'That's not the Zionism in which I believe.'

Speaking the truth to Jews

It is understandable that Jews might believe that their suffering is greater, more mysterious and meaningful than that of any other people. It is even understandable that Jews might feel that their suffering can justify the oppression of another people. What is harder to understand is why the rest of the world has gone along with it.

That Jews have suffered is undeniable. But acknowledgement of this suffering is rarely enough. Jews and others have demanded that not only should Jewish suffering be acknowledged, but that it also be accorded special status. Jewish suffering is held to be unique, central and most importantly, mysterious.

Jewish suffering is rarely measured against the sufferings of other groups. Blacks, women, children, gays, workers, peasants, minorities of all kinds, all have suffered, but none as much as Jews. Protestants at the hands of Catholics, Catholics at the hands of Protestants, pagans and heretics, all have suffered religious persecution, but none as relentlessly as Jews. Indians, Armenians, gypsies and aborigines, all have been targeted for elimination, but none as murderously and as premeditatedly as Jews

Jewish suffering is held to be mysterious, and beyond explanation. Context is rarely examined. The place and role of Jews in society—their historical relationships with Church and state, landlords and peasantry—is hardly ever subject to scrutiny, and, whilst non-Jewish attitudes to Jews are the subject of intense interest, Jewish attitudes to non-Jews are rarely mentioned. Attempts to confront these issues are met with suspicion, and sometimes hostility, in the fear that explanation may lead to rationalisation, which may lead to exculpation, and then even to justification.

The Holocaust, 'the ultimate mystery'

The stakes in this already fraught game have been raised so much higher by the Holocaust. Is the Holocaust 'The ultimate mystery, never to be comprehended or transmitted', as Elie Wiesel would have us

believe?[5] Are attempts to question the Holocaust narrative merely a cover for the wish to deny or even to justify the Holocaust? Was Jewish suffering in the Holocaust greater and of more significance than that of anyone else? Were the three million Polish Jews who died at the hands of the Nazis more important than the three million Polish non-Jews who also died? Twenty million black Africans, a million Ibos, a million Kampucheans, Armenians, aborigines, all have perished in genocides, but none as meaningfully as the six million Jews slaughtered in the only genocide to be theologically named, and now perceived by Jews and the rest of the Western world to be an event of near religious significance.

Whether there is anything special about Jews is not really relevant. What is relevant is that a large part of the Western world, even the most secular part, seems to believe that there is, or are not confident enough in their disbelief to say so. Similarly, whether the world believes that Jewish suffering is qualitatively and quantitatively different from all other suffering is also irrelevant. The fact is that most people seem compelled to agree that it is, or to remain silent.

Christianity occupies a central place in Western culture and experience and Jews occupy a central place in the Christian narrative, so it is no surprise that Jews and Jewish concerns receive a lot of attention. The Western world, though largely secular but still Christian in its cultural foundations, seems at times obsessed with Jews, and unable to see them for what, in the words of Richard Rubenstein, they may well be, 'a people like any other whose religion and culture were shaped so as to make it possible for them to cope with their very distinctive history and location among the peoples of the world.'[6] Jewish life seems at times to be at the very heart of Western concerns. And this goes way beyond the religious contexts. From Jewish history, stories of struggle from the Hebrew Bible, such as the Exodus from Egypt, have become paradigms for other people's struggles and aspirations. The emigration of Jews from Eastern Europe into their Golden Land in America has become as American a legend as the Wild West. Jewish folklore and myth, stereotypes of Jewish humour, food, family life—all are deeply woven into the fabric of Western, particularly American, life.

---

[5] Wiesel, Elie. 2000. *And the Sea Is Never Full: Memoirs, 1969*, translated by Marion Wiesel. London: HarperCollins.

[6] Rubenstein, Richard L. 1992. *After Auschwitz. History, Theology and Contemporary Judaism*. Baltimore: The Johns Hopkins University Press.

Christian attitudes towards Jews are complex and contradictory: Jesus was born a Jew and died a Jew, and yet, traditionally, His teachings supersede those of Judaism. Jesus lived amongst Jews, His message was shaped by Jews, yet He was rejected by Jews, and, it has been widely believed, died at the behest of Jews. So, for many Christians, Jews are both the people of God and the people who rejected God, and are objects of both great veneration and great loathing. Jewish suffering at the hands of the Christian majority is a matter of great shame and guilt. Yet still, in the minds of some Christians, and possibly buried deep within many more, are notions that the suffering of Jews is, for the killers of a God, deserved. This ambivalence is reflected in the secular world too, where Jews are widely admired for their history and traditions and for their creativity and success, yet are also regarded with some suspicion and dislike for their exclusivity and supposed sense of their own 'specialness'. Jews seem either loved or hated, and, now since the Holocaust, publicly at least, they seem loved, or at least if not loved, then certainly, indulged.

During much of their history in Europe Jews were persecuted, culminating most recently in the slaughter in the death camps. The relationship between that ultimate slaughter and the centuries of antisemitism that preceded it, the relationship of the Church to that antisemitism, and the intensity and duration of persecutions of Jews throughout history, all of this is appropriate for examination. The nature of those persecutions may also be investigated, and even the possible collusion by Jews themselves in their own victimhood, all may be subject to proper scrutiny. But, just as in the struggle between Israelis and Palestinians there can be no argument about who are the victims and who are the perpetrators, there can be no doubt that, for much of their history in Europe, Jews were victims. Western society, both Christian and secular, bears a heavy responsibility for Jewish suffering, and this responsibility is now rightly being taken very seriously indeed.

But what, when these legitimate feelings of responsibility are employed to conceal rather than reveal the truth? What, when Christian and other responsibility for Jewish suffering is used to justify the oppression of another people? What, when even the issue of who is the victim and who is the perpetrator becomes confused, when yesterday's victim becomes today's perpetrator, and when today's perpetrator uses its past victimhood to justify its present abuse of another people?

The establishment of the State of Israel in May 1948, coming just three years after the liberation of Auschwitz in January 1945, marks, for Jews, the transition from enslavement to empowerment. This empowerment of Jews took place not only with the establishment of Israel, but also continuously, from the mass emigration of Jews to the West in the late 19th and early 20th centuries, to the present day. Today in the West Jews enjoy unparalleled political, economic and social power and influence. Jews are represented way beyond their numbers in the upper echelons of all areas of public and professional life—politics, academia, the arts, the media and business. Even more than the political and economic power which Jews possess, however, is the social power. Jews have a moral prestige derived from their history and traditions as a chosen, and as a suffering people. In these more secular times, however, especially since the Holocaust, it is as a suffering people, that Jews occupy their special place in Western culture.

We see this in both public and private life. Public statements involving Jews or Israel so often include the almost obligatory reference to past Jewish suffering. And in private conversations whenever the subject arises, voices are lowered reverentially and words are carefully chosen. Who is able, when discussing the present suffering of Palestinians, to avoid inserting a reference to the past suffering of Jews? As if no matter what Jews do, account must always be taken of their own suffering. And who, when discussing the amount of Holocaust memorialisation that has taken place in the West—memorials, foundations, academic chairs at universities, study programmes, days of remembrance—who is able to avoid nervously inserting the words, 'quite rightly' into their sentences?

On being cursed as an antisemite

Jews have not been just passive recipients of all this special treatment and consideration. The special status accorded to Israel's behaviour in Palestine, and Jewish support for it, is not something that Jews have accepted reluctantly. On the contrary, Jews and Jewish organisations have demanded it. And at the heart of this demand for special consideration is the demand that the whole world, whilst recognising the uniqueness of Jewish suffering, should join with Jews in their fears about antisemitism and of its resurgence.

Antisemitism, in its historic, virulent and eliminationist form, did exist and could certainly exist again, but it does not currently exist in the West in any significantly observable form. Jews have never been so secure or empowered, yet many Jews feel and act as if they are a hair's breadth away from Auschwitz. And not only this, they require that everybody else feel the same. So soon after the Holocaust this is perhaps understandable, but less so when it is used to silence dissent and criticism of Israel and Zionism.

Jews, individually and collectively, use their political, economic, social, and moral power in support of Israel and Zionism. In their defence of Israel and Zionism Jews brandish their suffering at the world, accusing it of reverting to its old antisemitic ways. They claim that criticism of Israel and Zionism is in fact criticism of Jews. Just as the Jews were, in the past, the objects of classic antisemitism, so Israel, the state of the Jews, is the object of a new, modern antisemitism. They will concede that Israel, like any other state in the world, is not exempt from criticism, but they do claim that Israel's right to exist *as a Jewish state* is so exempt. In effect, we may criticise Israel for what Israel does, but not for what Israel is.

But what is Israel? Defenders of Israel claim that Jews, like any other people, are entitled to national self-determination and statehood, and that to deny Jews that which is granted to all other peoples is discriminatory. Thus anti-Zionism is, in effect, antisemitism. But, even leaving aside the fact that Israel was established on the expulsion and exile of the Palestinians, is Israel as a Jewish state merely giving to Jews that which is given to all other peoples? Is Israel, a state which officially defines itself as for one ethnic group alone, the same as other states? Israel is the state of the Jews and of only the Jews. In its immigration, land, planning and housing laws and practices, military recruitment regulations and many other laws, practices and customs, Israel officially and unofficially, overtly and covertly, discriminates against non-Jews. In any other context, with any other people this would be deemed discriminatory and perhaps even racist. Of course, one may agree or disagree with any of this but is such agreement of disagreement necessarily antisemitic?

Is a Jewish state acceptable in this day and age? Are the Jews a people who qualify for national self-determination, or are Jews a religious group only? Post-Holocaust, does the Jewish need for a state of their own perhaps even justify the displacement of the Palestinians? Are Jews who

wield power to serve what they perceive as their own ethnic interests and to support Israel to be held politically accountable? What is antisemitism? Is anti-Zionism antisemitism? All this and a great deal more could and should be debated. What need not be debated is this: that every complexity and ambiguity of Jewish identity and history, every example of Jewish suffering, every instance of anti-Jewish prejudice, however inconsequential, is used to justify the crimes of Israel and Zionism. Every possible interpretation or misinterpretation of language, and every kind of intellectual sophistry is used by Zionists to muddy the waters and label the critic of Israel and Zionism an antisemite. Words and phrases become loaded with hidden meanings, so that even the most honest critic of Israel has to twist and turn and jump through hoops to ensure that he or she is not perceived to be an antisemite.

And the penalties for transgression are terrible. For those who do not manage to pick their way through this minefield the charge of antisemite awaits, with all its possibilities of political, religious and social exclusion. No longer a descriptive term for someone who hates Jews simply for being Jews, 'antisemite' is now a curse to hurl against anyone who criticises Jews, and, increasingly against anyone who dares too trenchantly to criticise Israel and Zionism. And for those Jews of conscience who dare speak out, for them there is reserved the special penalty of exclusion from Jewish life and exile.

Zionism and the State of Israel now lie at the very heart of Jewish life and so many Jews, even if unaffiliated officially to Zionism, have supported it, and continue to support it in its aims. Indeed, almost all the organised Jewish establishments throughout the world, in Israel, Europe and North America have used, and continue to use their power, influence, and, most importantly, their moral prestige, to support Israel in its attempts to subjugate the Palestinians. And the rest of the Western world, by its support for these efforts, and by its silence, is complicit in these crimes.

Marc Ellis' 'ecumenical deal', which translates also into a political deal, says it all. It goes like this: To the Christian and to the entire non-Jewish world, Jews say this: 'You will apologise for Jewish suffering again and again and again. And, when you have done apologising, you will then apologise some more. When you have apologised sufficiently we will forgive you ... provided that you let us do what we want in Palestine.'

The situation in Israel/Palestine gets worse and worse. The hatred against Israel and the West grows and grows. Increasingly, Jews are

perceived as complicit with power and injustice. There is growing rage. Meanwhile Jews themselves retreat further and further behind the walls of a blind and misplaced group solidarity.

Albert Camus, at a gathering of Dominican friars, commenting on Pope Pius XII's manner of addressing the Holocaust, wrote,

> What the world expects of Christians is that Christians should speak out loud and clear, and that they should voice their condemnation in such a way that never a doubt, never the slightest doubt, could arise in the heart of the simplest man or woman.[7]

On 14 November 2001 Marc Ellis, addressing a meeting at the General Synod of the Church of England, closed with the words.

> Your responsibility … is not to patronise us, not to flee in fear from us, not to treat us as children, and not to repent endlessly for the Holocaust. Your job is to speak honestly to us, to even scold us, to point the finger in the way we pointed the finger at you, to tell us to stop before it's too late.

For those able to see it, the irony is breathtaking.

---

7 Camus, *Resistance, Rebellion, and Death*, 1995, in Mark Chmiel, 'Elie Wiesel and the Question of Palestine', *Tikkun* 17 (No.6 November/December 2002): 66.

THE RIGHT OF RETURN
AND ITS DETRACTORS
Naseer Aruri

The question of the Palestinian refugees[1] has not been central in what
came to be known during the past thirty-six years as the Middle East
Peace Process, an American diplomatic monopoly, which has merely
succeeded in perpetuating the 1967 occupation, while keeping the 1948
issues off limits. This has been a peace process largely driven by the
factor of geo-politics rather than the forces of international law. Had
international law, represented by countless United Nations resolutions
and other instruments, been allowed to become relevant to the peace
process, it could possibly have neutralised one of the major stumbling
blocks (the imbalance of power) which retarded the pursuit of a political
settlement in Israel/Palestine. Not only is there no military solution to
the Arab-Israeli conflict, but a political solution, which is rather remote
at present, will not be lasting if it emanates from a calculus of pure geo-
politics.

Since the inception of this problem in 1948 when Israel was
established on 78 percent of what used to be Palestine, the question of
refugee rights, among other components of the Palestine question (borders,
sovereignty, water, Jewish settlements, mutual recognition) continued to

---

[1] John Quigley points out the anomaly of referring to the Palestinians who fled in 1948 and
1967 as 'refugees'. Although that term is used also in the UN Security Council Resolution
242 (1967) it is inexact. In international practice, 'refugee' refers to a person who seeks the
right to reside in a foreign country because he does not want to reside in his own country
for fear of persecution. The United Nations convention on refugees defines 'refugee' in
this way. 'The Palestine Arabs, however, seek to return to their own country. Thus, they do
not fit the definition of "refugee". It is more accurate to refer to them as displaced persons,
that is, persons who, for reasons not of their own choosing, are living outside their own
country. Such persons have, under international law, a right of return. This right is based
on the attachment of the person to the person's native territory. That attachment is given
recognition in the law. Take, for example, a group of persons who flee a natural disaster,
such as a flood, and in order to escape the flood they cross an international border. Once
the waters have receded and it is safe for them to return to their country, they have a legal
right to do so. If the government of their country decides, for any reason, not to re-admit
them, it would be acting unlawfully' (Quigley 1998: 83-84).

bedevil the international community and particularly the permanent members of the United Nations Security Council. Numerous proposals for a settlement have emanated primarily from Washington since the June 1967 Arab-Israeli war, but almost all of them, from the Rogers Plan of 1969 all the way up to the Oslo Accords of September 1993 have ended in total failure.[2] Almost every single US plan removed the refugee component of the Palestine question to the sidelines during the past half-century. The Oslo Accords, signed at the White House on 13 September 1993, designated it as a 'final status' issue to be left until the very end of the negotiations.[3]

This essay demonstrates how the primacy assigned to geo-politics, as well as the efforts of various governments in the region and outside, have not only resulted in the marginalization of Palestinian rights, particularly refugee rights, but also have eroded the earlier consensus built around General Assembly Resolution 194(III) adopted on 11 December 1948.[4] Paragraph 11 of the resolution deals with the refugees by stating that the General Assembly:

> Resolves that the refugees wishing to return to their homes and live at peace with their neighbours should be permitted to do so at the earliest practicable date, and that compensation should be paid for the property of those choosing not to return and for the loss of or damage to property which, under principles of international law or in equity, should be made good by the Governments or authorities responsible.[5]

This resolution was voted upon every single year since 1948, but although it was reaffirmed annually until 1993, the year of the Oslo agreement, it was never implemented.

The right of return, as defined in resolution 194, became a rallying cry for grassroots organising throughout the 1990s and especially after the failure of the Camp David meeting, which was in effect, a failure of Oslo in July 2000.[6] An international solidarity movement, which

---

[2] For a discussion of these plans, see Aruri 1995 and 2003.
[3] For a discussion of the Oslo Accords, see Beilin 1999; Said 2000; Watson 2000.
[4] G.A. Res. 194, U.N. Doc. A/810, at 21 (1948).
[5] See partial text in Aruri 1983: 94–95.
[6] See Aruri 2003: Chapter 10.

had been working on behalf of the Palestinian cause since the early 1970s, and which had to step aside after the 'historic hand-shake' of Arafat and Rabin in September 1993, came back after the failure of Oslo in 2000, hoping to succeed where governments failed in ameliorating the plight of the Palestinians, particularly the refugees. This study will trace the developments which led to the present situation, where the fulfilment of the right of return seems more remote than ever, and where civil society assumes a more active role in the struggle for refugee rights.

An historical overview

In 1948, between 750,000 and 800,000 Palestinians, about 83 percent of the population, became refugees.[7] An additional 320,000 Palestinians became refugees as a result of the 1967 war.[8] There are today 5 million refugees, of whom, 3.7 million are registered with the United Nations Relief and Works Agency (UNRWA), and 1.3 million unregistered refugees.[9] Since the 1948 Palestinian Catastrophe *(al-Nakba)*[10] and its concomitant creation of the Palestinian refugee crisis, the issues of return, compensation, and restitution have taken a back seat to the discussions surrounding the overall question of Palestinian statehood.

During most of the past five decades, the issue of refugees has been marginalized, despite the fact that Israel's admission to the United Nations was made contingent on its compliance with United Nations General Assembly Resolution 194 of December 1948.[11] General Assembly Resolution 273 of 11 May 1949 made Israel's admission conditional on Israel's unambiguous commitment to 'unreservedly' respect UN resolutions pertaining to the Arab-Israeli conflict, including Resolution 194.[12]

---

[7] For figures, causes, consequences and other details about the 1948 exodus, see Morris 1987; see also Palumbo 1987, Flapan 1987 and Pappé 1992.

[8] Harris (1980) estimates that the West Bank lost 250,000 of its inhabitants, while the Gaza Strip's population lost 70,000.

[9] For details about the refugees, their villages, those registered with the United Nations Relief and Work Agency (UNRWA) and those who are unregistered, see Abu-Sitta 1998; see also UNRWA home page *at*: http://www.un.org/unrwa (accessed 22 March 2003).

[10] Also called the cataclysm, the events of that year included the mass deportation of Palestinians from their homes, massacres of civilians, and the levelling of hundreds of Palestinian villages. See generally Palumbo 1987.

[11] GA Resolution 194 (III) UN Doc. A/810 at 21 (1948); see also Mallison and Mallison 1979.

[12] G.A. Res. 273, U.N. Doc. A/RES/273 (III) (1949).

Israel was admitted to the United Nations without complying with its obligations to the Palestinian refugees, thus keeping alive and exacerbating the refugee crisis we face today. General Assembly Resolution 194 has been ritualistically reaffirmed numerous times.[13] Israel's non-compliance had impelled the General Assembly to adopt other resolutions calling on Israel to meet its obligations to the refugees. For example, Resolution 3236 of 22 November 1974 upheld the 'inalienable right of the Palestinians to return to their homes and property from which they have been displaced and uprooted.'[14] And in 1997, Resolution 52/62 reaffirmed that the 'Palestine Arab refugees are entitled to their property and to the income derived therefrom, in conformity with the principles of justice and equity.'[15]

With the emergence of the Palestine Liberation Organization (PLO) and the resumption of armed struggle during the 1960s, the issue of the refugees, rather than becoming the central human dimension of the revolutionaries' struggle to reverse the *Nakba*, was relegated to a humanitarian, charitable issue better left to organizations such as UNRWA. The Palestinian national movement declared its objective in 1968 as the creation of a single democratic secular state in all of Palestine, in which Muslims, Christians and Jews would live on the basis of equality before the law. In that setting, the Palestinian national movement assumed that the refugees would exercise their right of return, and be naturally accommodated in the future unitary state.

The 1967 war exacerbated the refugee crisis by creating a new generation of refugees. At the same time, the refugee crisis completely disappeared from the PLO agenda. The overarching objective of the PLO became global recognition of its status as sole legitimate representative of the Palestine people.[16] The PLO, however, perceived the plight of the refugees as a distraction from the 'important' issues. True, the refugees remained a humanitarian concern, but only to showcase the 'social' institutions, which the PLO built in Lebanon during the

---

[13] See Aruri 1983: 94–95.

[14] G.A. Res. 3236, U.N. XXIX 13th Sess., at 1(b)2 (1974). See also Aruri 1983: 95–96.

[15] G.A. Res. 52/62, U.N. Doc. A/RES/52/62, at sec. 1 (1997). For further information on restitution, see Kubursi 2001. See also Akram 2001. On restitution, see Kubursi 2001.

[16] For example, the Arab states meeting at summit conferences in Algiers in 1972 and Rabat, Morocco in 1974 recognized the PLO as the sole, legitimate representative of the Palestinian people. By the end of the 1970s, the PLO was recognized as such by most members of the non-aligned movement in the United Nations and the Communist bloc.

1970s, an infrastructure of a state-in-waiting.[17] Yet from the perspective of political rights, the refugee question continued to lack any political content and force.[18]

After 1972, as the armed struggle further gave way to a new form of diplomatic work, the refugee question became dormant. The arrangements formulated in Arab summit conferences in Algiers, Rabat, and Cairo during the mid-seventies, encouraged the PLO to promote itself with a programme of 'self-determination' in a mini-Palestinian state in the West Bank and Gaza, which constituted less than 22 percent of pre-1948 Palestine. In return for supporting the 'new' PLO, with such watered-down objectives, the Arab governments demanded an unwritten *quid pro quo*. The PLO would drastically scale down its guerrilla operations and cease its rhetoric about a democratic secular state in all of historic Palestine. In return, not only would the PLO be 'rewarded' with Arab diplomatic support in far-flung countries, but the Arab governments would also increase economic assistance to the organisation.

For the following two decades, this unwritten agreement, and the search for a 'two-state solution', would consume the combined energies of Palestinians and Arabs. The PLO quest for international recognition, both as the sole legitimate representative of the Palestinian people and as a solid bargaining partner for the creation of a mini-state, claimed the largest portion of Arab and Palestinian energies. This came at the expense of refugee rights and interests. And while the PLO achieved its goal of becoming the focal point of the Palestine question, ironically, in 1993 it became the first Arab party to sign an agreement that effectively deferred the internationally recognised refugee rights.[19] More drastically, it agreed in the meetings in 2000 at Camp David not to insist on the right of return.

The joint Arab-Palestinian pursuit of the two-state solution was never taken seriously by the United States and Israel, yet it was exploited by them repeatedly in their own attempts to marginalise the refugee issue and remove it from the active diplomatic agenda. The United States

---

[17] See Rubenberg 1983.

[18] See Aruri 2001, which describes the marginalization of the refugee issues in PLO-Arab dealings.

[19] See 'Declaration of Principles on Interim Self-Government Arrangements', 13 September 1993 signed by Israel and PLO, available at http://www.us-israel.org/jsource/peace/dop.html (accessed 22 March 2003).

assumed the role of chief arbiter, if not sole peacemaker in the Middle East since 1972.[20] All other would-be conciliators, including the United Nations, were held at bay. Indeed, the Arab-Israeli conflict was one of the very few that was effectively removed from the international arena of conflict resolution.

An overview of US policy towards the refugee question

The Palestine policy of the US in the 1940s can be described as inconsistent, if not altogether incoherent, vacillating between acknowledging self-determination for the Palestinians, and, alternatively, justifying its denial by colonial-settler Jews and a Palestinian Jewish minority. Until 1947, the State Department had acknowledged the Palestinians' rights to self-determination. But the US government lobbied strongly for the United Nations' partition plan,[21] which denied that right by proposing the establishment of a Jewish state in 55 percent of Palestine and an Arab state in 43.5 percent,[22] despite the fact that the Jews constituted less than one-third of the population and owned no more than 6 percent of the total land. By 1948, the US began to float the idea of replacing the partition plan with a UN trusteeship under Chapter XII of the UN Charter. When the partition plan failed to materialise, and the Zionist militias prevailed over the Palestinian resistance and the Arab fighters who came haphazardly to their defence, US policy began to shift towards support of a Jordanian take-over of the 22 percent of Palestine that did not fall under Israeli control. Jordan was also encouraged to absorb most of the refugees who were the victims of Zionist ethnic cleansing in 1948.

At the same time, the United States took an active part in drafting General Assembly Resolution 194 of 11 December 1948, stating that those 'refugees wishing to return to their homes and live in peace with their neighbours should be permitted to do so at the earliest practicable date.'[23] That resolution, which also called for compensation and restitution, established the United Nations Conciliation Commission on Palestine

---

[20] See Aruri 2003, especially Chapters 2 and 3.
[21] G.A. Res. 181(II), U.N. GAOR, at 131-132, U.N. Doc. A/310 (1947).
[22] G.A. Res. 181(II), U.N. GAOR, at 131-132, U.N. Doc. A/310 (1947).
[23] G.A. Res. 194(III), U.N. GAOR, at 24, U.N. Doc. A/810 (1948).

(UNCCP),[24] to help in economic rehabilitation, and to provide legal protection (Tadmor 1994).

Israel, however, proceeded to make its own rules despite the fact that its admission to the UN was linked to its own compliance with UN resolutions, particularly Resolution 194. Israel decreed that a comprehensive settlement in the region must precede any discussion of the refugee question. The Truman administration set a precedent by accommodating that position, thus allowing Israel to set the pace in Middle East policy. Despite expressing some misgivings about Israel's handling of the refugees, Truman approved an Israeli plan to repatriate about 100,000 on the basis of family reunification. The Truman administration also attempted to settle about 100,000 Palestinian refugees in Iraq. Resettlement of the refugees in Arab countries became effectively an American policy goal and remains so to the present, despite a *pro forma* endorsement of Resolution 194 on an annual basis at the General Assembly (Lee 1986: 532, 535). By late March 1949, the US administration announced that the refugee problem was problematic, and President Truman and Secretary of State Acheson announced that:

From the political point of view, the stabilization of the Near East is a major objective of American foreign policy. The refugee problem, therefore, as a focal point for continued unrest within the Arab states, a source of continuing friction between Israel and the Arabs, and a likely channel for Soviet exploitation, is directly related to our national interests (in Lawson 1995: 75).

Yet the administration failed to insist that Israel comply with the UN resolution, not only for the sake of legality, but also for the sake of US strategic interests.

By the time Lyndon B Johnson inherited the presidency, the refugee question had been down-graded in US policy planning, which veered much closer to the Israeli position of resettling the refugees in Arab countries. In fact, the Israeli position of 'resettlement' was incorporated into the platform of the Democratic Party on which Johnson was elected in 1964. The important new reality affecting US policy towards the refugee question was the Arab-Israeli war of June 1967 and

---

[24] See Akram 2001. Resolution 194 established the Conciliation Commission for Palestine composed of three member states: France, Turkey and the United States. The commission was given broad authority to carry out the functions previously entrusted to the UN Mediator, Count Folke Bernadotte, who was assassinated by the Jewish Stern Gang. See also Mallison and Mallison 1986: 177-79.

the new issues created by that war. The defeat of Arab armies in only six days elevated the role of Palestinian resistance to new heights, and shifted the focus away from the refugee issue, now deemed a charitable, humanitarian matter that paled next to the issue of PLO recognition.

After the 1967 War, any proposals emanating from Washington would address the refugee question in a mere ritualistic manner. The impact of that approach was to relegate the whole Palestine issue to the sidelines, while trying to find an acceptable Arab-Israeli formula based on land for peace. Consequently, the Palestinian right of return was subordinated to resolving issues that divided states in order to minimise the chances of a wider conflict with global ramifications.

A new chapter in the marginalization of the Palestinians' right of return came under President Jimmy Carter, who began his reassessment of Middle East policy with a specific reference to the Palestinian people who 'suffered so much and who were in need of a home.'[25] Ironically, however, Carter's 1978 Camp David peace plan redefined the refugees' right of return, in the words of the late Fayez Sayegh, as a *selective* privilege of readmission (see Sayegh 1979: 3, and Sayegh 1982: 24-25, 16-17). Carter's proposed 'self-governing authority,' together with Egypt, Israel, and Jordan, was empowered to decide on the modalities for admission of persons *displaced* from the West Bank and Gaza in 1967. As for the 1948 refugees, the Camp David plan merely called for a 'just solution,' with no mention of what that might entail.[26] The Palestinian dimension of Carter's Middle East policy was abandoned in favour of a separate peace between Israel and Egypt.

Although the PLO legitimately controlled representation of the Palestinian people for over ten years, and struggled for national self-determination with the support of a global consensus and UN General Assembly resolutions, Ronald Reagan considered Palestine as a problem of *mere* refugees. He also considered the PLO to be a terrorist organization, enrolled in the service of the 'evil empire'.[27]

---

[25] For discussion of the contents of Carter's 1972 speech regarding reassessment of Middle East Policy see Interview with Carter at http://www.gwu.edu/~nsarchiv/coldwar/interviews/episode-18/carter1.html.

[26] See Camp David Agreements, 17 September 1978, Egypt-Israel-U.S., 17 I.L.M. 1466 (signing 'A Framework for Peace in the Middle East'), available at http://www.israel-mfa.gov.il/mfa/go.asp?MFAH0f1z0.

[27] See Schultz 1985. For a comparison between the Sandanistas, the PLO, and Libyans see Boyd 1986.

From the outset of his administration, Reagan exempted Israel from the responsibility for the plight of the refugees, placing most of the burden of redress on Jordan, in accordance with the ideology espoused by revisionist Zionists, which assumes that a Palestinian state already exists in Jordan, notwithstanding the fact that the United Nations had divided Palestine, west of the River Jordan, in 1947 into a Palestinian Arab state and a Jewish state.[28] According to revisionist Zionist thinking, the former Palestine Mandate given to Britain by the League of Nations after World War I included all the area lying to the east of the River Jordan (now Jordan).

Reagan made only one reference to the question of refugees in his 1982 plan: 'The departure of the Palestinians from Beirut dramatizes more than ever the homelessness of the Palestinian people. Palestinians feel strongly that their cause is more than a question of refugees. I agree.'[29] Despite that agreement, however, Reagan later ordered his UN ambassador to reject a General Assembly resolution condemning the perpetrators of the massacre of Sabra and Shatila, and resolving that the Palestinian people should be enabled to return to their homes and property, in accordance with previous resolutions. The United States was joined by one other state: Israel.

With the advent of the Bush Administration, all attention was focused on Iraq and subsequently on the Madrid Conference of October 1991, with much of the emphasis being placed on an Israeli-Palestinian deal based on Carter's 1978 Camp David peace plan notion of Palestinian autonomy. Throughout the four years that Bush and Baker were at the helm, Israel and its US domestic supporters succeeded in placing Bush

---

[28] The founder of Revisionist Zionism, Ze'ev Jabotinsky wrote an article in 1923 entitled *The Iron Wall*, in which he wrote that Zionism should endeavour to bring about a Jewish state in the whole land of Israel (meaning Jordan and Palestine), regardless of the Arab response. See Flapan 1979: 117.

[29] The full text of the Reagan Plan is available at http://www.us-israel.org/jsource/Peace/reaganplan.html (accessed 22 March 2003). The departure of PLO military and civilian personnel from Lebanon in the autumn of 1982 was arranged by US Ambassador Philip Habib after the Israeli invasion of June 1982. The United States worked out an agreement between Israel and the PLO, whereby the besieged Arafat forces were given safe exit, and US guarantees of the safety of their dependents left behind. Despite that, however, Israel's right-wing Lebanese allies entered the Palestinian refugee camps of Sabra and Shatila on 16, 17 and 18 September and committed a massacre under Israel's watchful eyes. The largely civilian victims numbered between 2,500 and 3,000. Defence Minister Ariel Sharon was accused of 'indirect responsibility' by his own country's Kahan Commission, which was organized to investigate the massacres committed while Israel was occupying Lebanon.

on the defensive when a controversy erupted over the 10 billion dollar loan guarantees, which the Administration decided to link to the issue of building Jewish settlements in the occupied sector of the city of Jerusalem.[30] The issue of refugees remained dormant, if not tertiary, during the senior Bush's presidency.

Clinton continued Bush's policy of malign neglect of the refugee issue, but went further than any other previous president in embracing Israel's conditions overall on the question of Palestine. For example, a State Department White Paper dated 30 June 1993 entitled 'Declaration of Principles' implied that the US now considered the West Bank and Gaza to be 'disputed' rather than occupied territory.[31] When Clinton presided at the Oslo signing, on 13 September 1993, it became clear the refugee issue was in fact relegated to a 'final status' issue, not to be considered until after five years of a 'transition' period.[32] By the summit meeting at Camp David in July 2000, the most that refugees could realistically hope for was limited and regulated repatriation to the Palestinian entity, but not to their homes and certainly not to property in present-day Israel.[33] The latter, if available at all, would have only been open to token numbers and strictly in accord with what Israel would be willing to designate as 'family reunification'.[34] Barak's 'generosity' on the refugee issue at Camp David 2000 extended to allowing 4,000 refugees to enter what is now Israel each year within the framework of what he called *family reunions*, not the 'right of return': 'We cannot allow even one refugee back on the basis of the "right of return"… and we cannot accept historical responsibility for the creation of the problem.' [35]

Palestinian civil society and the refugees

Despite the exceedingly numerous meetings between Palestinian and Israeli negotiators held during the seven years since the signing of the

---

[30] For details of the controversy, see Aruri 1995: 273-75, 326-29.

[31] This Declaration of Principles should not be confused with the DOP, which refers to the Oslo Accords signed in the White House Rose Garden on 13 September 1993 by Israeli Prime Minister Rabin and Palestinian leader Yasir Arafat. For a discussion of the State Department DOP, see Aruri 1995: 333-35.

[32] For more details on Oslo and the refugee issue, see Aruri 2003: Chapters 6 and 10.

[33] For details on Camp David and the issue of refugees see Aruri 2003: 172-77.

[34] See Grech 2002.

[35] For relevant details about this issue, see Morris 2002.

Oslo accords, the input of the community of five million Palestinian refugees has never been sought. When the right of return began to resurface as a top item on the Palestinian people's agenda around 1999–2000, the role of the Palestinian Authority was minimal. In fact, the issue was placed on the public agenda not by the Palestinian Authority or by the PLO, but by various segments of Palestinian civil society.[36] In particular, grassroots organizations, new and old alike, seized the initiative by restoring the right of return to a central place in the discourse about Palestine.[37]

For example, on 16 September 2000, two demonstrations attended by several thousand activists were held simultaneously in Washington, DC, and London to promote the right of return. During the same period, similar demonstrations, most of which coincided with the eighteenth anniversary of the 1982 massacres at the Sabra and Shatila camps in Lebanon, were also staged in the Lebanese refugee camps, and in Palestine. Numerous conferences, workshops, and rallies were held in and outside the region since 2000, bringing together community leaders, activists, and scholars to discuss various strategies for reviving the right of return. Such gatherings, mass rallies, symposia, and public protests have been repeated numerous times in various cities and refugee camps in the region and around the world. Their leaders have vowed to continue such non-governmental actions until the right of return is dealt with in a fair and legal manner in any future settlement. The whole endeavour seems like a public reminder that the failure of the governments and the United Nations to produce any justice for the refugees made it incumbent on civil society to step in on behalf of the Palestinian refugees.

---

[36] The Palestinian Authority was created as a transitional government for the Palestinians by the Oslo Accord. It consisted of a council, and a chief executive who did not merit the title of president, but, rather, the Arabic title *ra'is*, which means chief, but not president with executive powers. The role of the PA was to administer the Occupied Territories during the transitional period. It was representative of Palestinians living in the Occupied Territories but not of the refugees. The PLO, on the other hand, had evolved into the national address of the Palestinian people as a whole. See Aruri 1995: Chapter 9.

[37] Among these organizations is the BADIL Resource Center for Palestinian Residency and Refugee Rights in Bethlehem, at http://www.badil.org (accessed 22 March 2003); A'idun ('We Will Return') in Lebanon and Syria; SHAML, The Palestinian Diaspora and Refugee Centre in Jerusalem, at http://www.shaml.org/ (accessed 22 March 2003); and Al-Awda (The Return) in the United States, at http://www.al-awda.org (accessed 22 March 2003).

Israel and the refugee question

If there were ever the slightest hope that the refugees could possibly attain even a modicum of their internationally recognised rights within the context of the Oslo framework, such hopes have been absolutely dashed. Under the unwritten rules of the 'peace process,' now defunct as a result of the September 2000 Palestinian *Intifada*, Sharon's inflexibility, and Bush's scant attention to Middle East diplomacy, it would be considered a sign of intransigence if Arafat, or any of his negotiators, were to bring up the right of return, Resolutions 194, or the 29 November 1947 Partition Resolution.[38]

For Israelis across the ideological spectrum, including members of the so-called peace camp, the return of refugees constitutes a clear and present danger, a real demographic threat to an exclusive Jewish state. Since they insist that their state remain exclusively Jewish, juridically and otherwise, such a position, although illegal and immoral, is nevertheless consistent with the Zionist framework of the state. The Palestinian refugees' right of return to their previous homes and property now in Israel is not only absent from the public Israeli agenda, and from the consciousness of the Israeli Jewish public, but it is also opposed by Israel's peace movement. For example, thirty-three prominent members of the Israeli Jewish peace movement addressed a message to the 'Palestinian Leadership' in a front-page advertisement in the Israeli daily *Ha'aretz*, saying in part:

> We recognize the true and urgent need to resolve the problem of the 1948 refugees, and we recognize the part of the State of Israel, also, in the creation of the problem. The refugees will have the right to return to their homeland, Palestine, and settle there. But, we want to clarify that we shall never be able to agree to the return of the refugees to within the borders of Israel, for the meaning of such a return would be the elimination of the State of Israel (*Ha'aretz*, 2 January 2001).

One of the signatories, the noted writer Amos Oz, wrote an article in the *New York Times*, 'Let Palestinians Govern Palestinians—

---

[38] See 'Bush and Sharon: Defining the Path', in Aruri 2003: Chapter 11.

Now', in which he praised Barak's government for offering to let the Palestinians govern themselves, while describing the Palestinian Authority as the real 'obstacle for peace' because it had raised the issue of the right of return:

> Implementing the Palestinian 'right of return' would amount to abolishing the Jewish people's right to self-determination. It would eventually make the Jewish people no more than an ethnic minority in the country, just as fundamentalist Islam would have it (Oz 2001).

The Israeli public seems united in its rejection of international law as it pertains to the rights of the Palestinian refugees. Thus, of all the issues to be addressed in Oslo's final round of negotiations labelled by the parties as 'final status negotiations'—borders, Jerusalem, settlements, water, refugees—the question of the refugees is certainly the most arduous.

From the point of view of the Palestinians, the conflict with Israel emerged in 1948, when Jewish/Israeli forces conquered nearly three quarters of Palestine (72 percent), and expelled, or caused 80 percent of the Palestinian population of the territory under its control to flee. Palestinian demand for repatriation includes return to their villages and towns inside Israel. In most instances they will not be able to return to their homes and towns as these have been razed by Israel. After the conquest of the rest of Palestine (the West Bank and Gaza) in 1967, Israel initiated a policy and practice of building Jewish colonial settlements on confiscated land in the 1967 Occupied Territories. Thus, over the years, Palestine has been reformed and reshaped little by little. Even if Palestinians return, they are not returning to the homeland of their expectations. Instead, Palestinian refugees would return to a homeland as defined by those who displaced them in the first place.

Since 1967, Israel's approach to the 'peace process' (before Sharon assumed power in 2001), was partially based on the notion that the conflict began in 1967 and not in 1948. Paradoxically, the 1967 borders, known as 'the green line', have continually been eroded by the insatiable appetite of successive Israeli governments for settlements. That ever-elusive 'green line' has, in effect, ceased to exist. Now, while Sharon is in his second administration, the conflict is being viewed in Israel as having started in October 2000, when the *Intifada* is presumed to have

shattered the *status quo*. Not only is the refugee issue absent from the table, but more refugees will be created as a result of Israel's Apartheid Wall, which is separating Palestinian communities from each other and from their land.[39]

Internal refugees

The refugees also include 'internal refugees', i.e., those Palestinians who live in the area in which the Jewish state was established in 1948, who can see their land, but cannot live on it, or make use of it. They are what Israel refers to as 'present absentees'. Many of these present absentees live in what are referred to as 'unrecognized villages', a term deriving from the fact that they cannot be found on any official map. They receive no municipal services, despite the fact that their inhabitants are Israeli citizens who pay the same taxes as all other Israelis. They are not entitled to water, electricity, schools, health facilities, or paved roads. The present absentees, including the citizens of unrecognized villages, certainly qualify for refugee status. Palestinian citizens of Israel who are internally displaced from their homes and villages—politically recognised, but legally denied their rights—number between 150,000 and 200,000. For example, the residents and home owners of two border villages, Iqrit and Kufr Bar'am, are not allowed to return to their homes, or work their agricultural lands, and have been forced to live elsewhere in Israel since 1948. The villagers and their descendants have attempted to pressure the Israeli government to permit their return, but to no avail.

The internal refugees constitute a significant sector of the Palestinian community who carry Israeli citizenship in Galilee, Negev, and in what are known as the 'mixed' cities (i.e., cities where there is not Jewish hegemony, such as the Haifa and Lydda areas) (Nir 2001). About half of Nazareth's Arab residents are internal refugees and their descendants, while more than half of Umm al-Fahm's residents belong to this group.[40]

Conscious of Arafat's propensity for making repeated concessions (see Farsoun and Zacharia 1997: 253-317), these internal refugees have

---

[39] See www.stopthewall.org.

[40] Ori Nir cites the work of Hebrew University professor Hillel Cohen, who put the number of the abandoned villages at 162 (Nir 2001).

organised themselves, and refused to have the Palestinian Authority assume responsibility for their future. According to the Israeli writer Ori Nir and Attorney Wakim Wakim (Secretary of the National Council for the Defence of the Rights of Displaced Persons in Israel), Arafat and his colleagues do not wish to have the present absenteea incorporate their cases into the 'peace' talks. Instead, they want the internal refugees themselves to wage their own legal, public, and political struggle within the framework of the State of Israel:

> We [internal refugees] don't want a situation to arise in which we end up being forgotten, and not included in an arrangement on the refugee problem. On the other hand, if such an arrangement is one in which the Palestinian leadership makes concessions about our basic rights, we wouldn't want any linkage between the diplomatic negotiations and our struggle as Israel[i] citizens (see Nir 2001).

More than a year after Wakim expressed this lack of confidence in the Palestinian leadership, Yasir Arafat reaffirmed an earlier concession on the right of return in a *New York Times* piece:

> In addition, we seek a fair and just solution to the plight of Palestinian refugees who for 54 years have not been permitted to return to their homes. We understand Israel's demographic concerns and understand that the right of return of Palestinian refugees, a right guaranteed under international law and United Nations Resolution 194, must be implemented in a way that takes into account such concerns. However, just as we Palestinians must be realistic with respect to Israel's demographic desires, Israelis too must be realistic in understanding that there can be no solution to the Israeli–Palestinian conflict if the legitimate rights of these innocent civilians continue to be ignored. Left unresolved, the refugee issue has the potential to undermine any permanent peace agreement between Palestinians and Israelis. How is a Palestinian refugee to understand that his or her right of return will not be honored but those of

Kosovar Albanians, Afghans and East Timorese have been? (Arafat 2002)

It must also be kept in mind that new refugees continue to be created by Israel's campaign of territorial domination in and around Jerusalem, underway since 1967, which continues to escalate. Residency cards are confiscated at will, and building permits are all but absolutely denied to Palestinians in all parts of the West Bank. This includes 'greater Jerusalem', a concept that has no juridical meaning and would appear to be a euphemism for Jewish land expansion and ownership via expropriation, eminent domain policies, and other methods of land domination. For example, Palestinian homes are being demolished on a wholesale basis. The bulldozer is the most lethal instrument of war against the Palestinian people (as it was in 1948).

The Palestinian Authority and the refugees: the Beilin-Abu Mazen Agreement

In the aftermath of the Israeli-Palestinian Interim Agreement on the West Bank and Gaza, concluded on 24 September 1995 (known as Oslo II), which divided the West Bank into three zones (A, B and C), Israel and the Palestinian Authority began to study possible modalities for a framework for the final status issues as mandated by the Declaration of Principles (DOP) from the Oslo Accords of 1993. A secret agreement was forged between Arafat's next-in-line (Mahmoud Abbas, known as Abu Mazen) and Yossi Beilin (a Meretz bloc leader close to Shimon Peres),[41] which envisaged solutions to the refugees question and other final status issues (the Beilin-Abu Mazen agreement). That agreement, however, was pushed to the sidelines due to the failure of Shimon Peres in his bid for re-election in the spring of 1996. The resurfacing of the agreement and the publication of the full text in *Newsweek Magazine* in September 2000 came in the wake of the unsuccessful Camp David talks in July 2000.

Dated 13 October 1995, this agreement, entitled 'Framework for the Conclusion of "A Final Status Agreement"' between Israel and

---

[41] Meretz is a left-liberal political group in Israel.

The Palestine Liberation Organization' (Framework Agreement), was regarded by its two authors (Beilin and Abu Mazen) as the document paving the way for a 'lasting and comprehensive peace.' Its importance was due strictly to the identity of its authors who at the time wielded considerable influence in the Israeli and Palestinian political spheres, but it had no legal standing whatsoever.

The 'Framework Agreement' was deemed essential in the sense that it declared 'null and void any agreement, declaration, document or statement which contradicts this Framework Agreement.' *Ipso facto*, presumably, it nullifies not only UN General Assembly Resolution 194,[42] but also all other international instruments and provisions of refugee law, human rights law, and humanitarian law in which refugee rights are enshrined, including Article 13 of the Universal Declaration On Human Rights,[43] as well as the 1949 Fourth Geneva Convention.[44] Article 13 provides, 'Everyone has the right to leave any country, including his own, and to return to his country.'[45] Moreover, the Beilin-Abu Mazen agreement also negates fundamental rights guaranteed by former agreements. For example, it appears that the provision of the International Covenant on Civil and Political Rights that 'no one shall be arbitrarily deprived of the right to enter his own country'[46] was eliminated, as was the provision of the International Convention on the Elimination of All Forms of Racial Discrimination that a state may not deny, on racial or ethnic grounds, the opportunity 'to return to one's country'.[47]

Surely, it does not take much legal research to discover that what Abu Mazen had signed on behalf of the five million refugees relinquishes fundamental rights that are well-established in numerous international instruments. Such instruments are well known to international

---

[42] See note 4 above.

[43] G.A. Res. 217A (III) (1948), available at http://www.un.org/Overview/rights/ (accessed 22 March 2003).

[44] Convention (IV) Relative to the Protection of Civilian Persons in Time of War (1949), available at http://www.us-israel.org/jsource/History/Human_Rights/geneva1/html (accessed 22 March 2003).

[45] G.A. Res. 217A (III)—see note 43 above.

[46] G.A. Res. 2200A (XVI), 21 U.N. GAOR, Supp. No. 16, at 52, U.N. Doc. A/6316 (1966), 999 U.N.T.S. 171 (1976), available at http://www1.umn.edu/humanrts/instree/b3ccpr.htm (accessed 22 March 2003).

[47] International Convention on the Elimination of All Forms of Racial Discrimination, 660 U.N.T.S. 195 (1969), available at http://www1.umn.edu/humanrts/instree/d1cerd.htm (accessed 22 March 2003).

lawyers and international law students everywhere. It is hard to imagine that they are not known to Abu Mazen.

Section I of Article VII of the Beilin–Abu Mazen 'Framework Agreement' requires the Palestinian side to reconsider the refugees' rights under international law in light of the changing realities on the ground since 1948:

> Whereas the Palestinian side considers that the right of the Palestinian Refugees to return to their homes is enshrined in international law and natural justice, it recognizes that the prerequisites of the new era of peace and coexistence, as well as the realities that have been created on the ground since 1948 have rendered the implementation of this right impracticable. The Palestinian side, thus, declares its readiness to accept and implement policies and measures that will ensure, insofar as this is possible, the welfare and well being of these refugees.[48]

Clearly, it must not have occurred to Abu Mazen, himself a refugee but now accustomed to luxurious living, that the 'welfare and well being' of 'these refugees', who constitute 63 percent of the eight million Palestinians in the world,[49] include their right of return, like all other refugees in the world.

In Section 2 of Article VII of the Beilin–Abu Mazen 'Framework Agreement', Israel acknowledges 'the moral and material suffering caused to the Palestinian people as a result of the war of 1947–1949,'[50] but in practice Israel accepts neither legal nor moral responsibility for that 'suffering'. In conformity with Oslo I, the Beilin–Abu Mazen framework removes the burden of redress from Israel: '[Israel] further acknowledges the Palestinian refugees' right of return to the Palestinian state and their right to compensation and rehabilitation for moral and material losses.'[51] The right of return as articulated by international law is, therefore, declared null and void in this clause, inasmuch as its implementation falls on the

---

[48] Text available at http://www.bitterlemons.org/docs/bielinmazen.html (accessed 22 March 2003).

[49] See, e.g., http://www.badil.org/statistics/population/pop1.htm (accessed 22 March 2003).

[50] See note 48 above.

[51] See note 48 above.

shoulders of the Palestinian Authority, with Israel shirking any and all of *its* responsibility (recognised by numerous international instruments) for the plight of the refugees. Moreover, according to the agreement, the right to compensation and restitution, another Israeli responsibility under United Nations resolutions, was to be dealt with, according to this framework, by a specially created International Commission for Palestinian Refugees (ICPR). The proposed commission was charged with responsibilities to fundraise, distribute payments, adjudicate between claims disputes, and to develop rehabilitation and absorption programmes. Its decisions would be final and subject to no appeal.

The ICPR would, in effect, shield Israel from its obligations under international law, and look elsewhere for means of redress. It would also protect Israel from any international litigation process. The Palestinian 'state', truncated as it may be, the Arab states, and international donors are, in effect, summoned by this framework agreement to assume Israel's liabilities. Not only would this obstruction of the judicial process be unusual and improper, but also its mechanisms are unlikely to provide the refugees reasonable redress. Their right of return to their homes and property would have been forever surrendered, and the most Israel would be willing to do would be to admit into Israel proper less than 100,000 refugees, strictly on a 'humanitarian basis' and under 'full peace conditions' (peace, that is, as defined by the victor).

Former Israeli Prime Minister Ehud Barak confirmed the gist of the Beilin-Abu Mazen framework as he was departing for the negotiations of Camp David 2000. He assured the Israeli public in a published message that Israel's 'red lines' included the right of return: 'Israel will not recognize any moral or legal responsibility for the Palestinian refugee problem.'[52]

Just as President Clinton was preparing to hand over the presidency to George W Bush, he proposed that both sides recognize the right of Palestinian refugees to return either to 'historic Palestine' or to 'their homeland'.[53] However, under the Clinton proposal, there was no specific right of return to what is now Israel. Instead, the refugees would have been forced to choose to go to the 'State of Palestine', that is, to the

---

[52] In *Yediot Aharonot*, 11 July 2000.

[53] The text was distributed by the Office of International Information Programs, U.S. Department of State, and is available at http://usinfo.state.gov (accessed 22 March 2003).

areas in one of the proposed 'land swap' schemes under discussion at that time, or to be resettled in Arab and/or other countries.

Current attempts to liquidate the right of return

The right of return has been one of the major stumbling blocks to a political settlement based on mutual recognition and self-determination for both people. Renewed attempts to continue that process by the Sharon government and Washington, with the implicit support of Arab and European governments anxious for an implementation of the so-called Road Map, have entered a new and serious phase. Emboldened by the occupation of Iraq and the prospects for a new US strategic hegemony in the region and beyond, the Bush-Sharon Axis seems poised to deliver a knock-out punch to any Palestinian insistence that refugee rights are an integral part of a peace settlement in Palestine.

The attempts to dilute and undermine the right of return have recently enlisted supporters in the compliant circles of the Palestinian leadership as well as key community activists in Palestine and elsewhere. Israeli and US insistence on linking any return to the negotiations table to a Palestinian agreement to appoint an 'empowered' prime minister who would 'dismantle the terrorist infrastructure', a term denigrating legitimate for Palestinian resistance, is based on an expectation that the right of return, among other basic components designated as final status issues, would be surrendered for the sake of a settlement. In fact, that surrender was one of fourteen reservations delineated by Sharon's cabinet as a condition for accepting the Road Map. Even Abu Mazin, who was seen as a Palestinian Karzi, or 'the Chalabi of Palestine', and who renounced the right of return in his agreement with Yossi Beilin, was not deemed capable of granting Israel the total surrender it desired.

The revival of the 'Ayalon-Nusseibeh Initiative' for a two-state solution, for Palestinians and Jews, instead of Palestinians and Israelis, makes Israel the state of the Jewish people rather than a state of its own citizens. Regarding the question of refugees and Israel's original sin in 1948, the document refers to the suffering of the Palestinians without mentioning Israel's part in creating that suffering:

Recognizing the suffering and the plight of the Palestinian refugees, the international community, Israel, and the Palestinian State will initiate and contribute to an international fund to compensate them.

Thus the 'recognition' of Israel's acts of ethnic cleansing, and the terrible catastrophe inflicted on an entire people becomes an international, even a Palestinian responsibility, rather than that of the perpetrator. The document, moreover, writes off individual rights of Palestinian refugees and disingenuously tries to find symmetry where symmetry does not exist:

Palestinian refugees will return only (*sic*) to the State of Palestine; Jews will return (*sic*) only to the State of Israel ... The international community will offer to compensate toward bettering the lot of those refugees willing to remain on their present countries.[54]

Meanwhile, it is certainly not coincidental that a series of workshops was organised recently by the British Royal Institute for International Affairs (RIIA) and the Center of Lebanese Studies on the Palestinian Refugee Question. The EU and Canada have at least partially funded these workshops, which are intended to undermine the right of return. Additionally, the Palestinian Center for Policy and Survey Research (PRS) published a major poll on 16 July 2003, claiming that the refugees themselves were no longer supporting the right of return, opting instead for meagre compensations.[55] The author of the poll, Dr Khalil Shikaki, was physically assaulted by refugees who converged on his Ramallah office, just as he was getting ready to announce the results to the media. Shikaki was accused of directing the kind of questions that would yield the answers he desired. Instead of giving the respondents the options that conform to international law and Resolution 194, Shikaki asked them to choose between

---

[54] See the discussion in Yehudith Harel, 'Holy Lands Peace & Justice—Urgent [Nusseibeh-Ayalon initiative support]' at http://list.haifa.ac.il/pipermail/alef/2003-March/000120.html (accessed 16 January 2004).
[55] *The Independent* (London) 16 July 2003.

—returning to Israel and obtaining Israeli citizenship,
—returning to an area in Israel that would then be swapped
with the Palestinian state,
—returning to the Palestinian state and obtaining citizenship
there, or
—resettlement in a third country with compensation.

His findings revealed that 54 percent of the respondents elected to live in a Palestinian state, while only 10 percent would live in Israel even with a Palestinian citizenship. According to the Badil Resource Center in occupied Bethlehem, an advocacy group for refugees, the refugees must be offered 'a free and educated choice between three major durable solutions: return + property restitution + compensation; integration in current host countries + property restitution + compensation; re-settlement in a third country + property restitution + compensation.'[56]

The most recent attempt to undermine the case of refugees is another unofficial agreement involving Yossi Beilin. This time, the Beilin-Abed Rabbo deal is equipped with an international sounding designation—the Geneva Accord—due, perhaps, to the fact that it was financed by Switzerland. It surfaced during October 2003, at a time of a crippling impasse, with Sharon having a free reign to kill, maim, destroy homes and farms, and build his wall, all in the name of fighting terror. This agreement, which has the blessings of Labour party luminaries, such as Amram Mitzna, Avraham Burg and author Amos Oz, as well as the implicit approval of Yasir Arafat and the younger Fatah leadership, does away completely and unequivocally with the right of return, giving Israel the prerogative of admitting whatever number of the refugees it deems tolerable. It is also interesting that during the last week of November 2003, a public opinion poll conducted by the Baker Institute at Rice University found that 53 and 56 percent respectively of Israelis and Palestinians support a peace accord along the lines of the proposed Geneva Agreement: two adjacent states, an almost total Israeli withdrawal from the territories occupied in 1967, division of sovereignty in Jerusalem, compensation for refugees, and an end to the conflict (see Rami Khouri 2003).

---

[56] Badil Resource Center, Bethlehem 15 July 2003. For a discussion of the Shikaki survey see http://www.shaml.org/ground/shukaki/ (accessed 16 January 2004).

Moreover the Palestinians would have to recognize Israel as a Jewish state and concede the major settlement blocs surrounding Jerusalem (Maale Adumim, Givat Zeev, and the Etzion Bloc)—all that in return for some sort of authority over the Jerusalem holy places. Despite that, however, the agreement incurred the wrath of Sharon, who accused the Israeli sponsors of being unauthorised agents who sacrifice Israel's security.[57]

Conclusion

The omission from Oslo's Declaration of Principles of the refugee question within the meaning of UN General Assembly Resolution 194 is the single most serious impediment to genuine redress of the refugees' grievances. It follows countless efforts by Israel and the United States throughout the past half century to utilise the peace process and other means for keeping the issue off the agenda. The Palestinian 'Legislative Council' created by Oslo, representing two million Palestinians living under Israeli occupation, will be neither able nor qualified to negotiate with Israel on the refugee question.

The creation of refugees in 1948 was intended to assure a permanent Jewish majority in the Jewish state. Today, more than a half century later, the overwhelming majority of Israelis consider the return of those refugees as a mortal danger, a demographic threat to Israel. Therefore, no change has occurred in the Zionist movement's reliance on ethnic cleansing as an instrument to insure that all of Palestine is its own domain, clean of non-Jews. Accordingly, the indigenous Palestinians can only be tolerated as a scattered minority living in enclaves under overall Jewish control. It was no accident that the Israeli architects of Oslo bestowed on Israel the control of 'external security', a euphemism for sovereignty. Nor was it a coincidence that the Palestinian Authority's Legislative Council and Arafat's executive were granted neither judicial nor legislative powers that could some day enable the Palestinians to enact a law of return of their own.

---

[57] See the Israeli Text and Context of the Geneva Accord (by Shiko Behar and Michael Warschawski) at http://www.merip.org/mero/mero112403.html.

The question of return has been marginalized also by the fact that it has already been considered by the DOP as a regional matter affecting *all* refugees, including Jews who left property in Arab countries. That is why both Camp David I (1978) and the DOP (1993) call for a committee consisting of Israel, Jordan, Egypt, and the Palestinian Council to settle that problem, with Israel retaining an effective veto.

We are now at a crucial juncture. The present Sharon government views 1948 as an incomplete phase that is perhaps now ready for completion, hence the campaign of the past three years to destroy the infrastructure of the Palestinian Authority and the institutions of civil society, together with the confiscation and destruction of Palestinian resources and property that might be in the way of the Zionist scheme of completion. Severe repression and economic strangulation are intended to make the Palestinians pursue 'voluntary transfer'. Standing in the way of the onslaught is the *Intifada inside* the Occupied Territories and the total refusal of the Palestinian diaspora and its supporters *outside* to renounce the right of return. The *Intifada*, which exacted a heavy toll on Palestinian society, has nevertheless demonstrated that Sharon has failed in his quest to offer security and prosperity. Meanwhile, outside, mobilising for refugee rights by NGOs and the International Solidarity Movement (ISM) has been a credible alternative to the empty rhetoric of organised governments and the failed legacy of the 'peace process'.

It is in this context that schemes such as those of Nusseibeh-Ayalon and Beilin-Abed Rabbo can be viewed. In such fashion, Sharon's detractors are using Palestinian figures and symbols to achieve goals similar to those which he himself has not been able to achieve for the Zionist movement. While Sharon tries to insure that a single sovereignty in the area lying between the Jordan and the Mediterranean Sea will be realised by brute force, Ayalon, Beilin *et al.* try to insure the same goal through offering the Palestinians a fractured existence, which their Palestinian interlocutors, together with the Quartet—US, UN, EU and Russia—can trumpet as a Palestinian state. Such a state might also fulfil the 'vision' of George W Bush, but it will not be the state that the Palestinians have struggled for, and are entitled to.

To foil these attempts, a truly representative Palestinian body, comprising all sectors—the refugee camps of Lebanon, Jordan, and Syria; from the West Bank and Gaza; from Israel proper; from the United States, Australia, and elsewhere—would have to bring together the

numerous endeavours on behalf of refugees, and reaffirm the refugees' rights under a single banner. This representative Palestinian body would re-establish the right of a reconstituted PLO to resolve the refugee question with Israel. Such a body, not Arafat's negotiators or Beilin's interlocutors, would decide which rights they would affirm and which, if any, they would relinquish. Such an enterprise would initiate the process of redress, the process of real confidence building, democratisation, and the process that could give a real voice to the voiceless.

References

Abu-Sitta, Salman H. 1998. *The Palestinian Nakba 1948. The Register of Depopulated Localities in Palestine* (with accompanying Map, *Palestine 1948 50 Years after Al Nakba. The Towns and Villages Depopulated by the Zionist Invasion of 1948*), London: The Palestine Return Centre

Akram, Susan. 2001. 'Reinterpreting Palestinian Refugee Rights under International Law', in Aruri (ed.) 2001: 165-94

Arafat, Yasir. 2002. 'The Palestinian Vision of Peace' (OP-ED), *New York Times*, 3 February, §4, 15

Aruri, Naseer. 1995. *The Obstruction of Peace: The U.S., Israel and the Palestinians.* Common Courage Press Box 702, Monroe, ME 04951

Aruri, Naseer. 2001. 'Towards Convening a Congress of Return and Self-Determination', in Aruri (ed.) 2001: 260-71

Aruri, Naseer. 2003. *Dishonest Broker: The U.S. Roles in Israel and Palestine.* Cambridge, MA: South End Press

Aruri, Naseer (ed.). 1983 (2nd ed. 1989) *Occupation: Israel Over Palestine.* Belmont, MA: Association of Arab-American University Students

Aruri, Naseer (ed.). 2001. *Palestinian Refugees and their Right of Return.* London and Sterling VA: Pluto Press

Beilin, Yossi. 1999. *Touching Peace: From the Oslo Accords to a Final Agreement.* London: Weidenfeld & Nicolson

Boyd, Gerald. 1986. 'Reagan Presses Hard for Contra Aid', *New York Times*, 7 June, A5

Farsoun, Samih K with Christina E Zacharia. 1997. *Palestine and the Palestinians.* Boulder, Co: Westview Press

Flapan, Simha. 1987. *The Birth of Israel: Myths and Realities.* London and Sydney: Croom Helm

Grech, Alain. 2002. 'The Broken Dream: Camp David Revisited', *Le Monde Diplomatique*, July 2002

Harris, William (1980) *Taking Root: Israeli Settlement in the West Bank, the Golan and Gaza-Sinai 1967-1980.* Chichester: Research Studies Press

Khouri, Rami. 2003. 'Time to consult the Israeli and Palestinian publics', *Daily Star* (Beirut) 28 November

Kubursi, Atif. 2001. *Valuing Palestinian Losses in Today's Dollars, in* , in Aruri (ed.) 2001: 217-51

Lawson, Fred H. 1995. 'The Truman Administration and the Palestinians', in Michael Suleiman (ed.), *US Policy on Palestine from Wilson to Clinto*n. Normal, Illinois: AAUG Press

Lee, Luke T. 1986. 'The Right to Compensation: Refugees and Countries of Asylum', *American Journal of International Law* 80: 532-67

Mallison , W Thomas and Sally V Mallison. 1979. *An International Law Analysis of the Major United Nations Resolutions Concerning the Palestine Question.* New York: United Nations

Mallison, W Thomas and Sally V Mallison. 1986. *The Palestinian Problem in International Law and World Order.* London: Longman

Morris, Benny. 1987. *The Birth of the Palestinian Refugee Problem, 1947-1949.* Cambridge: Cambridge University Press

Morris, Benny. 2002. 'Camp David and After; An Exchange', *New York Review of Books*, 12 June

Nir, Ori. 2001. 'The lost dreams of Sakhnin', *Ha'aretz*, 8 January

Oz, Amos. 2001. 'Let Palestinians Govern Palestinians—Now', *New York Times*, 6 January, A13

Palumbo, Michael. 1987. *The Palestinian Catastrophe: The 1948 Expulsion of a People from their Homeland.* Boston: Faber and Faber

Pappé, Ilan. 1992. *The Making of the Arab-Israeli Conflict, 1947-51.* New York: Macmillan/St Anthony's Press

Prior, Michael (ed.). 1998. *Western Scholarship and the History of Palestine.* London: Melisende

Quigley, John. 1998. 'The Right of Return of Displaced Jerusalemites' in Prior (ed.): 83-90

Rubenberg, Cheryl. 1983. *Palestine Liberation Organization: Its Institutional Infrastructure.* Belmont, MA: Institute of Arab Studies

Said, Edward W. 2000. *The End of the Peace Process: Oslo and After.* New York: Pantheon Books

Sayegh, Fayez A. 1979. *Camp David and Palestine: A Preliminary Analysis.* New York: Americans for Middle East Understanding

Sayegh, Fayez A. 1982. *Camp David and Palestine*, Monograph No. 1 Pleasantville, New York: The Fayez A. Sayegh Foundation, Inc

Schultz, George. 1985. *Terrorism and the Modern World. Terrorism:* 431-47

Tadmor, Yoav. 1994. 'The Palestinian Refugees of 1948: The Right to Compensation and Return', *Temple International and Comparative Law Journal* 8(2): 403-34

Watson, Geoffrey R. 2000. *The Oslo Accords: International Law and the Israeli-Palestinian Peace Agreements.* Oxford/New York: Oxford University Press

WAKING THE SLEEPING GIANT
Elizabeth Barlow

The displacement of one people by another in Israel/Palestine, involving shooting deaths, home demolitions, land confiscation, impoverishment and retaliatory suicide bombing, is taking place month by month, and day by day. And yet, the rest of the world makes no effective protest. Although world opinion is potentially a powerful force for change it has not yet engaged effectively in this issue. I shall review here instances in which world opinion has contributed to a resolution of other recent conflicts, and shall then examine the barriers to effective global mobilisation on the Palestinian-Israeli issue. Finally, I shall discuss ways to awaken the world community. In so doing I draw mainly on my own perspective as a US citizen—readers from other countries may apply what is said to their own situations.

Effective mobilisation of public opinion

In the last half-century alone people of conscience have made a great difference in public policy. This can be seen in the areas of US civil rights, the opposition to the Vietnam War, the protest against US involvement in Nicaragua, and the struggle against South African apartheid, and in other areas. Recalling these mass movements encourages one to hope that mobilisation on the question of Israel/Palestine could bring about corresponding improvements. Let us review the examples.

The US civil rights movement in the 1960s was led by black Christians and their allies, who spoke to a community which was largely unaware of the actual treatment of Blacks in the US, and which was confused about the relevant biblical message, and fearful of taking controversial stands. Though it took years of work, it finally became apparent that the US could not pretend to be a democracy if it did not allow *all* its citizens to vote, or if it provided inferior public services, including schools, to one race of people, or allowed them to be unequal

in its criminal justice system. The occasion for the changing of perspectives on the issue was the contrast visible in media coverage between the reasoned arguments of the Southern Christian Leadership Council and the brutal treatment of protesters by southern white leaders and law enforcement officials. The images portrayed black solidarity in Church rallies, where blacks first prayed for God's forgiveness of their oppressors and then went out to march for voting rights, only to be met with clubs, jeers, and fire hoses. In fact, many cite Atlanta Sheriff 'Bull' Connor's use of fire hoses to knock over 5-year-old children and 80-year-old ladies as being the devastating television image which brought about very solid support for a voter registration law, forbidding states' imposition of whimsical and unequal limitations on voter registration for one group of voters.

The opposition to US warfare in Vietnam—a US foreign policy issue—provides another example of the pressure of public opinion in the US on public policy. Here again, there was a long struggle to educate a very polarised US society on what was actually happening in Vietnam. This process also was facilitated by one striking image, the picture of a young Vietnamese girl screaming with pain after being napalmed by US planes. This image undercut all the noble official protestations that the US was fighting for democracy: I remember vividly the horror I felt when I saw this picture. While the government insisted that it was giving democracy what in fact was being delivered was napalm on a naked child's body.

In another striking example of US foreign policy, the US government during the Reagan administration was supplying death squads with arms and money, which were used to kill teachers and health workers in order to destabilise and overthrow the Nicaraguan government. This policy was accompanied by Cold War justifications. Some US Church leaders challenged the policy by offering sanctuary to citizens of Central America and by putting their bodies on the line, opening a wedge for discussion in the US, and focusing attention on the US 's official role in training Central Americans to torture and kill their own people, as well as US citizens, including nuns and priests. Pressure was strong enough to lead Congress to pass a law forbidding the transmission of US funds to Central American Contras. Reagan and his advisors, nevertheless, found a way through our equally disreputable policy in Iran to provide funds for Israel to transmit money to the Central American Contras, a fact which was not discovered until some time later.

Then, on the world stage, there was the mobilisation of world opinion against South African apartheid. The Boer leaders of South Africa portrayed the conflict as a war of civilisation against barbarism, which justified taking land and life from the indigenous population. The South African government stressed that everything was being done in a lawful way. Here again the images of dispossession and pauperization undercut the official claims, as viewers thought there must be something terribly wrong with a country that passes such unjust laws. A global educational campaign was launched which took some time, but in the end achieved solid global support. A divestment campaign throughout the world convinced investors not to support apartheid. Churches and universities were leaders in examining their portfolios to rid themselves of investments in companies that supported apartheid. Throughout the campaign supporters of apartheid used biblical arguments to underpin their position. Some Christians were frightened to speak out on a controversial issue. However, throughout the world South African entertainers and sports teams were not welcome, and global entertainers and sports teams did not perform in South Africa. Despite efforts to fragmentize the black population, South African government leaders were largely unsuccessful. Also, the black population insisted that they were not planning to drive out the whites, but that they only wanted equal rights. The black population projected a better future for all when apartheid would end. The South African white leadership appeared in sharp contrast to the black population which would, as they marched, sing in four-part harmony. The South African government, obviously afraid of demography and majority rule, would have preferred to continue their present system of apartheid and bantustans, but felt the isolation and global condemnation, and saw that their options could only get worse. They might not for long be dealing with a black population asking only for equal rights.

Other examples come to mind, but let us look at the lessons that can be drawn from the examples cited above. First, that images of what life is like under domination are extremely important, as many in the world simply do not know. Secondly, global citizens need to see the role our own countries have played in perpetuating inequity. Thirdly, solidarity within the oppressed population was important, as was the solid support around the world, with the result that the whole movement could work together. Finally, since people tend not to want to favour

one side over another, it needs to be stressed that the change will bring about a better situation for all—that change is indeed a win-win solution.

Barriers to advocacy in the Palestinian-Israeli conflict

I wish to draw attention to two major obstacles to engaging people in the Palestinian-Israeli conflict.

1. Lack of understanding, or misinformation, about the nature of the conflict

Why is the global community not making sufficient progress in the Palestinian-Israeli conflict? I suggest six contributory factors.

First, many people, certainly most Americans, still do not understand that there is an occupation taking place. They have accepted the Israeli explanation that it is simply 'disputed land', and are annoyed that the Palestinians will not 'compromise'. Americans must learn that there is indeed an occupation of one people by another, which has been protested by the United Nations immediately after the invasion in 1967, and almost annually since then. They must also learn that the occupation is in fact a very harsh and cruel one.

Second, Israel's occupation of Palestinian lands is tacitly or actively supported by other countries. Many people in the US see themselves as totally innocent, and see the problem as 'over there' between people who cannot seem to work things out. They do not recognize the crucial diplomatic support and the massive financial aid the US gives to Israel (about $100 billion since 1948, and currently well over $3 billion a year, plus $9 billion in loan guarantees). People in other countries have allowed the US to assume an undeserved and futile role as peace broker, marginalising other interested countries, the UN, the Fourth Geneva Convention and other aspects of international law.

Third, there are divisions within the Palestinian population and their supporters not only over tactics (suicide bombings, piecemeal negotiations, etc.), but also over goals (an attainable solution for refugees, and indeed whether there should be two states, or one state for all within mandatory Palestine, etc.).

Fourth, most people are reluctant to choose one side over another. Those of us working for justice and peace in the region need to make it very clear that we are simply asking them to choose life and justice. The peace with justice we espouse will be much better for both sides, and also better for the rest of the world. David Kimche, a devoted Zionist all his life, expressed the dilemma well:

> The Zionist ideal is now in danger. We are heading with the speed of an express train towards a binational state in which we, the Jews, will be a minority. Within five or six years the Palestinian Arabs will be in a majority in the land between the Jordan River and the Mediterranean. We will then be faced with a choice: either live as a minority in a democratic state characterised by 'one man (and woman) one vote,' or we will, as a minority, rule over an apartheid, non-democratic state. As a Zionist, I want neither. They do not fit into the ideology that brought me to this country.
>
> Yet unless we leave the territories the only other option will be the transfer of the Arab population, which is an unthinkable choice both for moral and for political reasons. There just is not any other option. We are not talking about something that might happen in the distant future; we are talking about a certainty that is just around the corner (Kimche 2003).

Fifth, many Israelis and Jews outside Israel hear any criticism of Israel as antisemitic, and as a prelude to another holocaust. We need to quote for them the many Israelis from the peace camp, as well as a growing number of soldiers who have committed acts of which they are ashamed, and political leaders and strategists who object to Israel's past and current policies of

—land confiscation: 72 percent of the West Bank declared Israeli 'state land'
—home demolition: 2,850 Palestinian homes, rendering 10,000 homeless
—school closures and road closures preventing people from getting to work, to schools, to healthcare, or to visit family

237

and friends
—unemployment: 65 percent in the West Bank and 70 percent in Gaza,
—per capita income: down 75 percent since 1993, and
—agricultural destruction: 150,000 olive and fruit trees have been uprooted (The Israeli Coalition Against House Demolitions [ICAHD], 2003).

Sixth, there is a lack of support, especially in the US, for the UN, international law and multilateral security. Existing international law and UN resolutions already provide the blueprint for a solution. The problem has been that Israel and the US have been trying to reach a solution at considerable variance with international law. Hanan Ashrawi expressed the need for a change of approach:

> Globally, the Palestinian question remains central to any human vision of globalization as a test of the collective will to intervene and to maintain a global rule of law based on operative principles of justice and historical redemption. Granted, the current dynamic is antithetical to the aspirations of peacemakers who had based their endeavors on the universality of human rights, parity before the law, positive intervention, and the non-violent resolution of conflicts through redress and the elimination of grievances. A serious paradigm shift is necessary for the restoration of these human values that have been subverted in the aftermath of September 11 and the triumph of the neoconservatives and the fundamentalist ideologues in key power centers (Ashrawi 2003: 3).

Let us hasten the paradigm shift!
Even though progress in the West on the matter is slow, we can take encouragement from clear signs of change of perception in Israeli society, even in places we might not expect. An increasing number of Israelis are realising that their dream to live in a peaceful Israel, one accepted by its neighbours, living where their children would not have to perform unspeakable deeds in the army or army reserve, is steadily turning into a nightmare.

Most recently, the protests of the Israeli peace camp have been joined by voices from an unexpected quarter. Four recent heads of Shin Bet, Israel's security service, have gone public. These very different individuals agree that Ariel Sharon's way is leading the country to a terrible disaster. Ami Ayalon, the Shin Bet chief from 1996 to 2000, in the joint interview said that,

> We are taking sure, steady steps to a place where the State of Israel will no longer be a democracy and a home for the Jewish people ... Many Israelis thought we could defeat the Palestinians by military means, and this would solve our problems. But this hasn't worked. Our economy is deteriorating and we have to change directions (in *Yediot Ahronot,* 14 November 2003).

The security chiefs pointed out that without a viable Palestinian state, there would soon be more Palestinians than Jews, and Israel would either have to deny Palestinians the vote in a single state (thereby losing its democratic character), or see the state lose its Jewish character. They also suggested that Sharon's continuing military attacks on Palestinians did not deter suicide bombings, but rather seemed to increase them.

In addition to these security chiefs, nearly 600 soldiers who have served as occupation troops before have signed a petition stating that they will no longer do so, because oppressing another people, in their words, will not lead to security. Additionally, 27 airmen and over 50 school graduates about to be drafted have announced that they will not serve. Even though many of these refuseniks are facing repeated prison terms for their conscientious objection to service for the occupation, the movement is still growing.

Moreover, Military Chief of Staff, Lt Gen Moshe Yaalon, in late October, told Israel's three leading newspapers that the road closures, curfews and roadblocks imposed on Palestine civilians were creating explosive levels of 'hatred and terrorism' among the populace. He said these tactics were against Israel's 'strategic interests' as they fostered militancy.

2. *Lack of understanding of religious imperatives*

Four areas strike me as being particular relevant to our discussion.

A. Ethnic cleansing. Zionists claim that the Holy Land belongs solely to the Jewish people, rather than to the indigenous population. Some Christians with casual familiarity with the books of the Torah assume that God has issued a directive that the Holy Land belongs solely to the Jewish people, and that all others should be driven out. Christians badly need basic training in how to read the Bible. Scholars tell us that the books of the Torah should be read as stories, not as history or political science. From archeological evidence we know that the time frame for the supposed biblical attacks by the Hebrew 'outsiders' simply does not work: many of the Canaanite cities that the biblical narrative describes as having been attacked by the Hebrews, e.g., Jericho and Ai, were uninhabited at the time of the supposed attack. Indeed, an increasing number of scholars argue that the evidence suggests that the 'Hebrews' were not outsiders at all, but had been living with the other groups of people in the Holy Land for some time, which suggests, of course, that historically there was no Hebrew 'conquest' in biblical times.

Furthermore, on the basis of this dubious biblical precedent, some argue that God commands believers to drive out, or kill indigenous peoples. Clearly, the biblical narrative mandating the genocide of the indigenous inhabitants of Canaan presents a moral problem for any reader of the Bible. The problem is compounded when it is acknowledged that that narrative has fuelled all kinds of improper behaviour towards a range of other indigenous peoples. In his *The Bible and Colonialism* (1997) Michael Prior has traced the biblical roots of ethnic cleansing, giving three examples, the Christian colonisers of Latin America, the Dutch Reformed theologians and Boer leaders in South Africa, and the Zionists in Israel. He examines the case of the Zionists in greater detail in his *Zionism and the State of Israel* (Prior 1999). Christians, who believe that God is a God of all people, face a serious challenge in claiming the authority of God for 19th-century nationalism and various practices of ethnic cleansing.

The situation came to a head in South Africa, where the Bible was held in great reverence by the Boers and many blacks. Having relied on some of its traditions—especially in the Book of Deuteronomy—to

justify apartheid the Church and South African nationalists came painfully, slowly and sometimes with considerable reluctance to the conclusion that apartheid was a heresy. Ironically the Bible itself also provided a corrective to its traditions which had been used in support of apartheid. Bishop Desmond Tutu explains that to counter the argument that God requires ethnic cleansing, he and others argued that, according to the Bible, 'what gave people their worth was the fact that they were created in the image of God—apartheid was evil, unbiblical and therefore unchristian' (Tobin and Tobin 2002: 260).

B. Christian Zionist fallacy. The Christian Zionist argument affects some denominations and some areas of the world more than others. It is strong among many, but not all evangelicals. In the US it is touted by televangelists Pat Robertson and Jerry Falwell. It appears that Christian Zionists are eagerly promoting the destruction of the world through an Armageddon disaster. They claim to find clues in the Book of Revelation that will chart the path toward destruction, and are working to hasten the ultimate end of everything. They say that Jews must return to Israel first, and then there will be a great conflagration. So they support Israel completely, without any tiresome examination of the issues. It does not really matter to them anyway, as they confidently hope to be among the 144,000 taken up in the rapture that will follow the total destruction, so for them law and moral values really are just a waste of time. A major question presents itself: does God, who created the world, really want humankind to hasten its end? Is this the God revealed to us through Christ? For a more detailed examination of the movement, see the writings of Don Wagner (e.g., Wagner 1995, 1999, and 2003) and Stephen Sizer (e.g., Sizer 1999).

C. The Christian duty to work for justice. Many Christians know that justice is at the centre of the Christian vision, but they are unclear as to their obligation to further justice. As Christianity is actually practised in the US there seems to be the view that while one might *pray* for justice one should only *work* for it if it encounters no controversies, or causes no hurt feelings. Yet virtually everything that is important may trigger controversies, or cause hurt feelings. But that should not stop people from trying to speak up on important issues. A prayer life that simply mouths prayers for an abstract justice without pulling one into the struggle is somewhat dysfunctional.

A good example of prayer life that leads to action is that of the Episcopalian Bishop of Boston, Thomas Shaw, who put on his clerical robes and with his fellow Episcopal bishops joined a protest in October 2001 at the Israeli Consulate in Boston against Israel's treatment of the Palestinians. Great criticism followed: 'How dare he take such a public position against Israel, which was a Jewish state?' Did not his action, therefore, constitute an Episcopalian attack on Judaism? 'How dare he become so "unbalanced"?' 'Had not the Palestinians made errors also?'

In the course of an explanation of his actions to his own people (in Tobin and Tobin 2002: 201-22), Bishop Shaw pointed out that his actions came as a result of daily prayer about the situation dating from the time he witnessed a murder of a Palestinian by Israeli security forces, and later a bus and passengers destroyed by a Palestinian suicide bomber.

> My witness before the Israeli Consulate that cold evening in late October was an extension of my prayer for peace, in which I was not only speaking to God but listening to God ... If the work that God calls us to do in our baptismal covenant, to 'strive for justice and peace among all people, and respect the dignity of every human being' is not advocacy, what is it? ... I came to the conclusion that advocacy on behalf of justice is deeply rooted in the Jewish and Christian tradition. Injustice has to be made visible if there is to be any reconciliation. Seeking justice and peace is not about avoiding conflict or protecting our brothers and sisters from themselves or unjust actions. It is about taking risks on behalf of the victims of injustice. That is what the prophets did in Israel, what Jesus did in the Roman Empire, what Gandhi did in India, what Desmond Tutu did in South Africa. The church is to be like that (in Tobin and Tobin 2002: 203-206).

Bishop Shaw examines the prophet Micah and the practice of Jesus in their advocacy. They are not striving for 'balance'. They are, instead,

> advocates for victims and the marginalized, wherever they may be. When Jesus acts against the institutional structures

of Judaism, or denounces the Pharisees and Scribes, he is not attacking the *faith* of the Jews, to its shame, as is often taught. In fact, he is holding up to the Jews the tradition of the Mosaic Covenant, calling them back to the prophetic faith of the Exodus (in Tobin and Tobin 2002: 209-10).

In the case of Boston, the protest against Israeli occupation led to interfaith discussions and trips to the Holy Land. The Christians in this case participated in continuing advocacy for justice while also undertaking discussions with Jewish groups. Sometimes the Jewish groups ask the Christians not to undertake any further work until the discussions with the Jewish partner is complete. Wisely, in the Boston case, the Christians did not agree to put their work for justice on hold.

Since those working for justice are being portrayed as one-sided, it is important to call attention to the fact that peace with justice is best not only for Palestinians, but for Israelis, and for the rest of the world as well. We should be sure to tell others about the many Israelis who are very uneasy about the current policy, the soldiers, the Shin Bet officials, the policymakers and the Israeli peace groups. It may in fact be easier for Jews, in view of the criticism they will experience from fellow Jews, to start by supporting the Jewish groups working for peace, such as the Israeli Coalition Against House Demolitions, B'tselem, Ta'ayush, and Rabbis for Human Rights.

D. Misunderstanding Islam. It has been easy for Christians to fall victim to attempts to dehumanise Muslims, as Islam and the history and culture of Muslim peoples is not well understood. Islamic civilisation, in fact, had long periods of cultural achievement and tolerance of diversity, at least of Jews and Christians. Violence in the contemporary Muslim world is best explained not by religion, but as resistance to the violence of domination and, in Israel-Palestine, also of occupation.

The way forward

There is already a global consensus on the best solution for the Israeli-Palestinian conflict, based on international law, human rights conventions, and UN resolutions—an independent Palestinian state on

243

all of the West Bank and Gaza, which is 22 percent of mandatory Palestine. This is already less than half the size of the area awarded by the UN Partition Plan on 29 November 1947. This proposal, then, already gives Israel 78 percent of mandatory Palestine, instead of the 55 percent actually awarded to it. The Israeli settlements in the Palestinian West Bank and Gaza, which were always illegal according to the Fourth Geneva Convention of 1949, have to be abandoned, although individual Israelis may remain if they wish, as long as they obey Palestinian law and do not expect Israeli soldiers to enter Palestinian areas to protect them. The Palestinians have said that they are willing to accept this. It should be noted that a major part of the responsibility for failure to reach a solution lies with the US, which has ignored international law, human rights conventions, and UN resolutions. It is the US which is totally isolated on this issue, except of course for Israel's support. In October 2003, the UN General Assembly adopted a resolution demanding that Israel 'stop and reverse the construction of the wall in the occupied territory'; the US was outvoted 144 to 4— only Micronesia and the Marshall Islands supported the US and Israel. Since the US controls the foreign policy of Micronesia and the Marshall Islands, it is hard to imagine a more forceful example of US isolation!

The global community might explain that if the parties prefer, they may choose a one-state solution, possibly with constitutional guarantees for minorities (Muslims and Christians now, but perhaps Jewish Israelis in another decade), and international supervision to make sure the minority is allowed to vote, and receives equal protection.

What the global community must rule out is expulsion of one people by the other, or the creation of non-contiguous bantustans that Prime Minister Sharon seems to favour. Either of these 'solutions' will simply create more violence, and make a lasting peace even harder to achieve.

The way forward has become easier, because of the many people in Israel who now understand that if Israel tries to hold on to the West Bank and Gaza, very soon the Palestinians living there could demand to vote—and they would soon outnumber the Jewish Israelis living in Israel and the territories. While the peace groups have made this point for many years, it is only recently that army officials, serving officers, would-be draftees, Labour Knesset members and even Likud leaders are now saying that Israel must leave the territories.

Sharon seems to have a plan of theoretically giving up the territories, while keeping Palestinians bottled up in little non-contiguous areas, where they cannot reach their own fields and orchards, sell their products, get to schools or hospitals, or visit relatives. For the sake of both Israel and the Palestinians, Sharon's solution must be firmly rejected by the global community.

Even though the solution suggested here is clearly best for both sides, one can expect that there will be a great deal of anguish. Will the US back this sensible solution? Let us look at the appalling confusion of US foreign policy in the area, and then consider what methods US and global citizens have to affect change in US policy.

1. *Images explain reality*

With so many people, particularly in the US, unaware of what life is really like for Palestinians, and to a lesser extent for Israelis, it is important to provide images through study tours, videos, talks by people from the region, and illustrations of what life is like with closure points and continual land confiscations, home demolitions and, now, the building of a wall twice as high as the Berlin Wall not on the border, but dividing Palestinian areas from one another. It is crucial to ensure that journalists are able to fully cover the occupied areas and send back their stories without censorship. It is also important that scholars are allowed to tell what they know without having lectures cancelled.

In addition, it is important that global citizens see the situation first hand. People can either arrange their own tours (groups like Sabeel, www.sabeel.org, will assist), or join pre-arranged tours, such as those sponsored by the Christian Peacemaker Team (CPT, www.cpt.org), or the Fellowship for Reconciliation (forusa.org). Some Christian denominations regularly plan trips. It is important, however, to stress that the groups should visit both Israeli and Palestinian peacemaker groups, such as, on the Israeli side, the Israeli Coalition Against House Demolitions (www.icahd.org), the human rights group B'tselem (www.btselem.org), Israeli activist groups, Rabbis for Human Rights (www.rhr.israel.net), Gush Shalom (www.gush-shalom.org) and Ta'ayush, Hamoked-Center for the Defense of the Individual (mail@hamoked.org.il), and Women in Black; and, on the Palestinian side, the Ecumenical Christian Center

Sabeel (www.sabeel.org), al Haq (www.alhaq.org), the Applied Research Center in Jerusalem (www.arij.org), Institute of Jerusalem Studies (www.jqf-jerusalem.org), Health, Development, Information and Policy Institute (www.hdip.org), Addameer Prisoners Support and Human Rights Association (www.addameer.org), Defense for Children International-Palestine Section (www.dci-pal.org), Law-The Palestinian Society for the Protection of Human Rights and the Environment, among others. Being 'one-sided' will not be helpful, and it is very important to engage with the perspectives of Israeli (Jewish) groups working for peace and mutual understanding.

For people who cannot go overseas, there are some very good videos, such as 'Palestine is STILL the Issue' by John Pilger (ordering information available from www.bullfrogfilms.com) and the ICAHD-produced video 'The Right to a Home and a Homeland' (see www.rebuildinghomes.com). The latter video shows Israeli Jews and Palestinians working together to rebuild Palestinian homes destroyed by the Israeli government. The harmony and mutual respect possible when among people of different communities, but who are committed to working together for justice is a vision not often seen in Western news media.

Church partnerships, or family adoptions are also methods of bringing understanding to those who do not live under occupation. The CPT group mentioned above promotes partnerships between families whose homes have been targeted for demolition by Israel and families in Europe, Canada, the US, or Israel. Another possibility is translating the situations faced by Palestinians to one's local context. For instance, in the US some student groups have illustrated closures by shutting down (temporarily) entrance to classrooms and dorms, forcing people to wait, empty their bags and endure a 'search'. Some groups were given prompt searches, while others were forced to linger. The unfairness of the situation, and the inability to predict when, or if, one will pass through, comes home to those who encounter these closures. The impact of by-pass roads can be described in a local area by explaining that the main thoroughfares are by-pass roads, and are designated for the sole use of the occupiers. The indigenous population must not cross these roads without a permit, for which the application fee is expensive, the process time-consuming, and the chances of approval are very slim, and the permit can be cancelled at any time. Moreover, the application fee is not returned.

Another way of bringing images of occupation home is to tie the issue to local observances. During the freezing temperatures of winter, people in higher latitudes are conscious of the vulnerability of the homeless. This is an appropriate time to talk about home demolitions in Palestine, and the sickness and inability to do school work that ensues. 30 March is 'Land Day' in Palestine, a time when one can explain the steady expropriation of land from Palestinians, even those who are citizens of Israel inside the Green Line. Easter may be an appropriate time to talk about Jerusalem, and what it means to Christians who are unable to reach it from Ramallah or Bethlehem, just five to eight miles away. Mothers' Day may be an occasion to talk about the difficulties of the Palestinian mothers, where 70 percent live below the poverty line, and homes continue to be demolished, and more than 60 percent of the workers are unemployed, and where children can be attacked with impunity by settlers or soldiers on the way to school.

Your own country's national day—for us in the US this is 4 July —may be an occasion for considering that the UN plan in 1947 was for two states in Israel and Palestine, but only one state has come into existence. Is it not time that the international community either worked to bring about the second state in the entire West Bank and Gaza or demanded a one-state solution with equal protection of the law for all its inhabitants? When children return to school, one could consider the plight of Palestinian children in their exhausting and difficult journeys across closure points to reach their schools. Labour Day might bring an examination of the rights of workers in Palestine. 29 November would be a reminder of the passage of the UN partition plan in 1947. Palestinians then wanted one state for all its citizens, instead of borders that would divide their families. It is well past the time when the Palestinians should either have their own state on all of the West Bank and Gaza, or be part of a larger state in all of mandatory Palestine with guaranteed equal protection of the laws, enforced by the UN. 10 December is the anniversary of the passage of the Universal Human Rights Convention in 1948, a time to bring its provisions to the attention of the global community and an opportunity to ensure that its provisions prevail. 28 December, 'Holy Innocents Day' in the Christian calendar marking the slaughter of the children of Bethlehem, can be the occasion to acknowledge that the continuation of this conflict is doing serious harm to both Palestinian and Israeli young people.

2. *A solution based on international law is best for all parties*

Advocacy will progress much faster if the public understands that it is in the interests of not only the Palestinians, but of the Israelis and the rest of the world as well. The sort of peace with justice that is being proposed here is a win-win situation. Since Israelis want to continue to live in the Middle East, it is important for them to be seen as a country which treats all its citizens in Israel in a fair manner, and which maintains cordial relations with its neighbours, and ends its occupation of the Palestinians in the West Bank and Gaza. Without justice, no peace will last. Continuing turmoil will devastate the Israeli economy, as well as the Palestinian economy. New immigrants will not want to come, or earlier immigrants to stay, in an Israel with a troubled economy, surrounded by hostility, and flouting international law and human rights. Since it was the UN which in 1947 decided to partition Palestine without consulting its population—albeit under fierce prodding by the US—it must now exert itself to achieve a measure of fairness for both Israelis and Palestinians.

3. *The absurdity of Israeli and US policy*

The absurdity of the present Israeli policy, and the mindless US support for it, needs to be exposed. Israel claims that it wishes to be at peace with its neighbours, and yet it permits soldiers to rampage in unnecessary killing sprees. Clearly, Israel bears some of the responsibility for the dire poverty imposed on Palestinians—through its acts of closure (preventing people from working, and goods from reaching markets), destruction of orchards, olive trees and farmland. It should also recognise that their dire straits may well be related to the growing number of Palestinians who choose to resist the occupation even at the cost of their own lives. In any case, Israel through its actions is increasing the number of families in poverty, and the number who are mourning the death of a family member.

And what about the United States? It claims that it wants a two-state solution, yet it has been funding, at a lavish level, settlements that it says are an 'obstacle to peace'. US-made attack helicopters, guns and tanks—also gifts from the American taxpayer—have been used for targeted assassinations, which occur without any judicial process, and have killed and injured in a single attack up to 100 civilians. As the number of civilians

mounts in this 'collateral damage' category, it is harder to believe that these are just accidents. The US claims that it needs stability and friendship towards the US in this most important region, both in principle, and in order to secure a steady supply of oil at reasonable prices, yet our policies are leading to turmoil, revolutions, war, and hatred, both for the US and for countries that are seen as its lackeys.

In the autumn of 2003, the European Union Commission Survey found that the US was (with Iran and North Korea) in second place, just behind Israel, as the most dangerous country to world peace. Its foreign policy is certainly confusing. The US claims that it wants 'democracy' in Iraq, but is working with Israel to withhold it from the Palestinians. The US argues that Israel will be safer if there are fewer Palestinians who have no hope, and therefore has undertaken programmes on its own and has encouraged the European Union to build up the Palestinian infrastructure, and then has watched silently as the Israeli army and settlers—using US-supplied weapons—destroy the very infrastructure that the US has paid for. If the US wants to throw away its money, it could burn it on the Mall in Washington without putting at risk the lives of Israelis, Palestinians, Americans and Europeans. This high-level waste of money in the US is occurring at a time when social service budgets, and school and university budgets are being pared to the bone.

The US continues to give money for settlements in the West Bank and Gaza. When these settlements are finally abandoned, the US will doubtless be asked to pay for their evacuation. Yet the settlements were always illegal, and Israel has been asked every year since 1967 to withdraw from the Occupied Territory. The US says it wants peace, but is laying the groundwork for endless wars. The US prizes its civil liberties, but, to silence reaction to its outrageous foreign policy, is now eroding constitutional guarantees. The US prides itself on its world leadership, yet, as Thomas Friedman expressed (*New York Times*, 20 November 2003), 'In the Mideast, now is the time for a fresh Bush diplomatic resolve to the Israeli-Palestinian conflict—the persistence of which is toxic for America's influence.' The US claims that a major duty of its State Department is to defend and protect American citizens abroad, yet it will not even conduct an inquiry into the death of the young American college student Rachel Corrie, deliberately crushed to death by an Israeli-driven Caterpillar bulldozer, another gift of the American taxpayers.

President George W Bush has embraced the so-called 'Road

Map' as a path to a peaceful settlement, which calls for no new settlements and no growth within existing settlements. Yet the growth continues. Once in a while there may be an unoccupied new settlement that is dismantled, and is so reported to Washington, but it pops up again in another place. The wall, which certainly violates the principles of the Road Map and would end any chance that the Road Map might bring about a final peace, grows apace for all to see, and the president has not been effective in stopping it. Indeed, he simply forks out more US taxpayer money. While the US may withhold $3 million of the amount it deems has been used on settlements from the promised $9 billion 'loan' guarantee, that will not stop settlement expansion. The US, if it means business, should stop funding entirely until there is an end to the occupation.

Israel seems to think that it has the US in its pocket. On 3 October 2001, Israel Radio (*Kol Yisrael*) reported that Israeli Prime Minister Ariel Sharon had boasted at a Cabinet meeting, 'I want to tell you something very clear, don't worry about American pressure on Israel. We, the Jewish people control America, and the Americans know it.'

Faced with the mess created by US policy in the Middle East, I take refuge in the poem 'Eagle Valor, Chicken Mind' by Robinson Jeffers, written of US policy some fifty years ago:

> Unhappy, eagle wings and beak, chicken brain.
> Weep (it is frequent in human affairs), weep for the terrible
>   magnificence of the means,
> The ridiculous incompetence of the reasons, the bloody and
>   shabby
> Pathos of the result.

4. Influencing the US

On 17 December 2003, Jonathan Katz, Associated Press, reported from Jerusalem that 43 percent of Americans feel Israel threatens world peace (lower than the 59 percent of Europeans who put Israel in the lead in August 2003, but still a rather high percentage for Americans). With images and maps that portray the reality of what is happening, and with arguments that explain that either a viable two-state solution, or a one-state solution are best for Israel, Palestine and the US, it should be possible

to explain to US citizens that this is an issue that deserves their support. Already the vast majority of American Jews have been recorded in numerous polls as favouring a two-state solution.

Because of failures in Iraq, US citizens may be more willing to take another look at collective security, international law, and the UN, but this may be an up-hill battle, as the UN and international law have been demonised since about 1967. If the US continues to obstruct a fair settlement of the Israeli–Palestinian conflict, there are several things that citizens in the rest of the world can do. Individuals in other countries can lobby individuals in the US, and can prod their governments to send strong communications. Occasionally countries are in a position to withhold favours until the US begins to understand how strongly the rest of the world feels about ending this conflict.

It may be possible to hold the US accountable for the loss of life and property which come as a direct result of its military gifts to Israel. These gifts, of course, appear to be illegal under two different US laws, which insist that military weapons can only be given to countries that do not flout human rights.

The world must plan an effective way of enforcing its will. If the UN Security Council is rendered impotent by a US veto, the General Assembly should take up the issue. The US itself created the precedent in 1950 during the Korean War. One hopes that the US will accede to a solution imposed by the General Assembly. If it does not, the world community should note that with about one third of US treasury debt owned by foreigners, and with its need to capture even more foreign investment for its growing debt, the US is definitely vulnerable to pressure.

5. Influencing Israel

Israelis are already busy discussing the issue, which because of demography seems immediate and pressing. Soldiers do not want to be occupiers. Gush Shalom, an Israeli peace group, has been explaining the laws of occupation to soldiers and warning them not to commit abuses, to prevent being labelled as 'war criminals'. Even if the government of Israel did not try them, they might find themselves unable to travel, lest they be arrested, and faced with a trial elsewhere. Women of the Machsom (Checkpoint Watch) group monitor soldiers' behaviour at checkpoints.

Several human rights groups are operating inside Israel. The group ICAHD, previously mentioned, seeks to protect Palestinian homes from demolition, and works to rebuild homes already demolished. The international community might most effectively support groups already at work inside Israel. This may very well be successful. That, one hopes, should be adequate to persuade Israel to act in its own best interests and end the conflict, something which most Israelis desire.

However, it is always possible that a government might react in a way which would be dangerous to Israel as well as to the international community. In that case, the world could insist that Israel live up to its obligations under the Fourth Geneva Convention, relating to the welfare of a civilian population under occupation. It could also insist that Israel pay damages for property damaged, and persons wounded, or killed, through its policies. Although hurting another country's economy is not a desirable situation, economic pressure is vastly preferable to allowing a situation to continue which results in deaths of both Palestinians and Israelis. So, the international community, if necessary, might urge international boycotts of Israeli products, and sponsor an educational campaign to alert the world business community not to support continued occupation. Artists and athletes could boycott Israeli events, and refuse permission to Israeli artists and sports teams to compete abroad.

The international community, in order to discourage any continuation of the present situation, may need to press human rights charges and monetary damages against individual perpetrators and the leaders responsible for army and settler violence against the Palestinians. I have not mentioned here Palestinian responsibility for damages from suicide-bombings. Legally, Palestine is now a reoccupied country, and because of Israeli attacks on Palestinian police posts and policemen, because of curfews and roadblocks, it can no longer be held responsible for what is happening in the West Bank and Gaza—that is now, in virtue of the occupation, Israel's responsibility. But when the occupation ends, the state of Palestine *must* curb hostile acts by its citizens.

Recently, the UN referred the building of the massive wall by Israel inside the West Bank to the international court for an advisory opinion. As advisory opinions do not enforce themselves, if the court finds that Israel abridged international law, the international community needs to find a way to hold Israel responsible for the damages wrought on the land and to people.

The European Union (EU) has taken action to prohibit imports from Israeli settlements in the West Bank or Gaza into Europe at the cheaper 'Israeli' rate. Since these imports were not accurately marked, the EU began to charge all Israeli products at the higher rate. For countries or individuals that wish to boycott Israeli settler goods from the West Bank or Gaza, the Jewish Peace Group, Gush Shalom, maintains a list of these products on their website (www.gush-shalom.org).

6. *Interim steps toward a solution*

Before a solution is in place, the Palestinian and international communities are in great danger. Israeli soldiers have killed UN officials, destroyed UN facilities and resources, killed Palestinian doctors treating the wounded and shot at ambulances. Sufficient pressure was brought on the Red Cross so that they have now departed from the West Bank and Gaza. The International Solidarity Movement, which observes and non-violently attempts to protect the Palestinian population has had several members attacked, imprisoned and killed. There must be effective world-wide attention until the occupation ends, preferably organised under the auspices of the UN.

7. *The urgency to act*

The urgency of the issue may help to focus global attention. In addition to the problems that a continuation of the conflict will cause to Palestinians and Israelis, an unresolved conflict could lead to religious conflagration throughout the world; global indifference to human rights, the UN, and the multilateral system of collective security; and, at some point, to a nuclear or biological/chemical war. The Israeli government at present has 200–400 nuclear weapons that we know about, and has refused international inspection. While, with the exception of Pakistan at the moment, no Arab or Muslim country has nuclear weapons, the imbalance, and a continuation of the conflict may create the perceived need to develop something credible to dissuade Israel (and possibly the US) from attacking them.

A strong global movement could bring us back to international law, human rights, the multilateral system of collective security, arms

control, regional and world peace and reduced arms budgets. All that is lacking is the will to act.

References

Ashrawi, Hanan. 2003. 'Peace in the Middle East: A Global Challenge and a Human Imperative', Acceptance Speech at Sydney Peace Prize Ceremony, 5 November. Full text at: www.palestinechronicle.com/ story.php?sid=2003111118593639

Ateek, Naim and Michael Prior (eds). 1999. *Holy Land—Hollow Jubilee: God, Justice, and the Palestinians.* London: Melisende

The Israeli Coalition Against House Demolitions and the Jerusalem Center for Social and Economic Rights. 2003. 'For a Just Peace Between Israelis & Palestinians', undated publication; websites: www.icahd.org and www.jcser.org

Kimche, David. 2003. 'A Genuinely Zionist Solution', *Jerusalem Post,* Opinion, 20 November

Prior, Michael. 1997. *The Bible and Colonialism: A Moral Critique.* Sheffield: Sheffield Academic Press

Prior, Michael. 1999. *Zionism and the State of Israel: A Moral Inquiry.* London and New York: Routledge

Shaw, Bishop M Thomas, SSJE. 2002. 'On Christian Advocacy', in Tobin and Tobin 2002: 201-222

Sizer, Stephen. 1999. 'Christian Zionism: A British Perspective', in Ateek and Prior 1999: 189-98

Tobin, Maurine and Robert Tobin (eds). 2002. *How Long O Lord,* Cambridge, Mass: Cowley Publications

Tutu, Bishop Desmond. 2002. 'A Clarion Call', in Tobin and Tobin 2002: 259-65

Wagner, Donald. 1995. *Anxious for Armageddon: A Call to Partnership for Middle Eastern and Western Christians.* Scottdale and Waterloo: Herald Press

Wagner, Donald. 1999. 'Reagan and Begin, Bibi and Jerry: The Theopolitical Alliance of the Likud Party with the American Christian 'Right' ', in Ateek and Prior 1999: 199-215

Wagner, Donald. 2003. *Dying in the Land of Promise. Palestine and Palestinian Christianity from Pentecost to 2000.* London: Melisende

SPEAKING the TRUTH